695

102 HIKES IN THE ALPINE LAKES, SOUTH CASCADES, AND OLYMPICS

Text: Ira Spring and Harvey Manning

Photos: Bob and Ira Spring

Maps: Helen Sherman

THE MOUNTAINEERS · SEATTLE

THE MOUNTAINEERS

Organized 1906

To explore and study the mountains, forests, and watercourses of the Northwest;

To gather into permanent form the history and traditions of this region;

To preserve by the encouragement of protective legislation or otherwise the natural beauty of Northwest America;

To make explorations into these regions in fulfillment of the above purposes;

To encourage a spirit of good fellowship among all lovers of outdoor life.

First edition, June 1971
Second edition, September 1974
Third edition, July 1976

Copyright © 1971, 1974
The Mountaineers, Seattle, Washington 98111
P.O. Box 122

Manufactured in the United States of America

Book design by Marge Mueller

Library of Congress Catalog Card No. 79-166974

ISBN 0-916890-24-4

Published simultaneously in Canada
by Mountain Craft, Box 5232
Vancouver, B.C. V6B 4B3

Cover photo: Gnome Tarn and Prusik Peak, Enchantment Lakes region—Hike 10
Title photo: Toleak Point—Hike 102

CONSERVATION AGENDA

A strict wilderness purism would forbid the publication of guidebooks as surely as the construction of roads, for absolute wildness depends on total secrecy. The Mountaineers, however, have come to realize the terrain of their favorite hikes, the traditional trips passed along from one club generation to the next by personal initiation and word of mouth, is not hidden from the latter-day frontiersmen whose mission is to "put nature to work."

This book, like its predecessors, admittedly is antithetical to the canons of purism, published as it is to lead more people onto the trails. Yet if the wilderness is to be protected from anachronistic frontiering, it must have more defenders, people who know it intimately and love it well in the way of the hiker and backpacker.

A duty—a moral obligation, in fact—falls upon the reader who profits from the half-century and more of Mountaineer experience distilled into these pages. To become a full and responsible citizen of the trail country, one must do more than walk and enjoy, one must join in the effort to preserve its integrity.

The following is a capsule summary of the current conservation agenda for the many provinces of the Cascades and Olympics to which the 102 hikes offer an introduction. Space does not allow more than a listing; for further information on any subject, write the Conservation Chairman of The Mountaineers.

Those who find this book a useful guide to hours and days of wandering the forests and meadows owe it to themselves, and to their children and grandchildren, to make the agenda their own.

How to begin? First, by giving up a "leave it to George" attitude and vowing to become involved in problems of land management. Second, by writing letters to Congressmen, Senators, other public officials, and newspapers supporting proposals to halt abuses. And third, by joining an organization, such as The Mountaineers or any of its allies, and sharing in the efforts to gain proper protection for threatened wildlands.

Alpine Lakes

Hikes 1-43 lie within a great "backyard wilderness" bounded north and south by the Stevens Pass and Snoqualmie Pass Highways, located minutes away from the homes of 2,000,000 residents of Puget Sound and Central Washington. "Central Park on the Outskirts," it has been called.

As of 1974, bills are before Congress to establish an Alpine Lakes National Recreation Area (under U.S. Forest Service jurisdiction) of some 926,000 acres with, as its core, an Alpine Lakes Wilderness of some 500,000 acres. The outer ring of the Recreation Area is designed to provide careful regulation of recreation and resource extraction and also to serve as a buffer zone for the inner sanctuary of the Wilderness.

Cascade Crest Trail

The route of the Cascade Crest Trail (part of the Pacific Crest National Scenic Trail) southward from Snoqualmie Pass should be designated as a no-logging strip, and protected from any further road intrusions.

The historic Naches Wagon Trail (Hike 46) deserves particularly urgent attention. The little that remains of the old emigrant route should be saved by placing it entirely off-limits to jeepers and trailbikers and logging.

Cougar Lakes

Hikes 47-52, 54, and 56 are in the 150,000 acres of the proposed two-section Cougar Lakes Wilderness; a bill to establish this area was introduced in Congress in 1970. The north section is bounded on the south by the Chinook Pass Highway, on the west by the Crystal Mountain Ski Area, and on the north by the lowering of the crest into wooded terrain. The larger south section includes the entire Cascade Crest between Chinook Pass and the White Pass Highway, bounded on the west much of the way by Mt. Rainier National Park, and extends eastward over valleys of virgin forests and ridges of flowers punctuated by such rugged peaks as Mt. Aix.

The Cougar Lakes Wilderness is needed as wild living room to complement increasingly-

Beargrass on Heather Mountain (John Spring photo)

crowded Mt. Rainier National Park and to prevent high-use road-oriented recreation (and logging) the fragile beauty cannot tolerate.

Mt. Rainier National Park

Ultimately the National Park boundaries must be pushed outward on the south, west, and north to take in the entirety of Mt. Rainier and all its flanking ridges and the intervening valleys; though many of these have been savagely clearcut, the Park is for the centuries and in time wounds will heal. Certain as yet unspoiled lands, notably in the Tatoosh Range, should be placed in the Park immediately.

On the north, where the Forest Service is thrusting logging roads almost to the boundary, logging should be halted, or at the very least, the roads "put to bed" when the cutting is complete in order to preserve the remoteness of Park meadows. Hunting should be controlled in all areas adjacent to the Park to maintain a complete summer-and-winter range for the animal population.

A majestic and imaginative proposal has

been made by Governor Dan Evans for an ice-to-saltwater Nisqually River Park reaching from the glaciers of Rainier the full length of the river to its outlet in the Nisqually Flats, one of only two estuaries of such size in Puget Sound still essentially in a natural condition.

South Cascades

The area sampled by Hikes 55-77 is large, varied, and badly abused. The Goat Rocks and Mt. Adams Wildernesses consist mainly of snow and rocks and meadows; boundaries should be adjusted outward to include more of the approach ridges and valleys.

The Mt. St. Helens area (Hikes 72-75) is one of the worst examples of mismanagement in the Northwest. Faced by an impossible checkerboard of private and public ownership, the U.S. Forest Service has capitulated to the exploiters. On three sides the graceful volcano rises above a sea of stumps, only the Spirit Lake side so far spared—and here the Service is plannning to log the , beautiful forest described in Hike 75. Further, the Service has opened the popular trails to motorized travel, so that children, old people, horses, and hundreds of hikers must compete with trailbikes. Because the Forest Service seems totally unwilling to radically alter its management philosophy, conservationists are now seeking a Mt. St. Helens National Monument.

The broad expanse of forested valleys and ridges between Adams and St. Helens has been criss-crossed with a spider web of roads in the years since World War II, obliterating hundreds of miles of trails. But small pockets of splendor remain relatively pristine and to preserve these a number of small Wildernesses are proposed.

Olympics

Hikes 79-102 are on the Olympic Peninsula, for the most part in Olympic National Park, most of which soon will be permanently classified as wilderness. The Park Service must be strenuously urged to acquire private lands within the Park, particularly in the Quinault Valley.

Eventually the Park must be enlarged along the eastern side, where, for example, the sum-mits of such peaks as Cruiser, The Brothers, and Constance lie exactly on the boundary, their east slopes and drainage valleys excluded. Looking west from Seattle to the Olympic horizon, the only portions of the Park that can be seen are the summits of several peaks. All the rest of the visible range is in Olympic National Forest, subject to logging, as can be vividly realized in winter, when snows demark the clearcuts, which grow larger year by year. To prevent further damage, Wildernesses must be established bordering the National Park on the northeast, southeast, and southwest.

Legislation is badly needed to extend the Park's ocean strip northward, thus heading off the threat of real estate subdivision on the wild coastline from the Ozette River to Point of the Arches, Shi-Shi Beach, and the Makah Indian Reservation.

Another grand plan, only now gathering momentum, envisions a Northwest National Seashore to save the still-unruined portions of the Strait of Juan de Fuca, Hood Canal, and the San Juan Islands.

The Mountaineers: An Invitation

The Mountaineers, with groups based in Seattle, Everett, Tacoma, and Olympia (and groups elsewhere in the planning stage) warmly invite the membership of all lovers of outdoor life who sympathize with the purposes of the organization and wish to share its activities.

The Mountaineers sponsor a year-around program of climbing, hiking, camping, ski-touring, snowshoeing, canoeing and kayaking, and bicycling. Many hundreds of outings are scheduled each year, ranging from afternoon walks to trips lasting 2 weeks or more. On a typical weekend as many as 50 excursions may be offered, from ocean beaches to the summit of Mt. Rainier. In addition, members engage in countless privately-organized trips of all kinds; the opportunity is boundless to make new friends with similar interests.

Enjoying wildlands is one side of the coin; the other is working to preserve the natural beauty of Northwest America. Here, The Mountaineers continue their role of leadership as they

Camp at Park Lake and Chikamin Ridge

have for 68 years, and seek new members to share the effort.

For membership application, and further information on club activities, write The Mountaineers, P.O. Box 122, Seattle, Washington 98111.

September 1974   HARVEY MANNING

A PLEA FOR FREEDOM FROM MACHINES

The Forest Service has no uniform, positive policy for administration of roadless areas, no clear notion of their highest and best uses. Guidelines ultimately must come from Congress, but until such time, we forest travelers must help shape Forest Service plans.

The Forest Service contains many dedicated men, some even ardent preservationists. However, most of them are more oriented to growing and cutting trees, and fitting in any and all other exploitations of commodity and recreational resources, than they are to protecting unique environments. The Supervisor of a National Forest walks a delicate line, trying to balance user demands from all sides. He really should not be in this position, or have such wide latitude to make major land-use decisions on a "political" basis, but should operate under very tight reins held by Congress. Under present circumstances, though, we forest citizens must make the best of a bad situation by letting the Forest Supervisors hear our individual voices loud and often. If every person who uses this book writes at least one letter a year, the trails can be saved from the invasion of machines and returned to the hikers.

Roadless areas are an increasingly rare and precious resource. Unfortunately, they are also a constant challenge to exploiters brought up in traditions of the frontier. But what challenge is there in building roads to the tops of high peaks or bridging canyons with cable cars? Such feats aren't even unusual anymore. The challenge of today is to value and preserve roadless areas. But the Forest Service continues in the old ways. Trails are obliterated by logging roads, some of them unnecessary even for the purpose of taking out timber, and hundreds of miles of foot trails are turned into motorcycle "roads." All this without consulting those who use and appreciate roadless country.

Three important reasons for hiking can be given. One is obvious—to enjoy scenery that can't be viewed from a car. Another is the physical challenge of doing something on your own that demands hard work. A third is to get away from the civilized world, away from the noise and stink of modern contraptions, and to gain a feeling of self-sufficiency. By mounting a machine, a forest traveler loses two of these three reasons not only for himself but for everyone else on the trail.

Motorbikers, of course, have their own reasons. They may enjoy the scenery, the same as a hiker. They like the challenge of wrestling a mechanical beast through tough terrain. Finally, they just have a lot of fun riding.

However, two of these three reasons for riding machines can be satisfied in non-hiking areas, such as abandoned gravel pits. As for the third goal of bikeriders, the scenery, they can get this the way the rest of us do, by **hiking** to beauty spots. The machine riders who claim they aren't able to hike because of some physical disability are not telling the truth. Except on a few raceways, more strength is required to get a bike up a trail than to walk.

Motorbikes are so cheap just about anybody can afford one. Sales figures show the craze is spreading like wildfire. In the Twisp River area, on the first 4 miles of the Entiat River trail, and elsewhere in the Cascades, there are already so many machines as to make hiking miserable. The worst is yet to come, because the Forest Service is developing gyro-stabilized trail machines, ideal for back-country administrative duties. But surely the Forest Service is not so blind it can't see ahead to the day when these machines which are now as awkward as trail bikes were 15 years ago, will be refined for family trail buses and individual use on and off trails. No terrain that can be walked will be too difficult for the gyro-bike.

Except for Forest Service maintenance work there is utterly no reason any machine should be allowed on any established hiking trails, which includes all the trails in this guide book. But while hikers were busy battling for the North Cascades National Park, motorbikers were multiplying and uniting in powerful clubs that are now demanding—and getting—better trails for their vehicles. Something got way out of proportion because the Forest Service, without any public hearings, arbitrarily allowed motor use of miles and miles of trails. Now the use is established, and public notices and hearings are required to **close** a trail to machines. Is this fair? Why not the reverse? Why didn't hikers get this consideration, so that no trail would be **opened** to machines without public notice and hearings?

It is now necessary for hikers to reclaim their trails one at a time. To do this, every hiker must write often—at least once a year—complaining to Supervisors of National Forests. In the North Cascades, the Supervisor of Wenatchee National Forest is going to be the hardest to convince, because unlike other Supervisors who detest machines on trails, the man currently in charge of Wenatchee likes machines and is providing them with a system of raceways.

Hikers stay away from trails they've found converted into motorcycle "roads." Rangers decide what to do with a trail on the basis of the kind of use it gets; they interpret a hikers' boycott of a trail as evidence it should be devoted entirely to machines.

Don't let machines drive you off your favorite trails. Keep hiking them. When you meet machines, make them obey the Forest Service trail courtesy rule, which is that **pedestrians have the right of way.** Stay in the trail and make the riders give you safe passage, but don't play "chicken" with a racing machine; you could get hurt. But if the rider doesn't obey the rules, be sure the Forest Supervisor hears about it in writing.

Wenatchee National Forest as a whole, and some ranger districts of Okanogan National Forest, have been the worst offenders in handing over trails to motorcycles.

Snoqualmie and Gifford Pinchot National Forests are the prime examples of another Forest Service fault—relentless road-building with very little thought to maintenance of roadless areas.

Certainly we need lumber as much as we need dedicated wilderness museums of virgin forest. And certainly there are areas that are well-suited to tree-farming and have lesser recreational values. But there are also large portions of National Forests where proper planning could make hiking and logging perfectly compatible. However, no such genuine "multiple-use" is possible with Forest Service networks of high-

standard, permanent logging roads. If they would only think it over, Forest Service officials could build a certain number of heavy-use trunk roads and do the actual logging from low-standard spurs that are "put to bed" when the harvest is complete. The trunk roads could be located away from the prime hiking routes; the trails would thus be out of use only during the several years of logging, a small part of the 50-80-year tree-growing cycle.

But Snoqualmie National Forest, with total blindness to the environment, built a permanent road next to the north boundary of Mount Rainier National Park, turning 3-day hikes into afternoon walks, and in one swoop ruined the only true wilderness within the Park. The trunk road could have been kept several miles from the Park and the boundary logging done on cat roads. This way the wilderness would have remained remote and truly wild. Another example of Snoqualmie Forest insensitivity is the East Fork Miller River road, a completely unnecessary desecration of a roadless area.

Gifford Pinchot National Forest is so thoroughly crisscrossed with roads that except for relatively small dedicated areas, only scraps remain of the vast and glorious trail country that existed 20 years ago. This is an efficient method of "tree farming" but a poor way to sustain the recreation resource. A far cry from genuine multiple use.

No National Forest ever should be given up as a lost cause. Pinchot seems a desperate case where roading is concerned and Snoqualmie not much better. At present Okanogan and Wenatchee seem to be managed less for hikers and more for trailbikes and every other variety of off-road machinery.

However, letters to Supervisors of Mt. Baker, Snoqualmie, Gifford Pinchot, Wenatchee, and Okanogan National Forests are read (and answered), and enough letters (and the need to write answers to specific complaints) can make the Supervisors change their minds about building high-standard roads up valleys which could be logged on temporary roads, and about leaving trails open to mechanized travel and improving them to make such travel easier.

The rule is: **each hiker must write at least**

one letter a year to a Forest Supervisor pleading for the preservation of roadless areas.

However, the only long-range security, the only final freedom from machines, lies in the continuing fight for more and larger wilderness areas dedicated by Congress and thus removed from the personal whims of transient Forest Supervisors. There are Supervisors (and other Forest Service personnel) who have an unsurpassed knowledge and appreciation of the land, and carefully and respectfully look after every quality of their beloved home terrain. These men we admire and trust as custodians of our national heritage. But the next Supervisor may be in office only a few years and raise havoc with hundreds of square miles of the American Earth.

If you, the readers of this book, agree with me, please start writing those letters. Only together, by a concerted effort, can we save our trail country from the machines.

September 1974   IRA SPRING

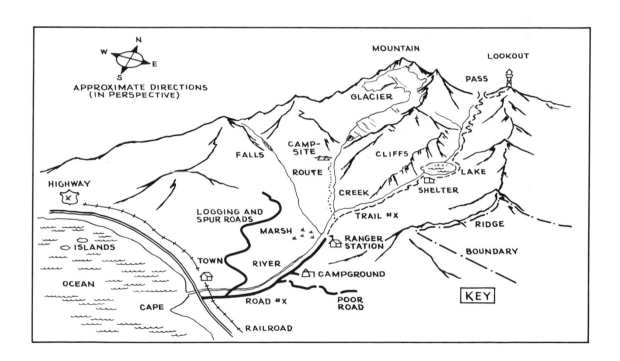

INTRODUCTION

The country sampled by the 102 hikes has many characteristics in common throughout, but also significant differences from place to place caused by variations in climate and geology and elevation and people-pressure. Three "provinces" may be distinguished.

First, the Alpine Lakes Cascades (Hikes 1-43), extending some 50 or so miles west to east from maritime greenery of Puget Sound lowlands to golden hills above the semi-arid Columbia River valley, and roughly 25-35 miles south to north from the Snoqualmie Pass Highway to the Stevens Pass Highway—beyond which lies the domain of a companion book, **101 Hikes in the North Cascades.**

On the windward slopes of the Cascades the precipitation is heavy enough to nourish near-rain forests. The leeward slopes, in the rain-shadow, often are sunny when the crest is lost in mists and drizzles, and the forests are generally more open. However, the range is much narrower here than it is to the north and the contrasts in climate from one edge to the other less marked. The hiking season is everywhere about the same because though snows pile deeper on the west, elevations average higher on the east. Past glaciation has left in all parts a legacy of sharp-sculptured peaks, plus cirque basins and scoured valleys now filled by lakes high and low—some 600 in all.

The second province, the Washington South Cascades (Hikes 44-78), is really an assemblage of quite diverse sub-provinces: the 25 miles south from Snoqualmie Pass, in which the Cascade Crest follows relatively low and heavily wooded ridges; the next 25-odd miles from north of Chinook Pass to White Pass, with the Crest rising to meadows and small crags of the proposed Cougar Lakes Wilderness; the 30 miles south from White Pass, where the Crest climbs more, from flowers to glaciers of the Goat Rocks and finally to the nearly 2½-mile-high summit of Mt. Adams; and a last 30 miles in which the Crest drops to the Columbia River. But the Cascade Crest is not the whole story: though the alpine realm of the Crest proper is rather narrow, west-

ward 35 miles from Adams over forested ridges is the graceful volcano of Mt. St. Helens; and of course, adjoining the Cougar Lakes area is the grandest volcano of them all, and the trail country described in a companion book, **50 Hikes in Mount Rainier National Park.**

The South Cascades offer isolated eruptions of spectacular violence—the volcanoes, the ice-plucked Goat Rocks and a few other peaks—but also the friendliest parklands of the entire range, and because of the distance from major cities, and the overshadowing fame of mountains farther north, some of the lonesomest.

The third province, the Olympic Peninsula (Hikes 79-102), extends some 55-85 miles from the Pacific Ocean east to Hood Canal and roughly 70 miles from the Strait of Juan de Fuca south to foothills, encompassing wilderness ocean beaches, west-side rain forests, a wilderness interior of glaciers and rock needles and flower gardens, and rainshadow ridges standing high above lowlands of Hood Canal and Puget Sound. Relatively little space is given the Olympics here, partly because they are more for the long-distance walker than the weekender, and mainly because Robert L. Wood's **Trail Country: Olympic National Park** covers the terrain in complete and loving detail.

Within these three provinces many varieties of trail experience are available. There are short and easy hikes that can be done by small children and old folks with no training or equipment for mountain travel. And also there are long hikes, and difficult hikes, and long-and-difficult hikes, which should be attempted only by experienced wilderness roamers.

Some trails are broad, well-graded, and clearly marked. Others are sketchy, ill-defined tracks built and maintained solely by hooves and boots. In this book, there are even described several non-trail routes which currently are strictly for the skilled brush-ape—though they will, surely, ultimately have trails, and popular ones, and that is why they are included.

There are hikes that can be done by any person capable of putting one foot in front of another for a morning or afternoon. And there are adventures that can take a party back through time to the frontier, into wildlands where the

Bogachiel rain forest (John Spring photo)

walker is utterly on his own, with no help from anyone if things go wrong.

Administration

The three provinces are administered by the National Park Service, by the U.S. Forest Service in the Snoqualmie-Mt. Baker, Wenatchee, Gifford Pinchot, and Olympic National Forests, and in small but important part by the Washington State Department of National Resources. Because regulations on use vary, hikers should be aware of which administrative units they are traveling.

Mount Rainier and Olympic National Parks have been set aside, to use the words of the National Park Act of 1916, "to conserve the scenery and the natural and historic objects and wildlife . . ." Each visitor must therefore enjoy the Parks "in such manner and by such means as will leave them unimpaired for the enjoyment of future generations." A good motto for Park users is: "Take only a picture, leave only a footprint."

Much of both Parks soon will be dedicated as wilderness, so that not only the National Park Act of 1916 but the Wilderness Act of 1964 will apply, giving a still higher degree of protection. Motorized travel on Park trails is forbidden and horse travel closely regulated. Hunting is banned —but not fishing. Pets are not allowed on trails, since their presence disturbs wildlife.

Camping permits are required for all overnight hikers in National Parks, and may be obtained at ranger stations on the entry roads.

Under U.S. Forest Service jurisdiction are the Goat Rocks and Mt. Adams Wildernesses (and hopefully, in the near future, the proposed Alpine Lakes and Cougar Lakes Wildernesses), where "the earth and its community of life are untrammeled by man, where man himself is a visitor who does not remain." Motorized travel is forbidden absolutely and horse travel is beginning to be regulated or even eliminated at some points; foot travel and camping are currently less restricted, though the back-country population explosion will require increasing controls to protect the fragile ecosystems. Wilderness permits, available at ranger stations and National Forest headquarters, are required for all travelers in dedicated Wildernesses.

Other portions of the National Forests are designated now, or may be in future, as recreation areas, scenic areas, roadless areas, or primitive areas, each of which has certain limitations on commodity exploitation and recreation. Multiple-use areas are devoted mainly to logging, though with some consideration of other uses; here things often change violently from one year to the next and the hiker may find roads and trails radically different from descriptions in this book.

Large areas of the Alpine Lakes and South Cascades are in a checkerboard ownership dating from the Northern Pacific Land Grant. The presence of private land intermixed with public land so far has interfered with trail use only here and there, but poses a future threat. The Forest Service is seeking to "block up" the public land by exchanges, but some private owners are uncooperative and the program is not moving as rapidly as could be wished.

Maps

Each hike description in this book lists the appropriate topographic maps (if such are available) published by the U.S. Geological Survey. These can be purchased at mountain equipment shops or map stores or by writing the U.S. Geological Survey, Federal Center, Denver, Colorado 80225. The USGS maps are the hiker's best friend.

The National Forests publish recreation maps which are quite accurate and up-to-date. These maps may be obtained free of charge at ranger stations or by writing the Forest Supervisors at:

Snoqualmie-Mt. Baker National Forest
1601 2nd Avenue
Seattle, WA 98101

Wenatchee National Forest
P.O. Box 811
Wenatchee, WA 98801

Gifford Pinchot National Forest
P.O. Box 449
Vancouver, WA 98660

Olympic National Forest
Federal Building
Olympia, WA 98501

Clothing and Equipment

Many trails described in this book can be walked easily and safely, at least along the lower portions, by any person capable of getting out of a car and onto his feet, and without any special equipment whatever.

To such people we can only say, "welcome to walking—but beware!" Northwest mountain weather, especially on the ocean side of the ranges, is notoriously undependable. Cloudless morning skies can be followed by afternoon deluges of rain or fierce squalls of snow. Even without a storm a person can get mighty chilly on high ridges when—as often happens—a cold wind blows under a bright sun and pure blue sky.

No one should set out on a Cascade or Olympic trail, unless for a brief stroll, lacking warm long pants, wool shirt or sweater, and a windproof and rain-repellent parka, coat, or poncho. (All these in the rucksack, if not on the body during the hot hours.) And on the feet— sturdy shoes or boots with rugged lug soles and a 5-9-inch top to keep out mud and dirt plus two pair of wool socks and an extra pair in the rucksack.

As for that rucksack, it should also contain the Ten Essentials, found to be so by generations of members of The Mountaineers, often from sad experience:

1. Extra clothing—more than needed in good weather.

2. Extra food—enough so something is left over at the end of the trip.

3. Sunglasses—necessary for most alpine travel and indispensable on snow.

4. Knife—for first aid and emergency firebuilding (making kindling).

5. Firestarter—a candle or chemical fuel for starting a fire with wet wood.

6. First aid kit.

7. Matches—in a waterproof container.

8. Flashlight—with extra bulb and batteries.

9. Map—be sure it's the right one for the trip.

10. Compass—be sure to know the declination, east or west.

Camping and Fires

Indiscriminate camping blights alpine meadows. A single small party may trample grass, flowers, and heather so badly they don't recover from the shock for several years. If the same spot is used several or more times a summer, year after year, the greenery vanishes, replaced by the dusty, muddy barrens of "slum camps." The respectful traveler always aims to camp in the woods, or in rocky morainal areas. These alternatives lacking, it is better to use a meadow site already ruined—a slum—rather than extend the destruction into pleasanter virginal places nearby. (If the site is messy, clean it up and feel the warm glow of virtue.) As time goes on and people pressure grows, more and more meadows necessarily will be posted against camping.

Particularly to be avoided are camps immediately beside streams or lakes. Delightful and scenic as such sites are, their use may endanger the water purity, as well as the health of delicate plants. Better to camp at a distance and leave the riverbanks and lakeshores undisturbed for all visitors to enjoy. In many jurisdictions camping is now expressly forbidden within 200 feet of lakes and streams.

Shelter cabins are on a first-come first-served basis, so always carry a tent or tarp. (But never ditch the sleeping area unless and until essential to avoid being flooded out—and afterwards be sure to fill the ditches, carefully replacing any sod that may have been dug up.) Most shelters are crummy and foul from years of abuse and are best avoided; in fact, many shelters are expected to be removed by land administrators in the next few years on the grounds that they are "attractive nuisances."

The bough bed, beloved of the frontier past, is so damaging to vegetation it is obsolete in areas worthy of preservation in a natural condi-

Junior Mountaineers cleaning up Trout Lake

tion, including all the country covered by this book. Instead, carry an air mattress or a foam-plastic pad.

The wood fire, another age-old tradition, also should be considered obsolete in the high country. At best, dry firewood is hard to find at popular camps; the easy wood was burnt years ago. What remains now is from picturesque silver snags and down logs, and in burning these one erodes the very beauty that makes the hike worth taking. Needless to say, green, living wood must never be cut; it doesn't burn anyway.

Both for reasons of convenience and conservation, The Mountaineers strongly urge the highland hiker to carry a lightweight stove for cooking and to depend on clothing and shelter (and sunset strolls) for evening warmth. The pleasures of a roaring blaze on a cold mountain night are indisputable, but for the sake of these pleasures a single party on a single night may use up ingredients of the scenery that were long decades in growing, dying, and silvering.

At remote back-country camps, and in forests, fires may still be built (for a while) with a clear conscience. Again, one should minimize impact by using only established fire pits and using only dead and down wood. When finished, be certain the fire is absolutely out—drown the coals

and stir them with a stick and then drown the ashes until the smoking and steaming have stopped completely and a finger stuck in the slurry feels no heat. Embers can smoulder underground in dry duff for days, spreading gradually and burning out a wide pit—or kindling trees and starting a forest fire.

Litter and Garbage and Sanitation

Ours is a wasteful, throwaway civilization—and something is going to have to be done about that soon. Meanwhile, it is bad wildland manners to leave litter for others to worry about. The rule among considerate hikers is: **If you can carry it in full, you can carry it out empty.**

On a day hike, take back to the road (and garbage can) every last orange peel and gum wrapper.

On an overnight or longer hike, burn all paper (if a fire is built) but carry back all unburnables, including cans, metal foil, plastic, glass, and papers that won't burn.

Don't bury garbage. If fresh, animals will dig it up and scatter the remnants. Burning before burying is no answer either. Tin cans take as long as 40 years to disintegrate completely; aluminum and glass last for centuries. Further, digging pits to bury junk disturbs the ground cover, and iron eventually leaches from buried cans and "rusts" springs and creeks.

Don't leave left-over food for the next travelers; they will have their own supplies and won't be tempted by "gifts" spoiled by time or chewed by animals.

Especially don't cache plastic tarps. Weathering quickly ruins the fabric, little creatures nibble, and the result is a useless, miserable mess.

Keep the water pure. Don't wash dishes in streams or lakes, loosing food particles and detergent. Haul buckets of water off to the woods or rocks, and wash and rinse there. Eliminate body wastes in places well removed from watercourses, and cover the evidence with loose dirt, humus, dead bark, or rocks. Increasingly, popular camps are provided with privies of sorts; use them.

Protect This Land, Your Land

The Cascade and Olympic country is large

and rugged and wild—but it is also, and particularly in the scenic climaxes favored by hikers, a fragile country. If man is to blend into the ecosystem, rather than dominate and destroy, he must walk lightly, respectfully, always striving to make his passage through the wilderness invisible.

The public servants entrusted with administration of the region have a complex and difficult job and they desperately need the cooperation of every wildland traveler. Here, the authors would like to express appreciation to these dedicated men for their advice on what trips to include in this book and for their detailed review of the text and maps. Thanks are due the Superintendent of Olympic National Park, the Supervisors of the Snoqualmie-Mt. Baker, Wenatchee, Gifford Pinchot, and Olympic National Forests, the director of the Washington State Department of National Resources, and their district rangers and other staff members.

On behalf of the U.S. Forest Service and National Park Service and the Washington State Department of Natural Resources and The Mountaineers, we invite Americans—and all citizens of Earth—to come and see and live in their Washington Cascades and Olympics, and while enjoying some of the world's finest wildlands, to vow henceforth to share in the task of preserving the trails and ridges, lakes and rivers, forests and flower gardens for future generations, our children and grandchildren, who will need the wilderness experience at least as much as we do, and probably more.

TABLE OF CONTENTS

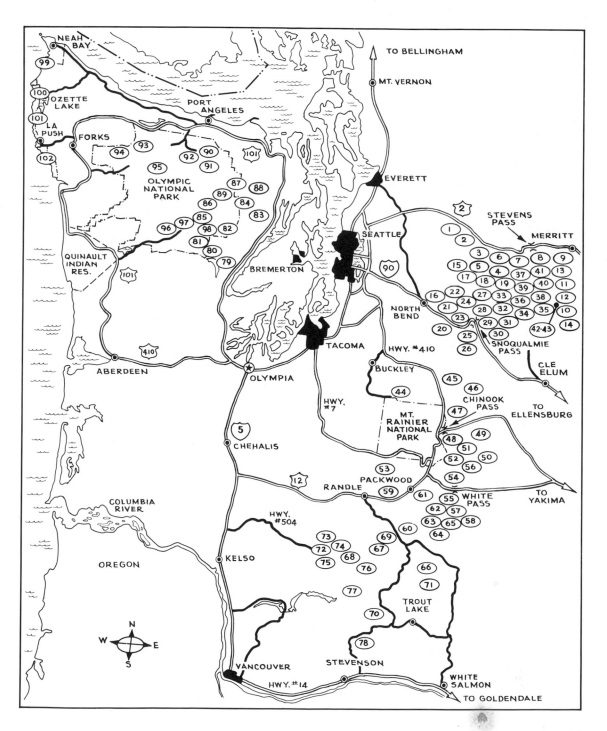

1   MOUNT PERSIS

One of the most dramatic viewpoints of the Cascade front range. A close look at the fierce west wall of Mt. Index. A breathtaking aerial view of the Skykomish River and the town of Index 5000 vertical feet below. A broad panorama westward over Puget Sound lowlands and saltwaterways to the Olympics. And a ring of peaks north, east, and south. If you're lucky enough to reach the summit on a clear day, be sure to have maps along to identify the cities and mountains.

This magnificence so close to the homes of millions of people should be enjoyed by thousands every year, but until the Forest Service builds a trail, only a handful will find their way to the top. Despite a forbidding north face, the mountain is too easy by its west ridge to challenge climbers, and without a trail the west ridge is much too tough for the average hiker. This leaves the peak to the few experienced in off-trail routefinding and willing to beat some brush.

Drive US 2 east from Goldbar 5 miles to No Name Creek (which also may not have a sign). A few hundred feet beyond turn right on an unmarked but well-used logging road. This private road lies on land owned by Burlington-Northern Railroad and often is gated or posted with a sign barring autos. In such case the hike must begin at the highway, elevation 400 feet.

Drive or walk the road, which climbs steeply from the highway, swings westerly around a ridge of Persis into the valley of Proctor Creek, alternately levels, climbs, levels, and finally climbs steeply below the logged-off slopes (mostly private land) of Persis. At 3.6 miles, about 2000 feet, take the second and most-used spur road. As of 1970 this spur could be driven a rough ½-mile farther and 300 feet higher. Car travel ends at a washed-out culvert.

Start hiking from here by 7 a.m. and carry water—there is no shade for the next 1½ miles and the mountain is dry. Climb the spur road to the top of the clearcut and follow it to the very end, about 3000 feet, on the steep west ridge, about 1½ miles from the car. Don't attempt a shortcut to the ridge crest—numerous cliffs are hidden in the trees.

The route is easy to find, staying on the ridge all the way, ascending very steeply. The first short stretch is through a tangle of blowdowns and a little brush, but after that the going is fairly open forest (except for two small patches of vine maple at about 4000 feet). On the descent beware of spur ridges left and right which end in cliffs.

At about 4500 feet the slope gentles. Climb over the top of the 4974-foot false summit (with looks at the awesome north wall of Persis) and drop to 4800 feet in a beautiful setting of rock, heather, gardens, and alpine trees. Lovely and lonesome camping here in early summer while snow water is available. Follow the meadows to the 5452-foot summit and gasp!

Round trip from highway about 14 miles
Hiking time 13-15 hours
High point 5452 feet
Elevation gain 5000 feet
Best June through October
One day
USGS Index

Round trip from road-end about 7 miles
Hiking time 8-9 hours
Elevation gain 3100 feet

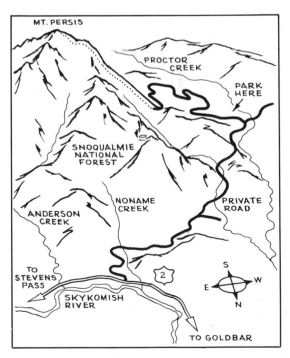

The north face of Mt. Persis. North and Middle Peaks of Mt. Index in the distance.

2 LAKE SERENE

Like Jack climbing the beanstalk, scramble up a ladder of roots from a busy valley of rumbling trains and speeding autos into the quiet haven of a lake held in a tiny scoop in the side of the giant, Mt. Index, whose rough walls leap a dizzying 3000 feet above the serene waters.

Drive US 2 east from Goldbar 6¾ miles. Just before the highway crosses the Skykomish River on a big steel bridge, turn right on the Mt. Index road. At .3 mile turn right on an **unmarked** and very poor one-lane road and drive or walk, passing an equally bad spur road to the right, and at 1½ miles, at an intersection marked "Private," park off the road. Elevation, 1200 feet.

Hike the right-hand road to the abandoned Honeymoon Mine and find the trail, probably unsigned, in brush and second-growth, bearing toward Bridal Veil Falls. The way climbs moderately at first, with views over the Skykomish valley, and then bumps against the foot of the forested cliff and the beginning of the ladderway. The trail was never "constructed," but was beaten out by boots of miners and fishermen and climbers, and scarcely can be recommended as an easy stroll for beginners. However, the tree roots provide convenient steps—plus handholds on the steepest sections—and there is no real danger. The ascent is strenuous but not long.

The trail soon passes an old mine and remnants of a cabin. Walk around the ruins for a close-up look at Bridal Veil Falls. The mine area has the last flat ground and the last drinking water before the lake. From here the way is straight up through forest on roots and rocks and mud, finally easing in grade at the lip of the basin.

Though the lake elevation is only 2509 feet, the Index-shadowed cirque is cold and snowy and alpine. For the most impressive inspections of the great precipice, wander westward and southward along the shores to large boulders fallen from above and to talus thrusting into the waters. (Watch out for falling rocks!) For views of the Skykomish valley, walk a short bit to the outlet, but don't bother going beyond—cliffs make a circuit of the east shore tough and tricky.

Campsites at the lake are heavily used, badly mauled, and thoroughly unappealing. If camping is planned anyway, be sure to carry a stove; the easy firewood is long gone.

The trail is usually free of snow in May, when the lake still remains frozen and partly covered by enormous avalanche fans. However, spring avalanches sometimes send rocks bounding into the woods and even down the trail. Forest Service rangers therefore recommend staying away until June.

Round trip 2 miles
Hiking time 4 hours
High point 2509 feet
Elevation gain 1300 feet
Best June through November
One day or backpack
USGS Index

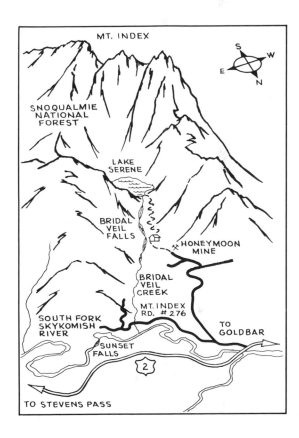

Lake Serene and towering cliffs of Mt. Index

3   TONGA RIDGE-MOUNT SAWYER

The easiest ridge walk on the west side of the Cascades, with grand views, beautiful meadows, and flowers throughout the summer.

Drive US 2 east from Skykomish 1.8 miles and turn right on the Foss River road. At 1.2 miles keep right on the main road. At 2.5 miles go straight ahead at the intersection just after passing under a railroad bridge. At 3.6 miles turn left on Tonga Ridge road No. 2605 for 6¾ miles. Turn right at a junction marked "Tonga Ridge" and continue 2¼ miles to the road-end, elevation 4400 feet.

The hike begins on an old fire trail climbing to the ridge crest. In a couple hundred feet the foot trail turns off the fire trail into forest, winds through woods a while, and then follows the ridge top in meadows. At about 1½ miles the trail leaves the crest to contour around Mt. Sawyer, finally dropping a bit to Sawyer Pass, 3 miles, 4800 feet, dividing the drainages of Burn Creek and Fisher Creek. Good campsites, and also the first water of the trip, in the gentle swale of the pass, a large green meadow (commonly called N. P. Camp) that turns a brilliant red in fall.

For a wide-view side-trip, scramble up 5501-foot Mt. Sawyer, the second large hill seen from the Tonga Ridge approach. Leave the trail wherever the slopes look appealing and plow upward in huckleberry brush, gaining 700 feet. Try it in late August and eat your way through delicious berries. The summit panorama includes Mt. Rainier, Mt. Baker, and Glacier Peak, plus Hinman, Daniel, Sloan, and more. Immediately below are two lakes of the Jewel Lake string, easily reached from Sawyer Pass by consulting a contour map.

The most obvious tread at Sawyer Pass is on the west side, but this is a fishermen's path toward Fisher Lake and soon fades out. The main trail stays to the east side of the pass, then descends 1600 feet into valley forest, crossing several small creeks, passing some logging activities, and joining the Deception Creek trail in 6 miles.

If pick-up transportation can be arranged, interesting one-way hikes can be made from here, exiting via Deception Creek (Hike 6), or Deception Lakes and Surprise Creek (Hike 7), or Deception Pass, a side-trip to Marmot Lake, and Hyas Lake (Hike 41).

Note: A major timber harvest on the east slopes of Mt. Sawyer and Sawyer Pass, above Deception Creek, will soon be complete, and road No. 2605 may then be open to public travel to the end; to get there, instead of turning right at the junction 6¾ miles from Foss River road No. 2622, one would continue on road No. 2605 for 11 miles to the trailhead below Sawyer Pass. Obviously this shortcut would give much quicker access to goals in and beyond upper Deception Creek. However, hikers seek challenges, not shortcuts, and it is therefore fervently urged (and demanded) that the Forest Service live up

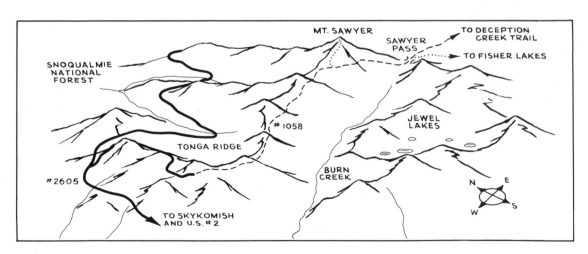

Tonga Ridge trail

to its "multiple use" theory by closing off the
last 3-4 miles of road No. 2605 once the cutting
is finished, thus preserving as trail country an
area that is very heavily used as such, and that
certainly doesn't need "improved" access by
automobile.

Round trip to pass 6½ miles
Hiking time 3 hours
High point 4800 feet
Elevation gain 400 feet
Best July through October
One day or backpack
USGS Scenic

4   NECKLACE VALLEY

A narrow alpine valley carved from the side of Mt. Hinman and appropriately named for its string of small gems—Jade, Emerald, and Opal Lakes. Nearby are Locket and Jewel Lakes. And others. Thanks to the long trail and difficult river crossing, this is much more lonesome country than the Foss Lakes area described in Hike 5.

Drive US 2 east from Skykomish 1.8 miles. Turn right on the Foss River road 3.6 miles to the Tonga Ridge junction, as described in Hike 3, and continue to the East Fork Foss River trail at 4.2 miles. On the left side of the road find a small parking area and the trailhead, elevation 1600 feet.

The trail sign reads 9 miles to Necklace Valley, but the Forest Service log says 8, the figure used here. Be prepared for 8 miles that feel like 9.

The first 5 miles gain only 600 feet and are very pleasant going through forest, following the valley bottom, passing the marshes of Alturas "Lake."

The trail this far is very worthwhile in its own

right, and can be hiked on a day walk or a weekend backpack in May and June when the high country is buried in snow.

The trail crosses the river which flows from the Hinman Glacier on Mt. Hinman and from the Lynch Glacier on Mt. Daniel. On the far bank the trail leaves the river and climbs into the hanging glacial trough, gaining 2400 feet in the 3 miles to the first gem of the necklace, Jade Lake, 4600 feet.

Necklace Valley is a delightful mixture of forest, heather, ice-polished granite—and of course, the lakes. Possibilities for roaming are endless. Campsites are available along the river and at most of the lakes.

From Emerald Lake, about ¼ mile up-valley from Jade Lake, cross a low saddle west to Jewel and Locket Lakes or cross the ridge east to Lake Ilswoot.

From the east side of Opal Lake, another ¼ mile up-valley from Emerald Lake, climb a short step up a tributary creek to Cloudy Lake.

Tougher to attain are La Bohn Lakes, set in granite bowls near the summit of 5600-foot La Bohn Gap. The off-trail route from the head of

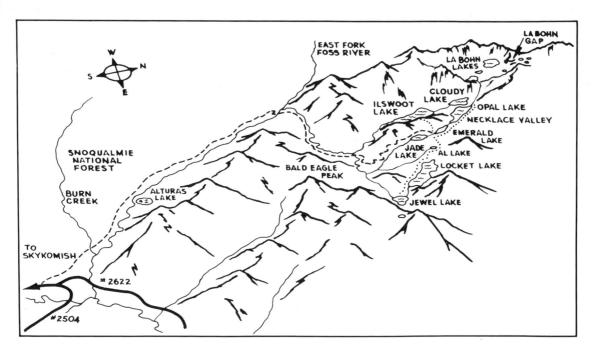

Necklace Valley, LaBohn Gap in distance

Necklace Valley goes abruptly up through cliffs, and though an easy way can be found, at least one hiker has been killed here, and the route cannot be recommended for any but experienced mountain travelers.

Round trip to Jade Lake 16 miles
Allow 2-3 days
High point 4600 feet
Elevation gain 3000 feet
Best late July through October
USGS Skykomish, Big Snow Mountain, Mt. Daniel

5   FOSS LAKES

Lovers of alpine lakes look at the Big Snow Mountain topog map and drool. Crowded onto this single sheet are 10 large lakes and numerous small ones, the rich legacy of ancient glaciers. The West Fork Foss River trail passes four of the lakes and fishermen's paths lead to others. Don't expect privacy—the area has long been famous and extremely popular for its numerous, unusually big, and readily accessible lakes.

Drive US 2 east from Skykomish 1.8 miles. Turn right on the Foss River road 4.2 miles to the East Fork Foss River trail, as described in Hike 4, and continue to West Fork Foss River road No. 2622 at 4.8 miles. Turn left 2 miles to the road-end and trailhead, elevation 1600 feet.

Hike an easy 1½ miles in cool forest to the first of the chain, Trout Lake, 2000 feet. Trees line the shore; through branches are glimpses of rugged cliffs above. This far makes a leisurely afternoon, and the trail is free of snow in May. Many campsites.

The steep, hot, 2-mile climb to Copper Lake, gaining 2000 feet, is something else in late summer. Water is plentiful but always out of reach —splashing in falls on the far hillside, rushing along a deep gully below the trail. The way at last opens into the cliff-walled basin of 3961-foot Copper Lake, surrounded by alpine trees and meadows and talus slopes. The campsites here are heavily used and crowded; others are available at the other lakes, but for any of them be sure to carry a stove.

Though much can be seen in a day or weekend, 3 days or more are needed for a satisfying

Copper Lake

exploration. Copper Lake is the beginning of high-land terrain, with miles of heather and blueberries amid groves of alpine trees, and glacier-smoothed rock knolls and granite buttresses. The crowds steadily diminish beyond Copper.

The lovely cirque of Malachite Lake, 4089 feet, is reached by a steep 1/4-mile path branching from the main trail 1/2 mile before Copper Lake.

Beyond Copper Lake the main trail climbs gently along a stream, passing the best and maybe the only flower display of the trip, to

4204-foot Little Heart Lake, 1 mile from Copper, then crosses a 4700-foot ridge and drops to 4545-foot Big Heart Lake, 2 1/2 miles from Copper.

The formal trail continues beyond the outlet of Big Heart Lake one mile over the end of the ridge to the outlet of 4609-foot Lake Angeline. Chetwoot Lake, 4905 feet, coldest and rockiest of the group, may be reached by leaving the formal trail at about its high point on the ridge and traveling south over the very summit of the high and narrow ridge between Big Heart and Angeline Lakes, down into a saddle, and up once more over the next ridge. The route is a bit rugged but quite feasible, with a beaten footpath much of the way. There is a campsite at Chetwoot from which the upper end of Lake Angeline is readily accessible.

There are also Delta, Azurite, and Otter Lakes, and a dozen or more smaller ones, many visible from the trail and each a jewel in its own right. Routes known to hardy fishermen exist to all of them, and even semblances of boot-beaten track, but essentially these lakes are for the experienced cross-country hiker.

Round trip to Copper Lake 8 miles
Hiking time 6-8 hours
High point 3961 feet
Elevation gain 2300 feet
Best July through October
One day or backpack
USGS Big Snow Mountain

Foss River trail skirting Trout Lake

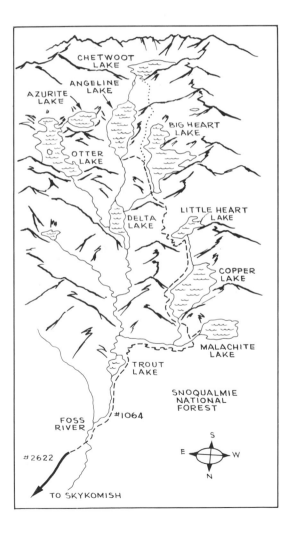

6   DECEPTION CREEK

There is no deception about Deception Creek except to those who believe river routes are always the easiest type. The trail gains and loses elevation constantly, and nears the creek only to cross to the far side—which it does four times in less than 6 miles. The maddening ups and downs and the tricky footlogs and all-summer mud may be discouraging; however, the valley offers the fullest and finest experience of virgin forest and wild water remaining in this portion of the Cascades.

Hikers may still enjoy the difficult valley trail. However, "multiple use" has removed the challenge. The Forest Service has recently built a logging road that allows a party to bypass the first 5 miles of the creek trail and quickly enlarge the mob already crowding Deception Lakes.

Drive US 2 east from Skykomish 7.8 miles to Deception Falls Picnic Area and to a road signed, "Deception Creek Trail." Turn right ½ mile on the powerline service road to the trailhead (no trail sign), elevation 2000 feet.

For the shorter route, follow directions for Tonga Ridge (Hike 3). Drive road No. 2605 4½ miles beyond the Tonga Ridge trail turnoff to where the road intersects trail No. 1058. The trail drops 600 feet in ¾ mile to join the Deception Creek trail near the 5-mile mark.

The hike begins with a down and a short but steep up, then levels off for ½ mile to a footlog crossing of Deception Creek. Now the way climbs above the stream and sidehills up and down through forest. At approximately 2 miles is a crossing of Sawyer Creek; the footlog is a lot higher in the air than the many others on the route; the creek rushes from a waterfall overhung with bushes and trees and gurgles over stones beneath.

At 3 miles Deception Creek is re-crossed on a log. A nice campsite here. The stream is close for the next ½ mile to the third footlog crossing of Deception Creek. After more ups and downs, at 5 miles is the junction with the trail from Sawyer Pass (Hike 3, and see note below). A bit farther is another good camp and in ¼ mile the trail crosses Deception Creek the fourth time, elevation 3200 feet. By now there are occasional views of Mt. Daniel at the valley head.

From this crossing the trail continues briefly in the valley bottom and then quits messing around and starts UP—climbing steeply from the stream, gaining 1200 feet to the Deception Lakes trail junction, 7 miles from the road, 4400 feet.

Here the hiker has a choice. He can stay on the Deception Creek trail, which drops 500 feet back to the creek and then climbs to 4500-foot Deception Pass, 10¼ miles from the road, and a junction with the Cascade Crest Trail; this low route winds through a string of subalpine meadows offering flowers and glimpses of peaks. Or, he can detour to Deception Lakes,

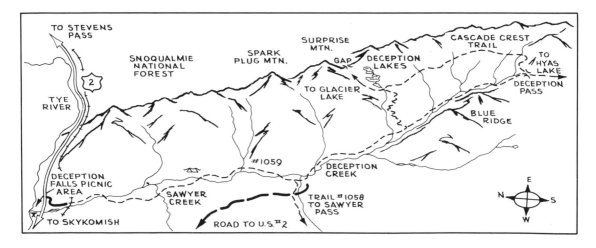

Trail crossing Deception Creek

climbing 700 feet in 1¼ miles, and follow the Cascade Crest Trail from there to Deception Pass; this route contours high on ridges with larger views of mountains and of Lake Clarice across the valley.

For multi-day trips, Deception Creek can be combined with Tonga Ridge (Hike 3), Surprise Lakes (Hike 7), or Marmot and Hyas Lakes (Hike 41).

Round trip to Deception Pass 20½ miles
Allow 2-3 days
High point 4500 feet
Elevation gain 3400 feet in, 900 feet out
Best July through October
USGS Scenic and Mt. Daniel
Round trip from road No. 2605 to Deception Lakes 9½ miles
Elevation gain 2900 feet in, 600 feet out

7   SURPRISE LAKE AND MOUNTAIN

Two alpine lakes surrounded by forest with mountain tops looming over the trees and reflected in the quiet water.

Drive US 2 east from Skykomish 10 miles to Scenic, the west portal of Burlington-Northern Railroad's Cascade Tunnel. Drive into the hamlet of Scenic, cross the railroad track, and in several yards turn right to a small parking lot at the trailhead, elevation 2200 feet.

Hike west along the old road beside the railroad tracks for approximately ½ mile to a powerline. The trail begins from the powerline service road, climbs through the hot-and-brushy clearcut area along the powerline, then enters cool forest. The tread is well-constructed and maintained but the nature of the soil makes for much mud in the first mile. In fact, a few horses can render the path unusable.

In 1 mile the trail fords Surprise Creek; if the water is high, look for a footlog a bit downstream. The steadily-ascending route is mostly in deep woods, but at around 3 miles climbs a rocky knoll with views back toward the Skykomish valley and up to Surprise Mountain. In 4 miles the way passes the old route of the Cascade Crest Trail from Stevens Pass; here too a path

Mt. Daniel from Surprise Gap

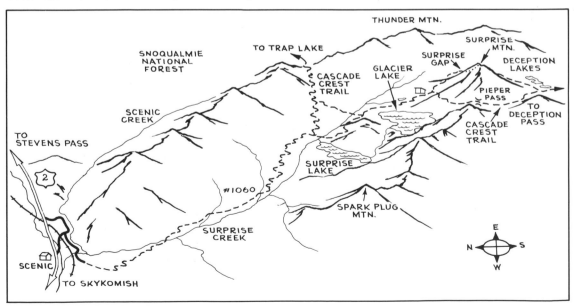

drops 100 feet to Surprise Lake, 4508 feet. Campsites at the lake, which also is a good destination for a day trip.

The valley trail continues uphill, in ¾ mile joining the new Cascade Crest Trail from Stevens Pass. At 1 mile from Surprise Lake is 4806-foot Glacier Lake and at 1½ miles are a lovely little meadow and a shelter cabin; camps here and at the lake.

Now the way opens from greenery into a granite basin under the cliffs of Surprise Mountain and ascends to a junction 2¼ miles from Surprise Lake. The new Crest Trail turns right, climbs to 5900-foot Pieper Pass, and swings around the south slopes of Surprise Mountain. The old trail switchbacks ¼ mile to 5780-foot Surprise Gap. North-slope snow patches linger until mid-July; proceed with caution.

Views from the gap are fine, but for really magnificent vistas find the lookout trail on the west side of the gap and climb 1 steep mile through meadows to the 6330-foot summit of Surprise Mountain. Look south across valley for-

ests of Deception Creek to glacier-gleaming Mt. Daniel and other peaks of the proposed Alpine Lakes Wilderness.

Deception Lakes lie 1 mile and 700 feet below Surprise Gap. They can also be reached by the new 10 percent-grade Crest Trail over Pieper Pass. From the junction, the distance to the lakes via the gap is 1¼ miles, via the pass (Crest Trail) 2¾ miles.

Round trip to Surprise Lake 8 miles
Hiking time 5 hours
High point 4500 feet
Elevation gain 2300 feet
Best late June through October
One day or backpack
USGS Scenic

Round trip to Surprise Mountain 15 miles
Hiking time 9-12 hours
High point 6330 feet
Elevation gain 4100 feet
Best late July through October
One day or backpack
USGS Scenic

8   LAKE JOSEPHINE

Roam fields of heather and blueberries on the Cascade Crest Trail. Linger at small lakes and large. Enjoy alpine trees and flowers and talus and streams and views over deep valleys. However, the trip is not all pure pleasure: the trail is partly obscured by ski slopes and the clearcut swaths of power transmission lines.

Drive US 2 to Stevens Pass and park near the Forest Service guard station, elevation 4056 feet. Pick up the Cascade Crest Trail on the far side of the parking lot and follow it through the ski area, making very sure to stick with the trail markers to avoid getting lost in the general confusion of the first ¼ mile.

Past the ski slopes the way ascends steadily in trees and rockslides to the Cascade Crest at 1 mile, 5100 feet, and then descends the east side 100 feet to the powerline clearcut and service road. (A somewhat shorter approach can be made by driving the Mill Creek road, which takes off from US 2 at 3 miles east of Stevens Pass, and hiking up the steep powerline maintenance road to intersect the Crest Trail.)

Again, the route through the powerline area may be very confusing. Go left down the road

Lake Josephine

about ½ mile, losing 300 feet, watching for trail markers leading away from the road and clearcut into a traverse through bits of forest, patches of well-watered meadow, and open talus with views out Mill Creek to the Nason Creek valley and Nason Ridge.

At 3 miles is 4595-foot Lake Susan Jane, a picturesque tarn (good camps) bounded by forest on one side and steep mountainside on the other.

From here shift into low gear and gain 400 feet to heather-and-berry meadows. Traverse gardens to the edge of a cliff and a 5000-foot junction, 3½ miles, with the Icicle Creek trail. Look down to the rock-and-forest cirque of Lake Josephine, 4681 feet, and beyond to the Stuart Range. Take the Icicle Creek trail and descend gently around the basin 350 feet to the lake

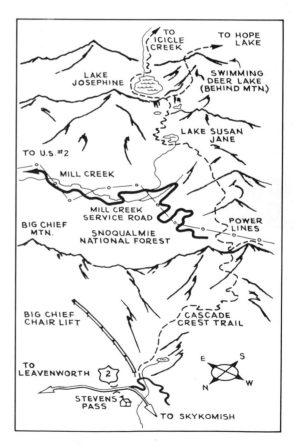

Cascade Crest Trail near Lake Susan Jane

and campsites near the outlet, 4½ miles from Stevens Pass.

The blue, sparkling lake is appealing, but so too are the high wanders. Before dropping to the shores, ascend heather slopes southwest to the 5500-foot ridge and long views. Or find the two small tarns in the meadow a few hundred feet west of the junction. Or follow the Crest Trail a mile from the junction to a view of Swimming Deer Lake.

If pick-up transportation can be arranged, a one-way hike can be made south on the Crest Trail to Surprise Lake (Hike 7), exiting at Scenic on US 2.

Round trip to Lake Josephine 9 miles
Hiking time 7 hours
High point 5500 feet
Elevation gain 1600 feet in, 850 feet out
Best mid-July through October
One day or backpack
USGS Stevens Pass

9 LARCH LAKE

A high mountain lake, rimmed by rocks and groves of larch, in the shadow of the tall and rugged Chiwaukum Mountains on the northeast edge of the Alpine Lakes area.

Tragically, much of the surrounding region is privately owned as a consequence of the infamous Northern Pacific Land Grant of 1864, and in 1973, despite strenuous efforts by conservationists, Wenatchee National Forest and Pack River Lumber Company began building a system of new roads to allow logging of both private and public timber. Take the hike—and return mourning the destruction and primed to fight to prevent butchering of still more of this superb wildland.

There are two approaches to Larch Lake: a well-graded trail over McCue Ridge; or a valley walk along Chiwaukum Creek, easy except for 2 very poor miles. Despite the rough stretch, the creek route is recommended. The forest is lovely (as long as it lasts), there are frequent charming views of the stream, and the way crosses three nice bridges, one of them just below a waterfall. Both approaches are the same length but the ridge trail climbs 300 feet higher going in and makes a 500-foot ascent coming out.

For the McCue Ridge route, which during the 1970s will be messed up by Pack River's logging operations, drive US 2 east from Stevens Pass 17 miles. Just opposite a highway rest area turn south around a pasture. There are numerous logging spurs but the correct way is well-marked. At 1.5 miles find Lake Julius trail No. 1584, elevation 2500 feet.

The trail follows Roaring Creek, climbing to a junction with McCue Ridge trail No. 1574 at 5½ miles, 5600 feet. Keep left, ascending to the ridge top at 5750 feet. At this point the ridge is timbered; for views, walk a path a few hundred feet east on the crest and look over a big patch of buckbrush, or snowbrush (ceanothus). Below is the vast Chiwaukum valley, west are the Chiwaukum Mountains, and south are Snowgrass Mountain and the Stuart Range. From the ridge the trail drops 550 feet to Chiwaukum Lake at 7½ miles; campsites along the shores (but **do not** camp right next to the water) and in a large, horsey area at the head of the lake in Ewing Basin. A way trail traverses the long

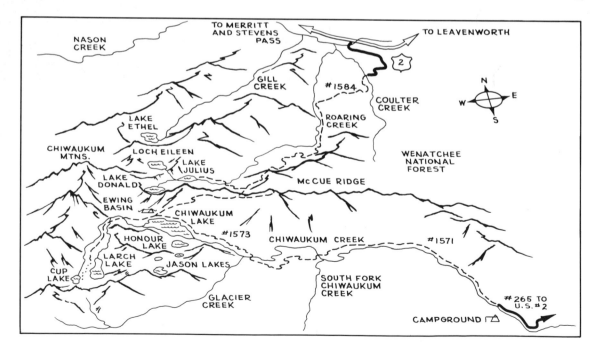

Larch Lake and Chiwaukum Mountains

basin and climbs steeply into meadowlands, at 10 miles reaching 6078-foot Larch Lake and many good camps.

For the Chiwaukum Creek route, drive US 2 east from Stevens Pass 25 miles and about ½ mile before reaching Tumwater Campground turn south on a rough road leading in 2 miles to a campground and trailhead, elevation 2200 feet.

Trail No. 1571 follows close by the creek in deep forest, gradually ascending. At 4 miles turn right on trail No. 1573 and at 5 miles begin climbing steeply, with many switchbacks, on a badly-eroded tread consisting mainly of loose schist, gaining 1200 feet in a little more than a mile. At 7 miles the unpleasantness ends as

5210-foot Chiwaukum Lake is attained. Follow the shore ½ mile to a junction with the McCue Ridge trail described above and continue to Larch Lake at 10 miles.

Among the possible explorations from Larch Lake are a scramble up among the 8000-foot Chiwaukum Mountains and a walk to tiny Cup Lake, set in a little north-facing cirque that doesn't melt free of snow until September, if then.

Round trip via Chiwaukum Creek 20 miles
Allow 2-3 days
High point 6078 feet
Elevation gain 3700 feet
Best mid-July through October
USGS Chiwaukum Mountains

37

10   ENCHANTMENT LAKES

A legendary group of lakes in rock basins over 7000 feet high amid the splintered Cashmere Crags of the Stuart Range; one of the most famous places in the entire Cascade Mountains. Large lakes, small ponds, gigantic slabs of ice-polished granite, flower gardens, heather meadows, groves of larch, lone trees gnarled and twisted by the elements, waterfalls, snow-

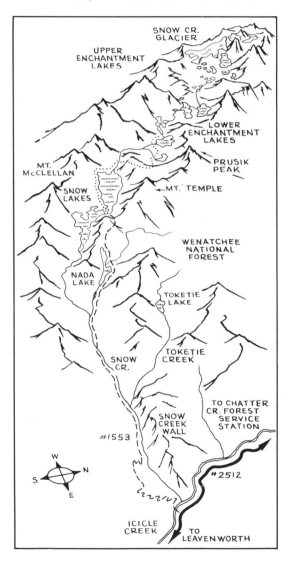

fields, and glaciers. Visit in summer for flowers, in late September to see the autumn gold of larch.

This is not a trip for beginners. The way is long, steep, and grueling. A strong hiker needs at least 12 hours to reach the high lakes. The average hiker takes 2 days. The rest never make it.

Drive US 2 east from Stevens Pass to Leavenworth. On the west outskirts of town turn south on Icicle road No. 2512. At 4 miles turn left into the Snow Lakes trail parking area, elevation 1600 feet.

Snow Lakes trail No. 1553 crosses the river and immediately starts up—and up. Motorbikes long have been prohibited, and now horses are not allowed prior to September 15. The way switchbacks upward in forest, with views in the early part to the granite cliffs of Snow Creek Wall. Small camps at approximately 2 miles, 2800 feet, offer a break in the journey for parties with heavy packs or not too much energy and wishing to make the approach in easy stages. At 5½ miles is Nada Lake, 5000 feet, and good camps. At 6¾ miles the trail ends in a large campsite between the two Snow Lakes at 5415 feet. To the north rises 8292-foot Mt. Temple and to the south 8364-foot Mt. McClellan. All beginners and most average hikers find this far enough, and these lakes magnificent enough—as indeed they are, but it just happens their beauty can't hold a candle to what lies above.

To continue to the Enchantments, cross the low dam between the two lakes. Pause to note this rather weird interference with nature: like a bathtub, water is drained through a hole in the bottom of the upper lake (which thus has a fluctuating shoreline) and is used to guarantee a pure intake for the Leavenworth Fish Hatchery; probably few people imagined, when the project was perpetrated back in the 1930s, that Snow Lakes would become as popular as they now are.

Follow a narrow path winding along the left shore. Go clear around the south end of the lake and cross the inlet stream. Then pick up a path marked by cairns leading straight up towards Mt. Temple. The first 700 or so vertical feet are in trees and brush, scrambling up steep granite boulders. Brush yields to a meadow mixed with boulders, still steep. From the top of the

Gnome Tarn and Little Annapurna

meadow at about 6800 feet the route traverses left to cross Trauma Rib, then proceeds over granite slabs towards a waterfall and the first lake. From here walking is a joy, and mostly very easy.

The nomenclature of the lakes, which until recently had only a group name, is disputed. The Starks, who know the area over many years, and in every season, proposed individual names appropriate to the theme of "enchantment," drawing on various mythologies. A lake and its sword-like rock peninsula became Lake Viviane and Excalibur Rock. Other lakes and tarns they called Rune, Talisman, Valkyrie, Leprechaun, Naiad, Lorelei, Dryad, Pixie, Gnome, Brisingamen, Brynhild, Reginleif, Sprite, and Titania. And there is Troll Sink (a pond), Valhalla Cirque, Tanglewood, and many more. The Forest Service, however, chose to decorate the map with trite, conventional names that immediately became "official"—for now.

Lower Enchantment Basin, at 7000 feet, is friendliest for camping—carry a stove because new regulations forbid native fuel fires in order to protect the beautiful silvered snags and logs.

Upper Enchantment Basin, at 7500 feet, has a wild, desolate splendor. Some of its lakes are clear and some are jade-colored by rock milk and some are frozen solid all summer. There are small glaciers, great slabs of ice-sculptured granite, and grand views of a cold high wilderness.

Round trip to Snow Lakes 13½ miles
Allow 2 days
High point 5415 feet
Elevation gain 3800 feet
Best July through mid-November
USGS Mt. Stuart and Liberty

Round trip to Lower Enchantment Lakes 20 miles
Allow 3-4 days
High point 7000 feet
Elevation gain 5400 feet
Best late July through mid-October

11   LAKE CAROLINE

Another famous beauty spot of the Alpine Lakes region. Meadows, a wealth of rugged granite crags, spectacular views—and lovely lakes, of course. A special treat is the great north face of 9415-foot Mt. Stuart, seen from close enough to make out crevasses in the hanging glaciers.

But again, the wreckers are at work. A logging road has shortened the trail 3 miles in the last 4 years, and this is only the beginning. Unless they can be halted by a mass uprising of irate hikers, the Forest Service and private landowners plan to push the road all the way to Little Eight Mile Lake, wiping out several more miles of superb forest and degrading the wilderness integrity of the entire area. Moreover, an outfit called Mt. Cashmere Inc. is seeking necessary state permits for a recreational subdivision in the very basin of Lake Caroline, on land "owned" by Pack River Lumber Company, the chalets to be attained by helicopter. Hike—then fight. Come back from the hills and write letters of protest to the Forest Service, congressmen, and senators.

Drive US 2 east from Stevens Pass to Leavenworth. On the west outskirts of town turn south on Icicle Creek road No. 2512. At 8.5 miles turn left across a new bridge on road No. 2412 up Eight Mile Creek, climbing steeply 3 miles to the trailhead, elevation 3800 feet. Logging operations make for a bit of confusion, but Eight Mile Lake Trail No. 1552, on the uphill side of the road, is clearly signed. A short loop road has been graveled into the old trail junction, providing limited parking.

The trail ascends moderately through splendid old forest—doomed, unless given a last-minute reprieve, to be hacked down and shipped to Japan—following along Eight Mile Creek 2½ miles to Little Eight Mile Lake, 4400 feet, and a junction. The left fork goes ½ mile up the valley to 4641-foot Eight Mile Lake and good camps. The lake is ringed by woods but awesome rock walls rise far above the trees.

The right fork climbs an endless series of switchbacks (hot and thirsty on sunny days) up from the valley, first in timber, then emerging into meadows. The labor is rewarded by steadily improving views to the jagged spires of the Stuart Range and finally the tall thrust of Mt. Stuart itself. At 5½ miles the way reaches the alpine basin of Lake Caroline, 6190 feet. The most attractive campsites are ½ mile farther and 200 feet higher at Little Lake Caroline, surrounded by meadows.

The best is yet to come. The 2-mile hike to 7200-foot Windy Pass, on good trail amid flowers and larches, is an absolute must. For broader views walk the ridge towards 8501-foot Mt. Cash-

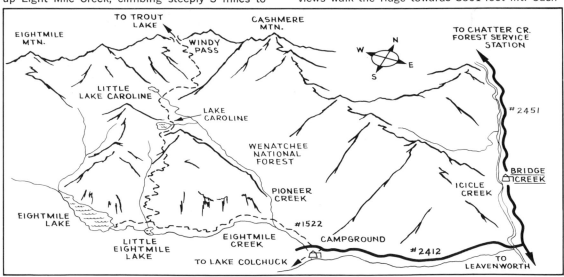

Mt. Stuart from near Windy Pass

mere—but don't try for the summit; the last pitches are strictly for climbers.

An alternate return route to civilization—though not to the starting point—can be made by going 8 miles from Windy Pass down the Trout Creek trail to Chatter Creek Guard Station.

Round trip 11 miles
Hiking time 8 hours
High point 6190 feet
Elevation gain 2400 feet
Best mid-July through October
One day or backpack
USGS Chiwaukum Mountains

Mt. Stuart from Lake Stuart

12   LAKE STUART-COLCHUCK LAKE

Two beautiful lakes amid alpine forests and granite cliffs of the Stuart Range. Hike to the emerald waters of Colchuck Lake and contemplate the towering crags above, decorated with two small glaciers. Or, to cure itchy feet, visit nearby Lake Stuart and explore onward to higher and lonesomer country and grand views of Mt. Stuart.

Unfortunately, the approach is through a checkerboard of mixed ownership where private and public land managers are cooperating to ravage the wilderness with logging roads. This is the tragic legacy of the Northern Pacific Land Grant, aggravated by a notorious example of "multiple-abuse." To take the hike—which grows shorter year by year—is to become very sad and very mad.

From Bridge Creek Campground (Hike 11) drive 4 miles on road No. 2412A to the trailhead, elevation 3600 feet. Find Lake Stuart-Colchuck Lake trail No. 1552A at a sharp turn of the road on the creek side.

The trail parallels Mountaineer Creek on a constant upward grade for 1 mile, then switchbacks up the steepening valley to a junction at 2½ miles, 4600 feet.

The left trail (a rough path) crosses Mountaineer Creek and ascends with many switchbacks, in open forest among numerous granite knolls, along the cascading waters of the East Fork Mountaineer Creek. During the final ¼ mile the way bypasses a waterfall, leaves the creek, and comes to a tiny, almost landlocked lagoon of Colchuck Lake, 5570 feet, 5 miles. Incredibly, this lovely blue-green lake, like others in the area, is drained for use by the Icicle Irrigation District. Camping at the lagoon or near the outlet.

The right trail proceeds gently up the main fork of Mountaineer Creek to the wooded shores, clear blue water, and tall cliffs of Lake Stuart, 5064 feet, 5½ miles. Campsites near the point where the trail first reaches the lake and around the south shore. For wandering, follow the trail ¾ mile beyond the lake to a marshy meadow under the towering cliffs of Mt. Stuart, then scramble rocks dotted with isolated larches to Horseshoe Lake, well above timberline at 6200 feet. Continue to the crest of Jack Ridge for better views of the north wall of 9415-foot Mt. Stuart.

Round trip to Colchuck Lake 10 miles
Hiking time 8 hours
High point 5570 feet
Elevation gain 2000 feet
Best mid-July through October
One day or backpack
USGS Chiwaukum and Mt. Stuart

Round trip to Lake Stuart 11 miles
Hiking time 7 hours
High point 5064 feet
Elevation gain 1500 feet
Best mid-July through October
One day or backpack

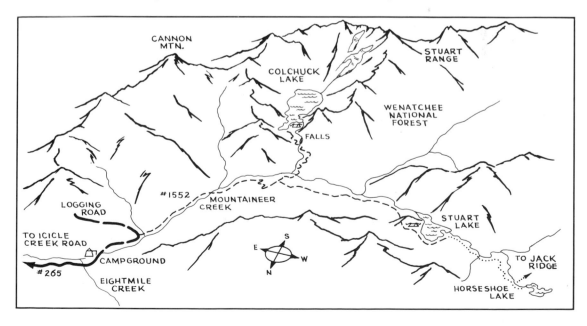

Icicle Ridge trail. Mt. Stuart in distance

13   LAKE MARY

Some hikers claim this is the loveliest part of the entire Alpine Lakes area. None denies the extraordinary beauties of the miles of flowers, grass, heather, and huckleberries, lakes and ponds and snowfields, and a succession of dream-like views—a highland designed for endless roaming.

Drive US 2 east from Stevens Pass to Leavenworth. On the west outskirts of town turn south on Icicle road No. 2451. At 8.5 miles pass Eight Mile junction and at 16.7 miles cross Icicle Creek on a concrete bridge. At 18.5 miles are the road-end and trailhead, elevation 2900 feet.

Icicle Creek trail No. 1551 goes upstream in forest, over several little creeks with campsites, to a junction at 2½ miles, 3000 feet. Turn right on Wildhorse trail No. 1592, cross Icicle Creek, and start up. Within a mile cross Frosty Creek (fill canteens—the next steep miles are long and waterless and can be scorching). Now comes a punishing series of switchbacks and hot traverses as the trail ascends the valley of Frosty Creek, gaining 3000 feet in less than 4 miles and leaving woods for parkland. At 6¾ miles pass a side-trail descending to tree-ringed Lake Margaret, and at 7½ miles attain the open crest of 5800-foot Frosty Pass and a junction with Icicle Ridge trail No. 1570.

Ascend the ridge trail east ½ mile along the alpine slopes of Snowgrass Mountain and find a short way trail dropping to Lake Mary, 6100 feet, a grand place for a basecamp. If the basin is crowded, go another long mile over a little pass to Upper Florence Lake, 6500 feet. Many other fine camps can be found elsewhere in the area.

Plan to spend a full, rich day wandering the Icicle Ridge trail to 6800-foot Ladies Pass, overlooking Lake Brigham and Lake Flora. The distance from Lake Mary is only 2 miles but the constant views of meadows and peaks and valleys slow the pace to the speed of a worm.

Other explorations abound: from Ladies Pass, ascend a path up a shoulder of Cape Horn and then scramble to the 7300-foot summit; also from Ladies Pass, take the trail traversing slopes of Cape Horn to the cold and rocky tarn of Lake Edna; from Lake Mary, follow the easy ridge crest to the very top of 7993-foot Snowgrass Mountain and a panorama of the Chiwaukum Mountains, the Wenatchee Mountains, the Stuart Range, and much more; from Frosty Pass, walk the Wildhorse trail north a bit more than a mile and then climb to 6242-foot Lake Grace. A week of rambling is scarcely enough.

If transportation can be arranged, a one-way trip can be made down the South Fork Chiwaukum Creek trail 12 miles from Ladies Pass to the road. Maps show a trail down Chatter Creek, but this route is not recommended: the trail was abandoned after a big slide and is now almost impossible to follow; several parties have lost the tread and gotten hung up in cliffs.

Round trip to Lake Mary 16 miles
Allow 2-3 days
High point 6200 feet
Elevation gain 3300 feet
Best mid-July through October
USGS Chiwaukum Mountains

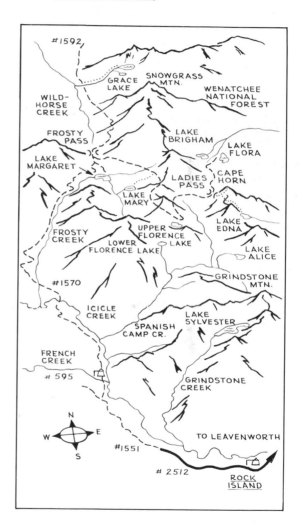

Ingalls Creek about 5 miles from the road

14   INGALLS CREEK

The longest wilderness valley remaining in the Cascades outside the far north, 16 miles of trail climbing from low forest to high meadows, passing constantly changing views of the spectacular Stuart Range.

Hike this trail the first week of June when the first 5 miles are lined with trillium, gold-colored paintbrush, and a few calypso orchids thrown in. If you're too early for trillium, there will be glacier lilies. If you're too late for trillium, there will be queen's cup.

Drive US 97 north from Swauk (Blewett)

Pass 12.5 miles and turn left on the Ingalls Creek road about 1 mile to the road-end and trailhead, elevation 1953 feet.

The trail ascends steadily but gently, alternating between groves of trees and patches of avalanche brush, mostly in sight and always in sound of roaring Ingalls Creek, with tantalizing glimpses of the rocky summits of the Stuart Range, and later, looks to fantastic spires.

In early June hikers usually will encounter snow patches from 4 miles or so, and difficult going beyond the vicinity of Falls Creek, 6 miles, 3200 feet. The lovely Falls Creek Camp is reached by a side-trail across Ingalls Creek, which is much too deep and swift to ford while melt-water is rushing. In any season this point makes a good turnaround for day-trippers.

The way continues upward along the al-most-straight fault-line valley (granite on one side, sediments and metamorphics on the other), the forest becoming subalpine and open, the views growing and shifting. Tributary creeks are crossed often enough to satisfy thirst; pleasant camps are frequent.

From Porcupine Creek, about 10 miles, 4100 feet, the path steepens a bit and sidehills above Ingalls Creek, the timber increasingly broken by meadows. Now the dramatic cliffs and but-tresses of 9415-foot Mt. Stuart, second-highest nonvolcanic peak in the state, dominate the scene.

At about 13½ miles, 4800 feet, the trail nears Ingalls Creek and commences a comparatively earnest ascent, climbing parkland and flowers and talus to Stuart Pass, 16 miles, 6400 feet. On the far side the tread descends Jack Creek to Chatter Creek Forest Station on Icicle Creek.

All along the upper valley the open country invites easy off-trail wanderings, such as to Longs Pass (Hike 42). From a camp in the de-lightful basin under Stuart Pass one can spend days exploring—begin by contouring meadows from the pass to 6463-foot Ingalls Lake (Hike 43).

Round trip to Falls Creek Camp 12 miles
Hiking time 6 hours
High point 3200 feet
Elevation gain 1200 feet
Best late May through November
One day or backpack
USGS Liberty and Mount Stuart

Round trip to Stuart Pass 32 miles
Allow 3-5 days
High point 6400 feet
Elevation gain 4400 feet
Best July through October

Trilliums

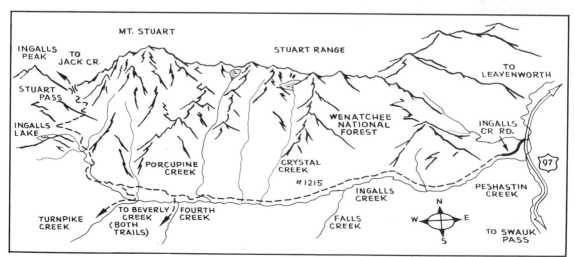

Anderson Lake, snow-covered in late June. Treen Peak, left, and Garfield Mountain, center

15   LENNOX CREEK

Waterfalls, broad slopes of heather meadows, views of peaks and valleys, and a quiet lake—all in a portion of the Cascades which has been ignored by public officials and thus, because of complicated and difficult access, has been little traveled. After lying in limbo for many years, this particular trail was reopened in 1970, and it won't be long before hikers discover the beauties of the North Fork Snoqualmie country and demand it be given deserved status by inclusion in the proposed Alpine Lakes Wilderness.

Drive Interstate 90 to North Bend, turn north on North Ballart Street (second street east from the stoplight), and proceed through town to the outskirts, where the street changes in name to North Fork Road (county), sometimes called the Lake Hancock Road. In 7.5 miles pass the Lake Hancock junction and at about 21 miles (mostly and increasingly rough) enter Snoqualmie National Forest; note a marked improvement in the road, now designated No. 250. At the boundary the road forks; keep right, cross Lennox Creek, and drive 4 miles to two small bridges over island-divided channels of Lennox Creek. About 1/4 mile farther is a fork; keep right on road No. 250B, heading up Cougar Creek drainage a short, switchbacking mile to the road-end at a hogback in a clearcut, elevation 2700 feet.

The trail (unmarked in 1970) starts steeply up the hogback on a bulldozer track, in less than 1/4 mile going from logged barrens into forest and passing a miner's cabin. Now the way contours the east side of Dog Mountain, traversing shoulders of a large avalanche chute. At about 2 miles the route enters a land of heather laced by numerous creeklets. Directly below the meadows and a bit hard to see is the spectacular waterfall of one of the tributaries of Lennox Creek.

At about 3 1/4 miles, 4600 feet, the trail gains a wooded saddle in the ridge. Enjoy the views down to Taylor River and across the valley to Treen Peak and a most unfamiliar aspect of Garfield Mountain.

From the saddle the trail switch-backs down 400 feet in a rough 1/2 mile to little Anderson Lake, surrounded by patches of heather and lots of trees. Camping is nice, and, as of 1970, quite private.

Round trip to Anderson Lake 7½ miles
Hiking time 5 hours
High point 4600 feet
Elevation gain 1900 feet in, 400 feet out
Best July to early November
One day or backpack
USGS Mt. Si and Snoqualmie Lake

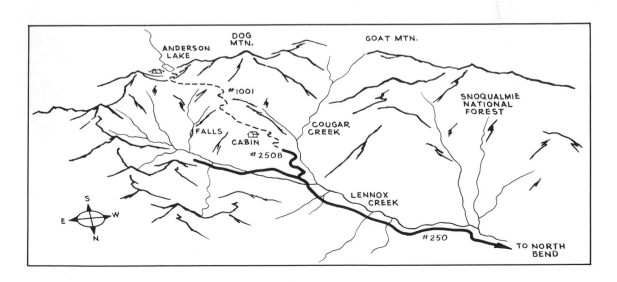

16   MOUNT SI

Climb steeply to the top of a fault scarp rising high above lowlands at the west edge of the Cascades. Look down to the Snoqualmie River meandering by the towns of North Bend and Snoqualmie and through green farms. If the smog isn't too thick, look west to Seattle and Puget Sound and the Olympic Mountains.

Si is a striking landmark at the gateway to the Cascades and is close to the city and therefore is perhaps the most heavily-traveled peak in the state. Mountaineers use the trail for conditioning, Boy Scouts come in troops, and families with little children, and elderly folk and young lovers and lone roamers—a cross-section of humanity (in fact, about 10,000 hikers a year) may be encountered on a typical Sunday.

By May of normal years the way is entirely clear of snow. Sometimes the mountain is briefly bare even in midwinter, and the trail usually can be hiked to high viewpoints in any month.
any month.

Drive Interstate 90 to North Bend. Exactly 1 mile from the east edge of town turn left on 432nd S.E. (Stilson Road), cross the westbound highway lane and continue straight ahead over the Middle Fork Snoqualmie River. Turn right at the first intersection. Drive 2.5 miles to a poorly-marked parking lot for 175 cars, a picnic area,

and the trailhead, elevation 650 feet. The trail is signed for hikers only.

The first ½ mile is in alders, then second-growth firs 60-70 years old. At 1 mile is a vista point on a big rock alongside the trail. At 1¾ miles enter Snag Flat, covered by a mixture of old snags and huge fir trees, some 8 feet in diameter, that survived the fires. Water here about 200 feet off the main trail on a spur going ½ mile to a viewpoint.

The trees get smaller but views are scarce until the old trail is intersected at 3 miles, just below the ridge, a mile from the top. The way follows a rocky shoulder with broad panoramas to Haystack Basin, at the foot of the cliffs of the final peak. The Department of Natural Resources, which relocated the trailhead and built the new path after the old one was partially obliterated by logging operations, plans to install pit toilets and primitive campsites. However, there is no water after the last snow melts, usually in May, so carry enough for cooking or else hike up after dinner, enjoy the night on top—thousands of lights below and millions of stars above—and return to the car for breakfast. There are no other camps on the route.

The Haystack can be climbed by crossing the basin to the northeast side and scrambling a steep, loose-rock gully, but the ascent is a bit

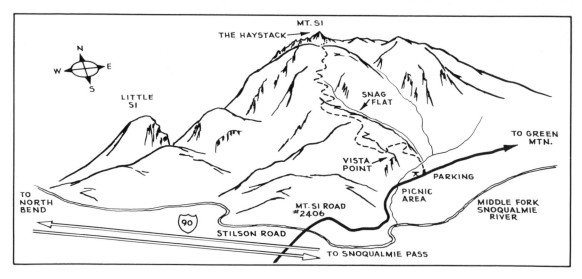

North Bend from edge of Haystack Basin

difficult and quite hazardous, and the summit view is only slightly better than that from the basin.

Round trip 8 miles
Hiking time 8 hours
High point 4167 feet
Elevation gain 3500 feet
Best April through November
One day
USGS on the corner of Mt. Si, Snoqualmie, North Bend, and Bandera

17 SNOQUALMIE-DEER-BEAR-DOROTHY LAKES

A short forest trail to four large subalpine lakes that for many decades, even when the hike was very long, were popular with fishermen and Boy Scout troops seeking a wilderness exper-ience. Now that logging roads have pushed far up the valleys, family groups, including tiny children, have joined the Sunday-afternoon throng. All the lakes offer good but heavily-used campsites.

Drive Interstate 90 east from North Bend 4 miles. Turn left at the second road (Edgewick

Upper end of Lake Dorothy (John Spring photo)

Road) beyond Ken's Truck Town Service Station and cross the west-bound highway lanes onto Middle Fork Snoqualmie River road No. 2445, signed "Taylor River Campground." Drive 15 miles to the Taylor River junction and turn left on the very rough (drive with caution) Taylor River road No. 2445 for 6.2 miles to a large clearcut and the road-end and Snoqualmie Lake trailhead, elevation 1865 feet. **Note:** Eventually the road may be closed at Otter Falls, adding 1 mile and 200 feet of elevation gain to the hike.)

The trail begins by sidehilling a logged-off slope. Entering deep shadows of virgin forest, the often-muddy path switchbacks steadily upwards (with many shortcuts), going near the roar of Nordrum Falls, remaining in lovely trees the entire way to Snoqualmie Lake, 2¼ miles, 3147 feet. Most people, whether day hikers or campers, stop here.

The trail swings around the north side of the basin, climbs to Deer Lake (3 miles, 3583 feet), levels out along the shores, climbs a bit to Bear Lake (3½ miles, 3610 feet), and goes by the lake on the flat to 4 miles.

Now the path rises into patches of heather and huckleberries among the trees, at 4½ miles topping out on the 3800-foot ridge dividing the drainages of the Taylor and Miller Rivers. No trip to the area is complete without these views down to the largest lake of the group, island-dotted Dorothy, set amid forests and gray-white cliffs, and views north to the Miller River valley, and views southeast to the dominant peak of the vicinity, 6670-foot Big Snow Mountain.

The trail drops 1 mile from the divide into a big, soggy meadow at the head of 3058-foot Lake Dorothy, crosses the inlet stream (by boulder-hopping or wading), and follows the east shore through trees 2 miles to the outlet.

To approach Lake Dorothy from the Skykomish River:

Drive US 2 east 17½ miles from Goldbar and just before the highway tunnel turn right on the road past Money Creek Campground. In 1 mile join the Miller River road and drive to the end, 9.3 miles from US 2, and the trailhead, elevation 2100 feet.

The trail shortly crosses the Miller River on a bridge and follows the west bank a few

hundred feet before turning abruptly towards the lake, reached in 1½ miles.

Round trip to Taylor-Miller divide 9 miles
Hiking time 6 hours
High point 3800 feet
Elevation gain 2000 feet
Best July through October
One day or backpack
USGS Snoqualmie Lake

One-way trip from Taylor River road to Miller River road
9 miles
Hiking time 6 hours

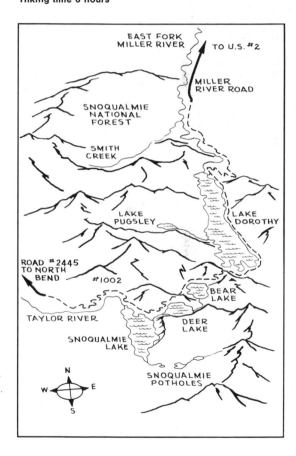

Hester Lake trail

18   HESTER LAKE-MYRTLE LAKE

Two high lakes, one offering some scenery and lots of solitude, the other lots of scenery—and people. However, the fishermen crowds don't climb the ridge where the views and meadow-wandering are.

Drive the Middle Fork Snoqualmie River road (Hike 17) to the Taylor River junction. Keep right on road No. 241 for 6 miles to the tiny Dingford Campground and the Dingford Creek trailhead, elevation 1400 feet.

The trail switchbacks steeply and hotly upward 1 mile through second-growth trees seeded after logging operations in the late 1940s, then gradually gentles out in cool virgin forest of tall, old Douglas fir and hemlock, going along constantly close to the tumble and roar of Dingford Creek. At about 2 miles, 2600 feet, is a ford of Goat Creek and an unmaintained fishermen's side-trail climbing a rough 1 mile to Horseshoe Lake and Goat Lake. At 3 miles, 2900 feet, the trail forks; a nice campsite here beside the creek.

The right fork, to Hester Lake, is in poor shape and will be allowed to stay that way for

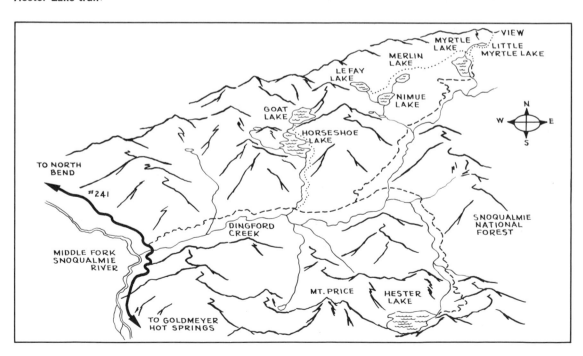

Oyster mushrooms growing in forest along the Middle fork Snoqualmie River

people wanting to get away from people. The trail crosses Dingford Creek, ascends moderately at first in subalpine meadow-marshes and patches of trees, then goes straight uphill to Hester Lake, 3888 feet, 2 miles from Dingford Creek. The deep blue lake is set in a cirque gouged in the side of 5600-foot Mt. Price; impressive cliffs rise from the shores, around which are good camps.

The left fork, to Myrtle Lake, is being improved for hikers and horses. The trail ascends easily in open forest, passing several meadows; the biggest difficulty (in season) is making any progress at all through the delicious blueberries. At 3 miles from the forks is Myrtle Lake, 3777 feet, amid clumps of alpine trees interspersed with huckleberry-covered meadows. Campsites at the lake and on higher benches.

For explorations, go around the east shore and find (if possible—it's not easy) a faint trail to Little Myrtle Lake. Continue another ¼ mile to the 4400-foot top of the ridge and views north to Lake Dorothy and south to Big Snow Mountain, 6670 feet. Alternatively, climb the slopes west from Myrtle Lake and roam the ridges and fields of blueberries to Merlin, Niume, and LeFay Lakes.

Round trip to Myrtle Lake 10 miles
Hiking time 7 hours
High point 3777 feet
Elevation gain 2400 feet
Best July through October
One day or backpack
USGS Snoqualmie Lake

Round trip to Hester Lake 9 miles
Hiking time 7 hours
High point 3886 feet
Elevation gain 2500 feet

19   DUTCH MILLER GAP- LA BOHN GAP

Hike the Cascade Crest Trail through a glorious valley of forests and meadows and waterfalls, rockslides and cliffs and jagged peaks, to wilderness headwaters of the Middle Fork Snoqualmie River. Then follow either the main trail to Dutch Miller Gap, named for an early prospector, or a way-trail to La Bohn Gap, where he dug his holes in the ground.

Drive the Middle Fork Snoqualmie River road (Hike 17) to the Taylor River junction. Keep right on road No. 241, going 12 miles to the road-end parking lot and trailhead, elevation about 3000 feet. Due to logging operations on private land (patented mining claims), the trailhead has varied in location in recent years. The Forest Service hopes soon to establish a permanent parking area and trailhead on the west side of Hardscrabble Creek.

The Cascade Crest Trail enters forest and ascends gently with ups and downs, passing a riverbank camp at 1½ miles.

The transition from low country to high is abrupt: at about 4 miles the trail switchbacks up a step in the valley, going by a splendid cataract of the river, and at the top emerges into heather, grass, flowers, large talus slopes, and views of craggy peaks. The way is flat and frequently marshy and muddy to 6 miles, where the river is so wide and slow and meandering as almost to be a lake, surrounded by a broad meadow. Here, at superbly scenic Pedro Camp, 4100 feet, the trail crosses a branch of the river on a bridge; shortly beyond prowl around to find remnants of an old miner's cabin (Dutch Miller's?).

The way goes moderately upward in heather and alpine trees another ½ mile to a junction with the Williams Lake—La Bohn Gap trail, an easy ¾ mile to the heather-fringed lake.

For the main event, follow tread a long mile or so and then climb rockslides and/or snowfields to a magnificent basin of cold little tarns set in granite bowls, of flower patches and waterfalls, and of the mineral outcroppings and diggings and garbage of Dutch Miller's old mine—and his contemporary successors. Climb a bit more to the 5600-foot crest of La Bohn Gap (2 miles from the junction) and more tarns and views of Bears Breast Mountain and down into Necklace Valley (Hike 4). Experienced roamers can walk to panoramas from 6585-foot La Bohn Peak west of the gap or make a more difficult scramble to the summit of 7492-foot Mt. Hinman. Many delightful camps in the basin and in the gap.

One-half mile from the Williams Lake junction the Cascade Crest Trail fords the river and as-

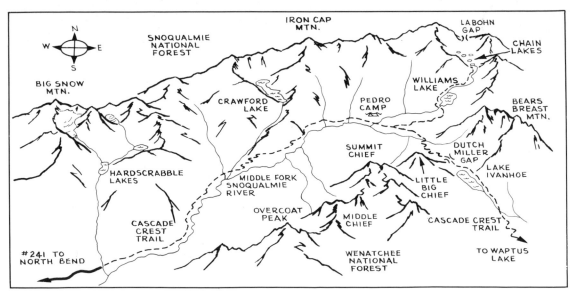

Williams Lake and Little Big Chief Mountain

cends between the walls of Bears Breast and Little Big Chief, with grand views of Little Big Chief, Summit Chief, Middle Chief, and Overcoat, to the gardens of Dutch Miller Gap, 7½ miles, 5000 feet. Look immediately below to Lake Ivanhoe and out the valley east to Waptus Lake. Look westerly back down the long Snoqualmie valley. The trail drops ½ mile to rock-shored Ivanhoe, 4652 feet, at the foot of the cliffs of Bears Breast. Good camps at the shelter by the lake. The trail continues down to Waptus Lake and the Cle Elum River (Hike 36).

Round trip to Dutch Miller Gap 15 miles
Allow 2 days
High point 5000 feet
Elevation gain 2200 feet
Best mid-July through October
USGS Big Snow Mountain and Mount Daniel

Round trip to La Bohn Gap approximately 16 miles
Allow 2 days
High point 5600 feet
Elevation gain 2800 feet
Best late July through October

Snoqualmie Pass Highway, logging roads, powerline, and railroad from summit ridge of McClellan Butte

20 McCLELLAN BUTTE

The sharp little peak looks formidable from I-90, and because of avalanche snows in a gully it is dangerous until early July. However, a steep and rugged trail climbs to a viewpoint only 50 feet below the rocky summit for panoramas west over lowlands to Seattle, Puget Sound, and the Olympics, south over uncountable clearcuts to Mt. Rainier, and east to Snoqualmie Pass peaks. The lower part of the route contains numerous scars and artifacts of man's present and past activities; the recorded history of the area dates to 1853, when Captain George B. McClellan journeyed approximately this far up the valley during his search for a cross-Cascades pass suitable for Indian-fighters and immigrants. The trail is very popular even though rough in spots, being maintained with the help of Boy Scout Troop 379, Highline. Considering the heavy use, it is remarkable the Forest Service hasn't maintained the path better.

Drive Interstate 90 east from the center of North Bend 12 miles and turn right at the overpass to forest road No. 222. Immediately beyond the Snoqualmie River bridge, turn right to the trailhead and parking lot, elevation 1500 feet.

The trail follows remnants of a wire-wrapped wooden waterline to a bridge (built by Scouts) over Alice Creek, climbs a bit, crosses a powerline swath, enters woods again, reaches a long-abandoned, overgrown railroad grade, and at ½ mile crosses the Milwaukee Railroad tracks and enters a vast clearcut. The loggers destroyed the original tread and the present path, badly eroded in places, dodges around stumps and debris. In the woods again, the trail passes mouldering mining relics and at 1 mile, 2000 feet, crosses a private (gated) logging road. Find a little spring left along the road — the last sure water after July.

The way steepens, going by a sometimes spring in a cool grove of large trees, then switchbacks up the wooded north face of the butte. At about 2½ miles the trail rounds the east side of the butte and crosses an avalanche gully with a treacherous snowbank that usually lasts into July. From here, with numerous switchbacks, the way sidehills below cliffs and occasional views, attaining the south ridge of the peak at 3¼ miles, 4900 feet. The trail follows the crest a short bit, with

looks down into Seattle's Cedar River watershed, rounds the east side of the mountain, drops 100 feet to a small pond (possible campsites) and climbs again, passing recent mining garbage to a magnicent viewpoint on the ridge crest about 50 vertical feet from the summit.

Ancient cables of doubtful security give shaky handholds for an exposed scramble to the actual summit. As in the case of nearby Mt. Si, the majority of hikers are content with the ridgetop view and leave the summit for experienced mountaineers.

Round trip 8 miles
Hiking time 8 hours
High point 5162 feet
Elevation gain 3700 feet
Best July through October
One day
USGS Bandera

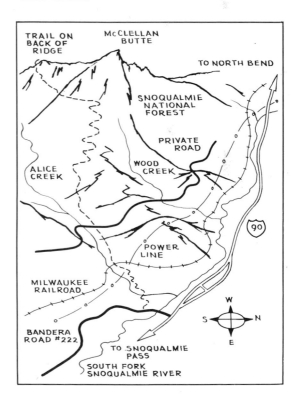

21   BANDERA MOUNTAIN

Even though there is no trail, just a boot-beaten track and follow-your-nose scramble, Bandera offers the easiest-to-reach summit panoramas in the Snoqualmie area, with superb views to the valley and lowlands, into the Alpine Lakes wilderness, and up and down the length of the Cascades. Because of the southwesterly exposure, snow melts off early; the ascent can be made when trails to nearby peaks are still buried in winter white.

In the summer of 1958 a fire started by loggers swept Bandera to timberline. Long before that, in the past century, the upper slopes were burned (probably by nature's lightning, not by man's carelessness) and forest has not yet begun to come back. Thus the entire ascent is in the open, and can be hot. To compensate, scenery is continuous every step of the way.

Drive Interstate 90 east from the center of North Bend 15 miles to Bandera Emergency Airfield. Turn left, crossing the westbound highway lanes, onto Forest Service road No. 2218, heading westward parallel to the highway. (Access will be confusing and difficult until completion of I-90 construction here.) At a junction in a short mile, go straight on road No. 2218A, signed "Lookout Point." Continue upward around a big switchback

to the east, climbing steeply and spectacularly to the airy road-end in an enormous clearcut and burn 6 miles from the highway, elevation about 3300 feet. Parking space is severely limited; be sure to leave room for others to turn around, since a traffic jam here could be disastrous. (Inexperienced mountain drivers are advised to park at the big switchback, 2200 feet, and walk the final 1½ miles of scary road.) Fill canteens at the roadend creek; there is no water above.

Begin by scrambling uphill near the creek, on meager boot-built tread, a short bit to a bulldozer track. Go rightward up the road a few hundred feet to a point where green timber at the margin of the burn is very close above. Climb the bank (where others obviously have done so) and a few yards of sparse brush to the edge of timber and there intersect the rough path hacked out by the fire-fighters of 1958.

Ascend the rude, steep tread with hands and feet to the upper limit of the burn, then strike directly upward, first over and around down logs, then in low greenery of small shrubs and bear grass. Admire picturesque bleached snags from the 19th century blaze. Off to the left, see a lichen-gray granite talus; listen for marmots whistling there.

Depending on the line of ascent chosen, the ridge crest is attained at around 4400-4700 feet;

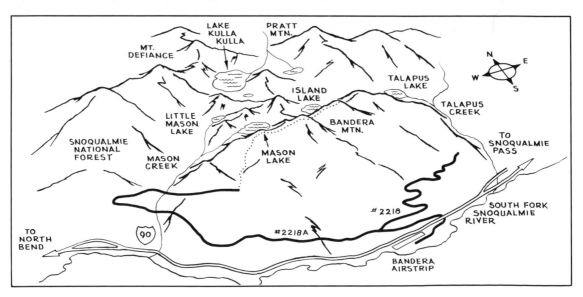

Island Lake from Bandera Mountain

immediately below on the far side is Mason Lake. The ridge is a good turnaround point for those who've had enough; the views are nearly as broad as those from the summit. The route to here often melts free of snow in early May.

Climb east on the crest through subalpine trees, then scramble granite boulders up a step in the ridge to the first summit, 5150 feet, and down-and-up a bit farther to the highest summit, 5240 feet. Look north to lakes in forest bowls below and far away to Glacier Peak and Mt. Baker, northeasterly to Snoqualmie peaks, south down to the highway, and beyond to omni-present Rainier, and west past the portal peaks of Washington and Defiance to lowlands. Civilization is near, but also wilderness.

Round trip 4 miles
Hiking time 5 hours
High point 5240 feet
Elevation gain 1900 feet
Best mid-May through November
One day
USGS Bandera

22 PRATT LAKE

Miles of deep forest and a lovely lake amid subalpine trees. A network of trails leads to other lakes and to meadow ridges and high views. From a basecamp hikers and fishermen can spend days exploring.

Drive Interstate 90 east from the center of North Bend 17 miles to a U-turn signed "Denny Creek." Turn left onto the westbound lanes and go ½ mile to the trailhead parking lot, elevation 1800 feet. (Upon completion of I-90 construction, access may be slightly changed.)

The first steep mile gains 800 feet in cool forest to a junction with the Granite Mountain trail; just beyond is a nice creek for drinking and resting. Turn left and sidehill upward on a gentler grade in young forest, through patches of twinflower, Canadian dogwood, salal, and bracken, by many good examples of nurse logs, to Lookout Point, 3 miles, 3400 feet, site of a demolished shelter and still a much-used camp. A rough fishermen's track drops ½ mile to Talapus Lake in the narrow valley below.

At 3½ miles is a short side-path down to

Pratt Lake from Pratt Mountain

Olallie Lake, around whose basin the main trail swings in open subalpine forest to a 4100-foot saddle, 4 miles, a logical turnaround point for day hikers. Lots of huckleberries here in season, plus a view south to Mt. Rainier, and a junction with the Mt. Defiance trail (see below). The Pratt Lake trail switchbacks down a steep hillside of much mud, some of it covered with new puncheon, flattens out and contours above the lake, then drops to the outlet, 5½ miles, 3400 feet, and popular camps.

Now, for explorations. (These are only a few; connoisseurs of the country have many other private favorites.)

In a short ½ mile from Pratt Lake is Lower Tuscohatchie Lake, 3400 feet, with a large shelter and a choice of three directions for wandering: A fishermen's path beats brush 1½ miles to 4023-foot Tuscohatchie Lake. From the outlet of Lower Tuscohatchie a trail ascends gently then steeply 3 miles, in trees with glimpses outward of alpine scenery, to 4500-foot Melakwa Lake (Hike 24). Also from the outlet of Lower Tuscohatchie, a less-used trail climbs northward to 4800 feet and drops past little Windy Lake to 3900-foot Kaleetan Lake, 3½ miles. The way is entirely in forest, with only occasional views over the Pratt River valley, logged in the 1930s, but the lonesome lake has a splendid backdrop in the cliffs of Kaleetan Peak.

From the Olallie-Pratt saddle (see above), the Mt. Defiance trail ascends westward through beargrass and heather and huckleberry meadows (fine views 1100 feet down to Lake Talapus) on the side of Pratt Mountain, whose 5099-foot summit is an easy scramble via huge boulder fields on the southwest side, passes Rainbow Lake (Island Lake lies ½ mile away on a side-path and actually is a more rewarding objective for hikers than Pratt Lake), comes near Mason Lake, traverses high above Lake Kulla Kulla, and climbs in flower gardens almost to the summit of 5584-foot Defiance, about 3 miles, and broad views. The trail continues westward on the ridge a mile, drops to Thompson Lake, 3400 feet, 5½ miles, and descends to the Granite Creek road, 7 miles.

Round trip to Pratt Lake 11 miles
Hiking time 8 hours
High point 4100 feet
Elevation gain 2300 feet in, 700 out
Best July through October
One day or backpack
USGS Snoqualmie Pass and Bandera

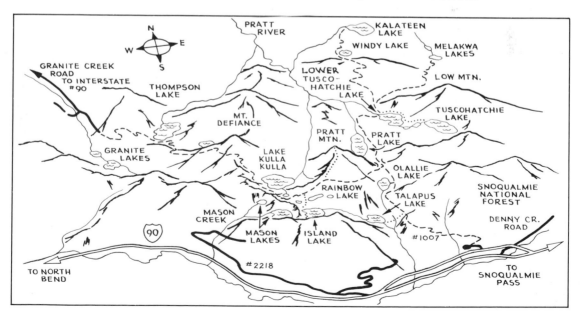

23   GRANITE MOUNTAIN

The most popular summit trail in the Snoqualmie region, and for good reason. Though the ascent is long and in midsummer can be blistering hot, the upper slopes are a delightful garden of granite and flowers and the panorama includes Mt. Rainier south, Mt. Baker and Glacier Peak north, Chimney Rock and Mt. Stuart east, and infinitely more peaks, valleys, and lakes.

Drive Interstate 90 east from the center of North Bend 17 miles to a U-turn signed "Denny Creek." Turn left onto the westbound lanes and go ½ mile to the trailhead parking lot, elevation 1800 feet.

The first steep mile on the Pratt Lake trail gains 800 feet in cool forest to the Granite Mountain junction and a creek for drinking and resting. Be sure to fill canteens; this may be the last water.

Go right from the 2600-foot junction, traversing in trees ½ mile, then heading straight up and up in countless short switchbacks on an open south slope where fires and avalanches have inhibited the growth of forest. (On sunny days, start early to beat the heat.)

At 4000 feet the trail abruptly gentles and swings east across an avalanche gully—an area of potentially extreme danger perhaps through May. Hikers seeking the summit before Memorial Day of cold springs should be very wary of crossing this gully; a better alternative in avalanche season is to leave the trail and climb directly to the peak on the rough but safe granite felsenmeer ("rock sea") of the southwest ridge, which melts free of snow while the trail route has another month of winter whiteness left.

Beyond the gully the trail sidehills through rock gardens, passing a waterfall (early summer only) from snows above, and then switchbacks steeply to grass and flowers, reaching the summit ridge at 5200 feet. In early summer the route beyond here may be too snowy for some tastes; if so, wander easterly on the crest for splendid views over the Snoqualmie Pass peaks, down to alpine lakes, and through the pass to Lake Keechelus.

The trail ascends westward in meadows, above cosy cirque-scoop benches, and switchbacks to the fire lookout, 5629 feet, 4½ miles, and full compensation for the struggle.

Experienced highland rovers depart from the trail on secret routes to solitudes of hidden lakes and alpine nooks. It is possible to camp near the summit, either for the sunset and dawn views or to allow time for exploration.

The hike has special appeal in early summer when flowers are blooming and in fall when blueberries are ripe and the slopes are flaming.

Round trip 9 miles
Hiking time 8 hours
High point 5629 feet
Elevation gain 3800 feet
Best June through November
One day
USGS Snoqualmie Pass

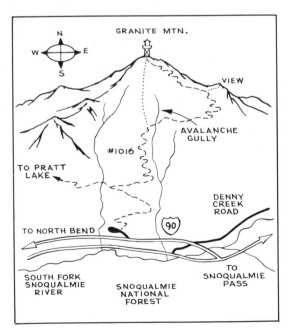

Snoqualmie Pass from Granite Mountain

24 MELAKWA LAKE

The most spectacular alpine scenery of the Snoqualmie Pass vicinity, with snowfields and walls of Kaleetan, Chair, and Bryant Peaks rising above the little lake, one shore in forest, the other in rocks and flowers.

Drive Interstate 90 east from the center of North Bend 17 miles to a U-turn signed "Denny Creek." Turn left over the westbound highway lanes onto the Denny Creek road and continue 3 miles to Denny Creek Campground. Just beyond, turn left on a road over the river and follow it ¼ mile, passing private homes, to the road-end parking area and trailhead, elevation 2300 feet. (On busy summer weekends it may be necessary to park before crossing the Snoqualmie River bridge.)

The trail ascends moderately along Denny Creek in forest, crossing the stream on a bridge at ¼ mile and recrossing at 1 mile, 2800 feet, on water-smoothed slabs of a lovely cataract. (During high water of early summer the torrential flow will turn back most hikers.) The way leaves forest and strikes upward in avalanche greenery to Keekwulee Falls, 1½ miles.

The next ½ mile of tight switchbacks must be hiked with great caution, especially by parties including small children, and particularly in darkness. The route is up a cliff, and though the tread is wide and trees give a sense of security, one false step can—and has—led to sudden death.

At 2 miles, 3500 feet, the path flattens out above Snowshoe Falls into the upper basin, shortly crosses the creek, goes from trees to low brush to trees again, and switchbacks to wooded Hemlock Pass, 3½ miles, 4600 feet. From here the trail drops a bit in forest to the outlet of Melakwa Lake, 4 miles, 4550 feet.

Enjoy views of talus, snowfields, and cliffs falling abruptly from the 6200-foot summits of Kaleetan and Chair. Good camps are numerous—those on a peninsula across the lake are sunniest.

For explorations, roam meadows and boulders to tiny Upper Melakwa Lake and 5300-foot Melakwa Pass. Experienced cross-country travelers can descend past Iceberg (Chair Peak) Lake to intersect the Snow Lake trail (Hike 27) for an alternate return to the highway.

For another way back to the highway, and for lonesome walking, take the 3-mile trail from Melakwa Lake to Pratt Lake (Hike 22).

Round trip to Melakwa outlet 8 miles
Hiking time 6 hours
High point 4600 feet
Elevation gain 2300 feet
Best mid-July through October
One day or backpack
USGS Snoqualmie Pass

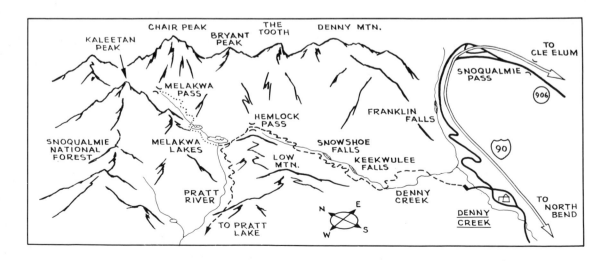

Keekwulee Falls from the Melakwa Lake trail

25 ANNETTE LAKE

A very popular and often crowded little sub-alpine lake, with cliffs and talus of Abiel Peak above the shores of open forest, pleasant for camping. Boy Scouts of the Chief Seattle Council are helping the Forest Service maintain and improve the trail. For lonesome walking here, try early summer or late fall.

Drive Interstate 90 east from the center of North Bend 17.7 miles and just past the highway bridge over the river turn right into the Asahel Curtis Nature Trail parking lot. Drive west on Bandera road No. 222 a few hundred feet, crossing Humpback Creek, turn left and climb 1/4 mile on road No. 22015, then left again on a powerline service road and park near Humpback Creek, elevation 2200 feet. (Alternatively, park at the highway and start on the nature trail.) After the hike, in order to enter westbound lanes of Interstate 90 from the parking area, it is necessary to drive west on Bandera road No. 222 about 7 miles to a freeway entrance.

The way begins by crossing Humpback Creek (not easy in early summer; when meltwater is rushing it is best to begin on the nature trail from the highway) and ascending service road, then trail through the powerline swath, with views back to Granite Mountain. Soon the path enters woods and at 3/4 mile crosses the Milwaukee Railroad tracks, 2400 feet.

Now comes the hard part, switchbacking steeply upward in nice, old forest on the slopes of Silver Peak, occasional talus openings giving looks over the valley to Humpback Mountain. After gaining 1200 feet in 1 1/2 miles, at the 3600-foot level the way flattens out and goes along a final mile of minor ups and downs to the lake outlet, 3 miles, 3600 feet.

Wander along the east shore for picnic spots or camps with views of small cliffs and waterfalls.

Some cross-country hikers continue to the summit of Silver Peak via the draw between Silver and Abiel Peaks, a good but quite brushy route.

Round trip 6 miles
Hiking time 4 hours
High point 3600 feet
Elevation gain 1400 feet
Best June through November
One day or backpack
USGS Snoqualmie Pass

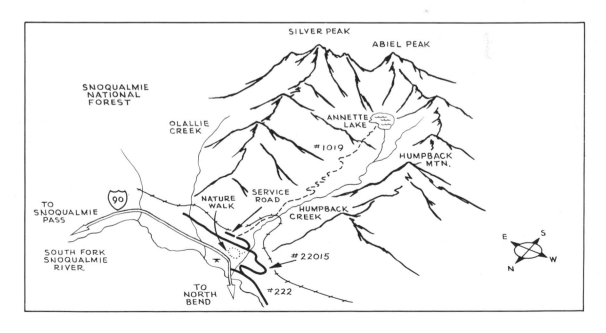

Annette Lake and cliffs of Abiel Peak

26   SILVER PEAK

Hike the Cascade Crest Trail through sub-alpine forest, then wander easily up heather and flowers to a rocky summit with views north to Snoqualmie Pass peaks, east to Lake Keechelus, south over rolling green ridges to Mt. Rainier, and west down to Annette Lake and out to the Olympics.

However, though some beauty remains, long gone is the sense of remoteness and solitude that 50 years ago, and even 15 years ago, made this one of the most popular hikes in the Snoqualmie Pass vicinity. Much of the way is within the roar of Interstate 90 and the route is cut by powerlines, a radio relay, a road, and several logging spurs—including one up Cold Creek to within ½ mile of Olallie Meadow.

Silver Peak can be approached in four different manners: via Lodge Lake-Olallie Meadow, 6 miles of trail one way plus the summit scramble; from the Snoqualmie Summit Ski Area, 7½ miles of trail, not recommended because of the depressing tow-hill devastation; from a powerline road, 3 miles of trail; and via Lost Lake and Cottonwood and Mirror Lakes, 3 miles of trail.

Lodge Lake trail (officially, Silver Peak trail) No. 1040 begins beside a fenced-in waterfall across Interstate 90 from a turnout 2.3 miles west of Snoqualmie Pass summit. Since left turns over the westbound lanes are forbidden, drive to the summit interchange and return west to the turnout parking area, elevation 2500 feet. Cross the highway to the trailhead—a dangerous and virtually impossible feat on a busy weekend.

Climb 500 feet in ½ mile (passing a short side-trail to Lodge Lake) to join the Cascade Crest Trail, which contours and ascends a bit to Rockdale Creek and then intersects the powerline road and follows it ¼ mile to the end, 2½ miles from Interstate 90. (For this shorter approach see instructions below.)

From the powerline road-end the Cascade Crest Trail re-enters woods and climbs gradually to campsites in forest-ringed Olallie Meadow, 3800 feet (3 miles from the waterfall beside Interstate 90), and swings upward around the east side of Silver Peak. At about 5½ miles, 4400 feet, below the saddle between Silver and Tinkham Peak, find unmarked Gardner Mountain trail No. 1018 heading west and uphill. (Here is the junction with the approach via Lost Lake.)

Ascend the Gardner Mountain trail about 500 feet in ½ mile to heather meadows on the south ridge of Silver Peak. Leave tread and pick an obvious route to the top, first on a wide slope

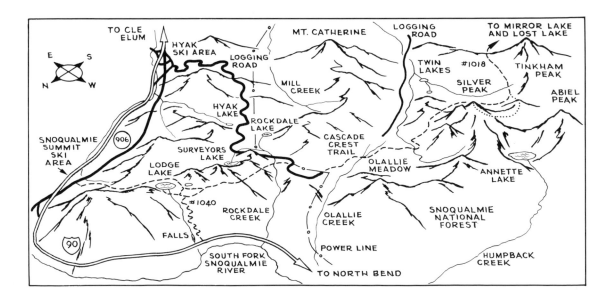

Mt. Rainier from Silver Peak. Abiel Peak on right.

of flowers, then on a narrow crest of heather and trees; when the trees are too thick, keep to the east side. The final 200 feet are steeply up shattered rock to the 5603-foot summit.

To start the hike from the powerline road, drive Interstate 90 east 2 miles from Snoqualmie Pass and take the Hyak exit. A short bit before the entrance to the Hyak ski area turn right several hundred feet, then left onto a logging road which climbs through the ski area, past Hyak Lake (the logging road becomes the powerline road) to the road-end 3 miles from the highway, elevation 3400 feet.

To reach Lost Lake, drive Interstate 90 east from Snoqualmie Pass 10.5 miles and take the Stampede Pass-Lake Kachess exit. Turn right toward Stampede Pass 1 mile, then right 4 miles to a five-way intersection at Lost Lake. Take the road on the north side of the lake for a very rough 2 miles (best to walk the last ½ mile) to the end, elevation 3600 feet. Hike 1½ miles to the Crest Trail at Mirror Lake, then 1½ miles north on the Crest Trail to the Gardner Mountain junction.

Round trip via Lodge Lake trail 13 miles
Hiking time 8 hours
High point 5603 feet
Elevation gain 3100 feet
Best early July through October
One day or backpack
USGS Snoqualmie Pass

Round trip from Lost Lake road 8 miles
Hiking time 5 hours
Elevation gain 2000 feet

27   SNOW LAKE

The largest alpine lake (more than a mile long) in the Snoqualmie Pass area. On one side cliffs rise steeply to Chair Peak, and on the other forest slopes fall into the broad gulf of the Middle Fork Snoqualmie River. The trail and lake are extremely popular, but there is plenty of room to escape crowds.

Drive Interstate 90 east from the center of North Bend 21.7 miles and turn right on the Snoqualmie Pass exit, then left 2 miles on the Alpental road through the ski area and sub-division to the parking lot and trailhead, elevation 3100 feet.

The trail climbs a bit in forest to intersect the generations-old hiking route from the pass, obliterated by the Alpental subdividers, and ascends gradually, sometimes in cool trees, sometimes on open slopes with looks over Source Creek to Denny Mountain, now civilized, and to The Tooth and Chair Peak, still wild.

The way swings around the valley head above the 3800-foot droplet of Source Lake and switchbacks a steep ½ mile in heather and flowers and parkland to the saddle, 3½ miles, 4400 feet, between Source Creek and Snow Lake. Day hikers may well be content with the picnic spots in blossoms and blueberries and splendid views.

The trail drops sharply ½ mile from the saddle to meadow shores of Snow Lake, 4 miles, 4016 feet. Many good—but usually mobbed—camps along the lake, which often is partly frozen through July. More secluded sites in the saddle and at various secret places.

The Cascade Crest Trail (alternate route) rounds the north side of the lake and descends the Rock Creek valley to the Middle Fork Snoqualmie.

To get away from overpopulation, follow a faint fishermen's path west from the Cascade Crest Trail, over the Snow Lake outlet, and up to 4800-foot Gem Lake. This is alpine roaming country at its best. With map and compass and a sharp eye, experienced wanderers can find easy routes to Upper and Lower Wildcat Lakes, to the summits of Wright Mountain and Preacher Mountain. And more.

Round trip 8 miles
Hiking time 6 hours
High point 4400 feet
Elevation gain 1300 feet in, 400 feet out
Best July through October
One day or backpack
USGS Snoqualmie Pass and Bandera

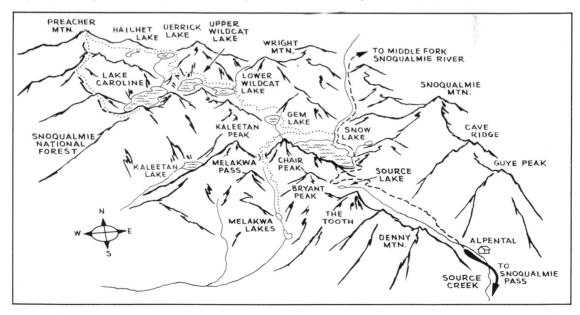

A church hike at Snow Lake

28   COMMONWEALTH BASIN

Those who have watched the accelerating degradation of Snoqualmie Pass over the past 25 years can barely stand the pain of a visit. However, the wildness of Commonwealth Basin remains intact—so far—and a short walk leads from scenes of brutal desecration into peaceful subalpine forest, beside cold creeks, perfect for leisurely afternoon strolls with tiny children—even though the path, strangely ignored by the Forest Service despite its use by thousands of hikers annually, is rough and sometimes muddy. The trail continues upward to meadows and high views.

Drive Interstate 90 east from the center of North Bend 21.7 miles, take the Snoqualmie Pass exit, and turn left on the Alpental road. Some 300 feet beyond the westbound freeway entrance find the parking lot and trailhead, elevation 3000 feet, signed "Red Mountain."

The trail starts in woods, crosses a small logging clearing, and reenters timber. At 1/4 mile the way opens into a large clearcut and ascends a logging road. At the lip of the basin, roughly 3/4 mile and 3400 feet, the trail plunges into woods and escapes the vistas southward over desolation.

Now the outrage and sorrow can be submerged in pleasure, walking in forest shadows, glimpsing peaks through trees, crossing Commonwealth Creek in about 1 1/4 miles and soon recrossing; campsites at both places. The path climbs a couple hundred feet and sidehills slopes of Kendall, returning to the valley floor at about 2 miles, 3800 feet, and crossing the east branch of the creek.

Here the work begins, ascending the spine of a sparsely-wooded ridge in numerous short switchbacks, with steadily growing views, the rough, hot way finally flattening out in heather gardens and alpine trees of a cirque basin at the foot of Red Mountain. A few steps away on a side-trail is Red Pond, 3 miles, 4900 feet. Eat a picnic lunch, tour the bouldery and flowery shores, listen for marmots whistling, walk to the edge of the cirque and look over the valley and the rimming peaks and south to Mt. Rainier. Campsites are over-used but pleasant; carry a stove and don't hack the shrubbery.

The trail swings up talus and rock buttresses almost but not quite to the saddle and follows the ridge west to Red Mountain Pass, 3 1/2 miles, 5400 feet, and views to the deep Middle Fork Snoqualmie valley, the sharp tower of Mt. Thompson, the rugged Chimney Rock group, and far horizons.

From the pass the Cascade Crest Trail (scheduled to be re-routed to a more easterly line in the 1970s) plunges down a narrow gully from which snow seldom melts to allow safe travel before late August.

For broader panoramas wander westward from the pass on a boot-beaten track up heather benches and blueberry fields to the 5700-foot summit of a nameless little peak next to Lundin.

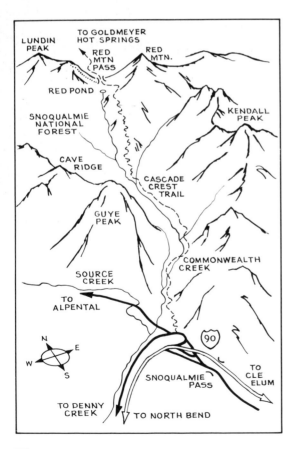

Dutch Miller Gap and Mt. Thompson from trail on Lundin Peak

Round trip to pass 7 miles
Hiking time 5 hours
High point 5400 feet
Elevation gain 2400 feet
Best mid-July through October
One day or backpack
USGS Snoqualmie Pass

Huckleberry Mountain

29   GOLD CREEK

Miles of rushing streams, tall trees, vine maple, and slide alder under the steep walls of Rampart Ridge to the east and equally steep cliffs of Kendall Peak to the west. Then rugged paths to either of two beautiful alpine lakes—and views—and highland roaming.

However, the route is among the toughest in this book and definitely not for the average walker. Once there was an excellent trail all the way from Lake Keechelus, as evidenced by bits of stonework over rockslides, ancient puncheon, and short stretches of smooth tread in the woods. Indeed, the tread must still be there under massive blowdowns and impenetrable thickets. But the Forest Service abandoned the trail years ago and though Mountaineer parties several times cleared the track it was a losing battle in the absence of government help. The existing path

has been beaten out by boots, with constant ups and downs around brush patches, continual climbing over, under, and around logs, and much smashing through chest-deep huckleberries (don't take the hike on a wet day). At least there are no motorbikes and darn few horses—something to think about when climbing under or over the 49th log. In 1975 or so the new Cascade Crest Trail may traverse the head of Gold Creek, but until then the valley is strictly for experienced wilderness travelers.

Drive Interstate 90 east 2 miles from Snoqualmie Pass to the Hyak interchange and find forest road No. 22034 on the north side of the highway. Cross Gold Creek and turn north on road 22019. In ½ mile the road branches four ways. Take the second fork from the right and drive ½ mile more. As of 1970 the road was gated at this point, elevation 2600 feet, by a recreation home subdivision. Park and walk the remaining ½ mile to the road-end, first on blacktop, then on gravel, keeping right at most junctions and avoiding side-roads to houses and one that climbs to clearcuts high on the mountain. In 1970 the correct road was marked by small arrows of red paint. All mileages are estimates, very possibly distorted by the difficulties.

The rough trail starts on the east side of the valley, alternating between woods and brush, with one pleasant and easy passage along a gravel bar. Clearcuts can be seen across the river, but soon the limit of logging is reached and the forest scene becomes wild and pure. At about 3 miles cross Gold Creek (on a footlog or by wading) and continue up the west side of the valley, at about 3½ miles crossing Silver Creek. At 3¾ miles is the last of numerous riverside camps. At 4½ miles cross Alaska Creek and ¼ mile beyond, in a tiny grassy, marshy meadow, find an unmarked junction, 3000 feet. Campsites here, and views to Alta Mountain and Chikamin Ridge and Peak.

The left fork climbs a steep mile up a tributary through vine maple and slide alder and finally a rockslide to 4200-foot Alaska Lake.

The right fork proceeds up the main valley, contouring and climbing through avalanche greenery, then trees, another mile around the base of Alaska Mountain. Now the way turns steeply uphill, gaining 1000 feet in ½ mile, passing two lovely waterfalls on a hazardous staircase of rocks, roots, and trees. Be particularly cautious on the descent—a slip could cause a serious fall. Near the top is a fine view down Gold Creek to Lake Keechelus and Mt. Rainier. At last the route abruptly flattens out for a short, level romp to the shores of 4624-foot Joe Lake, set in an alpine cirque beneath the spire of 6300-foot Huckleberry Mountain and the heather-and-forest slopes of Alaska Mountain. Over the ridge to the west can be seen the tower of 6554-foot Mt. Thompson, and across the valley to the east, the fluted walls of Chikamin Ridge.

Any hikers capable of negotiating this trail will be experienced enough in cross-country travel to return, if they wish, by contouring open slopes on the west side of Alaska Mountain and descending to Alaska Lake.

Round trip to Alaska Lake 11 miles
Allow 2 days
High point 4200 feet
Elevation gain 1600 feet
Best mid-July through September
USGS Snoqualmie Pass

Round trip to Joe Lake 12 miles
Allow 2 days
High point 4624 feet
Elevation gain 2000 feet

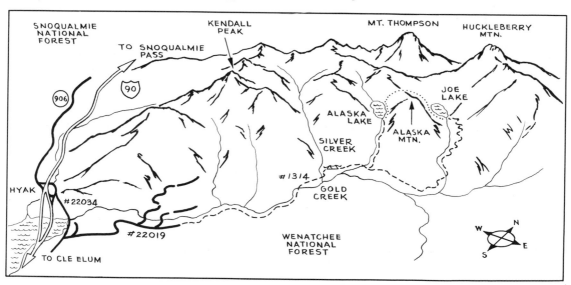

Lake Lillian and Rampart Ridge

30   MOUNT MARGARET-
LAKE LILLIAN

A short climb to a little mountain with big views, then onward in meadows to a secluded alpine lake, a fine basecamp for highland roaming on Rampart Ridge.

Drive Interstate 90 east from Snoqualmie Pass 2 miles to the Hyak interchange and find forest road No. 22034 on the north side of the highway. Follow this road about 2½ miles to Rocky Run Guard Station and immediately turn right on a gravel road. Drive upward on a confusing system of logging roads that defies verbal description, especially since the situation changes as more logging is done. Small rock cairns mark the way at some intersections. Most cars will be stopped by a washed-out switchback about 1½ miles from the highway, elevation 4000 feet. Park here and continue on foot.

The road climbs through recent logging operations. In about ¼ mile a spur road goes straight toward the timber and crosses Wolfe Creek. This spur may be flagged with plastic streamers. **This is an old, abandoned trail.** It does lead to the Mt. Margaret ridge crest, but is faint in spots and plagued by considerable deadfall. Trail markers show the way—sometimes. This route is probably a little shorter than the road walk, but only those expert at trail-finding and willing to crawl over logs should take it.

For the easier (but more uninteresting) route, continue on the main logging road, zigzagging for 1 mile up clearcuts and finally deadending in brush. The meager trail ducks into timber at the upper lefthand corner of this final clearing, ascends ½ mile to the ridge, 5000 feet, and there intersects the old trail. The way goes through subalpine trees near the crest, soon passing a side-trail dropping to 4800-foot Margaret Lake, then contours Mt. Margaret at the 5200-foot level. Strike upward on any of several convenient lines to the 5500-foot summit ridge and views west to

Snoqualmie Pass peaks, north to the jagged Chimney rock group, down to Lake Keechelus and smaller lakes, and in every direction to forests motheaten by logging.

The trail, at present unmaintained, sidehills around Mt. Margaret and descends meadows to tiny Twin Lakes (scenic campsites) at 3 miles, 4700 feet. Rough tread undulates across steep slopes of subalpine forest and talus. At 4 miles, 4800 feet, is lovely Lake Lillian, amid rocks and heather and flowers and alpine trees and pleasant camps.

For wanderings, investigate lonesome little meadow basins, or climb Rampart Ridge for broad views, or continue north to Rampart Lakes (Hike 31).

Round trip to Mt. Margaret 6 miles
Hiking time 5 hours
High point 5520 feet
Elevation gain 1500 feet
Best late June through October
One day
USGS Snoqualmie Pass

Round trip to Lake Lillian 7 miles
Hiking time 6 hours
High point 5200 feet
Elevation gain 1300 feet in, 500 feet out
Best July through October
One day or backpack

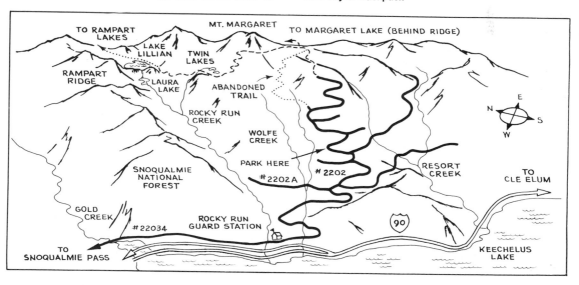

31 RAMPART RIDGE

A cool and green valley forest, a large alpine lake walled by glacier-carved cliffs which drop straight into the water, and a heaven of rock-bowl lakelets and ponds, gardens of heather and blossoms, and ridges and nooks for prowling. On summer weekends hundreds of hikers throng the shores of Rachel Lake—which is magnificently beautiful even amid a crowd. For a chance to be lonesome, go higher.

Considering the tremendous amount of use, this trail should be one of the best, but isn't. The tread was never built, but simply beaten into existence by thousands of feet. The way goes around, up, or down to avoid obstacles, and

Lila Lake and Hibox Mountain

hardly knows how to switchback. However, there are compensations. The trail is so poor (though regularly brushed out, at least) that the Forest Service has posted it for foot travel only. So don't complain; if the going were easy there would be horses picketed in every decent campsite and motorbikers razzing around in their pursuit of total idiocy.

Drive Interstate 90 east from Snoqualmie Pass 12½ miles, take the Lake Kachess exit, and follow signs 5 miles to Kachess Lake Campground. Turn left 4 miles on Box Canyon road No. 2214 to a junction. Turn left ¼ mile to the bridge over North Fork Box Canyon Creek. Just before the bridge is the Rachel Lake trailhead, elevation 2800 feet.

The hike begins with a mile of moderate ascent to a mandatory cold drink and rest stop by water-carved and pot-holed and moss-carpeted slabs. The trail levels out along the creek for 1½ miles, occasionally brushy and muddy. In an open swath of avalanche greenery, look above to 6032-foot Hibox Mountain. At 2½ miles the valley ends in an abrupt headwall and rough tread proceeds straight up, rarely bothering to switchback, gaining 1300 feet in a cruel mile. Suddenly the angle eases and forest yields to meadows and at 4 miles, 4700 feet, is Rachel Lake.

Follow fishermen's tracks around the lake, admiring blue waters ringed by trees and cliffs— and numerous campsites. For privacy go left past the narrows to the secluded south bay.

To visit the higher country, turn right at the shore on a boot-built path climbing above the cirque, with views down to the lake and out Box Canyon Creek. (Note the fresh logging which menaces the wildland integrity of this entire area.) After a steep ½ mile the trail flattens in a wide parkland saddle, 5200 feet, and reaches an unmarked junction offering a choice.

Go right 1 mile to 5200-foot Lila Lake, or ramble the easy ridge to the summit of 6240-foot Alta Mountain. Experienced alpine pedestrians can find a route north to Park Lakes and Chikamin Ridge (Hike 32).

Go left an up-and-down mile to 5100-foot Rampart Lakes. Examine in detail each of the little lakes and tiny ponds, the surrounding buttresses, waterfalls, and peaceful mountain homes. Note the mixture of basalts, con-

glomerates, and rusty mineralized lobes. Snoop into a flowery corner, climb a heather knoll, think about roaming the short but rough way south to Lake Lillian (Hike 30), and before you know it, arrive on the crest of 5800-foot Rampart Ridge and enjoy views down to Gold Creek, west to Snoqualmie Pass, south to Rainier, east to Stuart, and north to Three Queens and Chimney Rock.

Round trip to Rachel Lake 8 miles
Hiking time 6 hours
High point 4700 feet
Elevation gain 1900 feet
Best mid-July through October
One day or backpack
USGS Snoqualmie Pass

Round trip to Rampart Lakes 11 miles
Hiking time 8 hours
High point 5200 feet
Elevation gain 2400 feet

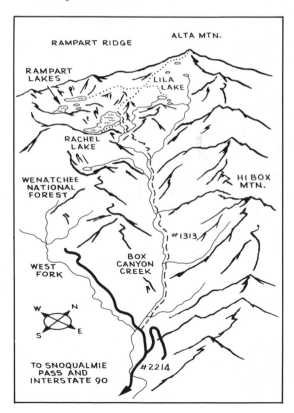

32 MINERAL CREEK PARK

Heather and huckleberry meadows surrounding alpine lakes, mountains to climb, and views. The trail is tough and not many fish are in the lakes, so the area currently offers more solitude than nearby Spectacle and Rachel Lakes.

Once upon a time—until 1968, in fact—the trip began with a lovely walk along Kachess Lake. Now, in the name of progress, a logging road has intersected the route right in the middle, cutting the hike in half. Since the challenge and satisfaction of traveling the entire distance in unmarred wilderness have been lost, the most practical plan probably is to use the new road as an approach to the upper half and maybe some other day walk the lower half.

To reach the halfway point, drive to Cooper Lake (Hike 33) and keep left on road No. 228A climbing over Cooper Pass and dropping into the Kachess valley. At 11 miles from the Cle Elum River road, shortly after crossing the Kachess River, find the trailhead, elevation 2400 feet. The path goes through a broad valley-bottom clearcut to a footlog crossing of Mineral Creek and on the far side ascends to join the trail from Kachess Lake.

Just in case there are die-hard hikers willing to ignore the new road to recapture a semblance of the old wilderness experience, the trip will be described here from Kachess Lake.

Drive Interstate 90 east from Snoqualmie Pass 12½ miles, take the Kachess Lake exit, and follow signs 5 miles to Kachess Lake Campground. Proceed .7 mile to the northernmost (uplake) point one can drive and find the trailhead in the tent-only camping area, elevation 2254 feet.

Little Kachess trail No. 1312 follows the lake more than 3 miles to its head, never over 200-300 feet above the water, but seldom level and with so many ups and downs that about 1000 feet of elevation are gained and lost. At the end of the lake the footpath merges into a mining road built in the days of the Model T and now abandoned. At about 4½ miles the route turns up Mineral Creek trail No. 1331, climbing steeply; here is the junction with the old Cooper Pass trail which joins the logging road in about ¼ mile; this latter trail is the beginning of the short version of the trip.

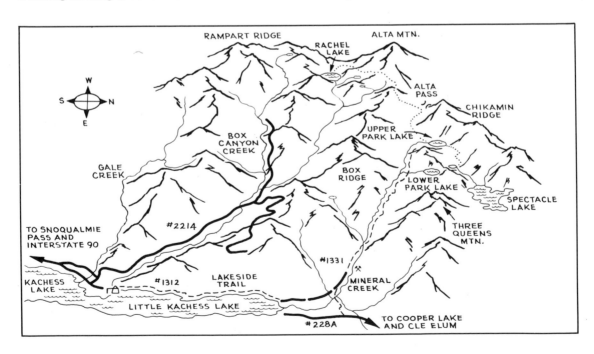

Chikamin Ridge from high route between Park and Rachel Lakes

The mining road continues 1¼ mile to an end at a group of dilapidated buildings. From here on the tread was never constructed, but just grew, going up and down and around, never flat, often very steep. Most of the way is brushed out—thankfully so, for much of the route is on slopes of slick alder and vine maple. Beyond the mine buildings ¼ mile the trail crosses Mineral Creek, and at about 3¾ miles from the Cooper Pass logging road, crosses the outlet stream from the lower Park Lake. At about 5 miles the path reaches upper Park Lake, 4700 feet, and the edge of meadow country. Excellent camps here; more private ones a mile to the north over a low divide by a small lake under Three Queens Mountain.

For wide views wander in parkland up the steep 5600-foot ridge to the west. Look down into Gold Creek and across to Joe Lake, Huckleberry Mountain, Mt. Thompson, and Snoqualmie Pass peaks. Look north along the ridge to Chikamin Peak.

When complete, the new Cascade Crest Trail will allow an easy hike from Park Lakes to Spectacle Lake (Hike 33).

Experienced cross-country navigators can enjoy the gorgeous high-level trek to Rachel Lake (Hike 31). The going is not difficult, but finding the right way requires a bit of luck. From Upper Park Lake traverse south at the base of the Mineral Creek-Gold Creek Ridge, then scramble up heather and rock to Alta Pass. Keep climbing up the ridge to a 6000-foot high point and panoramas north, west, and east. Look down on Rachel Lake, then pick the route, first dropping down a steep meadow before contouring around cliffs to the right.

Round trip from Cooper Pass road 10 miles
Hiking time 8 hours
High point 4700 feet
Elevation gain 2300 feet
Best July through October
One day or backpack
USGS Snoqualmie Pass and Kachess Lake

Round trip from Kachess Lake Campground 20 miles
Allow 2 days
Elevation gain 3300 feet

83

Three Queens Mountain and Spectacle Lake

33   SPECTACLE LAKE

Only a scattering of miniature glaciers remain of the huge frozen streams that gouged out the Alpine Lakes region of the Cascades. However, the handiwork of ancient ice lies everywhere, and is beautifully exhibited by this delightful lake in a basin of glacier-polished rock.

Drive Interstate 90 east from Snoqualmie Pass about 27 miles and take the Salmon la Sac-Roslyn exit, following Highway 903 through Roslyn and Ronald and along Lake Cle Elum. At 15 miles from Roslyn and 1 mile short of Salmon la Sac turn left on Cooper road No. 228A. At 4.7 miles from the junction turn right on Cooper River road No. 235, go by the recreation area, cross the river on a wooden bridge, pass the campground, and follow the main road, climbing steadily. At 8.3 miles is the road-end and Pete Lake trailhead, elevation 3400 feet.

The trail begins by descending 500 feet in ½ mile, first on the edge of a clearcut, then in timber, to intersect the old Cooper River trail—an easy enough way to start the hike but a murderous finish. With the usual valley ups and downs the route follows the river in deep forest and at 2½ miles reaches Pete Lake, 2980 feet, and much-used and often-crowded campsites. Unravel a confusion of paths at the shelter cabin and find the main trail, which climbs slightly over a rocky rib and drops to a double crossing of two swift creeks at about 4 miles. Both must be crossed—don't be misled by a way trail heading up the valley. Footlogs may be available; if not, the boulder-hopping can be difficult in high water of early summer.

Shortly beyond the two creeks join a new 10-percent grade trail (a segment of the relocated Cascade Crest Trail currently under construction piece by piece) that bypasses marshy Spectacle Meadows and switchbacks up toward Chikamin Ridge. The way is mostly in forest and views are scarce but occasionally Three Queens can be seen through the trees. At 5¾ miles the new trail proceeds onward toward the pass between Spectacle and Park Lakes and the Spectacle Lake trail branches right and climbs straight up the hillside with trees and roots for footholds. This is, and will remain, a hikers-only path; the Forest Service promises that horses never will be allowed at the lake.

The steep ascent is difficult but only ½ mile long, soon passing a lovely waterfall spilling from the lake, 4200 feet. For the best camps cross the outlet just above the falls and walk the south shore. The lake is like an octopus with a half-dozen arms, which makes the shoreline difficult to traverse but provides many glorious camps. To the south rises Three Queens, about 6800 feet. To the northwest is Chikamin Peak and to the north the spectacular spires of 7512-foot Lemah Mountain.

Splendid as the lake is, even better country for wilderness hikers lies beyond; 3-4 days is a minimum stay to sample the good things waiting. A rough, tough mile farther is 4700-foot Glacier Lake. There is no trail—go around the south shore of Spectacle Lake to the inlet stream coming from the direction of Glacier Lake and follow it upward. Most exciting of all is ice-fed Chikamin Lake at 5180 feet, another 1½ miles beyond Glacier Lake.

The Forest Service plans eventually to close the road at Cooper Lake, adding about 2 miles each way to the hike.

Round trip 12½ miles
Allow 2 days
High point 4200 feet
Elevation gain 1300 feet in, 500 feet out
Best August through October
USGS Snoqualmie Pass and Kachess Lake

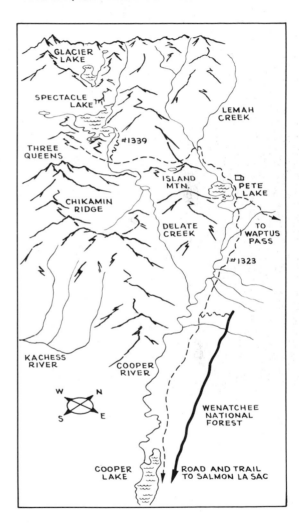

34   POLALLIE RIDGE

A splendid hike to a high ridge overlooking Cooper Lake, with spectacular views of Dutch Miller Gap peaks, Mt. Hinman, and Mt. Daniel. A 6-mile round trip to the ridge top can be made, or if transportation can be arranged, a one-way trip for miles along the open crest, then more miles down through forest. The trail can be very hot and dry in sunny weather; be sure to carry water and start early.

Drive 7.3 miles on the Cooper road, then the Cooper River road (Hike 33) to the bridge over Tired Creek. A few feet beyond are the parking

Pete Lake and, left to right, Chikamin Peak, Lemah Mountain, and Chimney Rock from Polallie Ridge

area and trailhead, elevation about 3300 feet. (To do the one-way trip, a party must first leave a car in the Salmon la Sac Campground.)

Tired Creek trail No. 1317 starts on a bulldozed fire trail climbing steeply around a clearcut and at the top joining the old trail, a rough but adequate path ascending steadily with many switchbacks. Views begin at the road and get better as elevation is gained. At about 1¾ miles two switchbacks on the edge of a ridge offer a look west to Pete Lake. At 2 miles forest yields to meadowlands as the trail traverses under the ridge and aims for a wooded pass at the head of Tired Creek.

The best views are from the top of this ridge, a logical turnaround for day hikers and an absolutely mandatory side-trip for those continuing on. Leave the trail at any convenient spot, scramble to the crest, and walk to the highest point, 5300 feet, a great place to soak up scenery and spend the day watching shadows move along distant mountains.

Many goodies remain in store for hikers choosing the one-way trip. Regain the trail from the view crest and contour to the wooded pass, 3 miles, 5400 feet, and a junction. The left fork drops 2 miles to Waptus Pass; for a 10-mile loop trip, one can return to the car via this pass and Pete Lake (Hike 33). Turn right on the Polallie

Ridge trail, traversing the ridge crest a mile, then going onward in high forest, meadows, and marshes to a possible campsite at tiny Diamond Lake, 5½ miles, 5200 feet. The lake is mostly surrounded by trees but there is a good view of the rounded top of 5295-foot Cone Mountain. At about 6 miles the ridge starts dropping rapidly. The trail more or less keeps on the crest, joining the Cooper River trail at 8½ miles and at 9 miles reaching recreation homes and the road near Salmon la Sac Campground.

The Forest Service plans eventually to close the road at Cooper Lake, adding about 2 miles of hiking.

Round trip to ridge top 6 miles
Hiking time 4 hours
High point 5300 feet
Elevation gain 2000 feet
Best late June through November
One day
USGS Lake Kachess

One-way trip from Tired Creek to Salmon la Sac
   12 miles
Hiking time 5 hours
High point 5547 feet
Elevation gain 2200 feet, not counting side-trip to
   ridge crest
Best July through November
One day or backpack

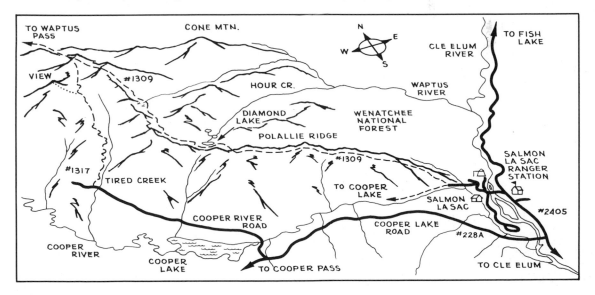

35 JOLLY MOUNTAIN

An eastern outpost of the Alpine Lakes Cascades with 360-degree views east to Mt. Stuart and the freeway leading into Ellensburg, north to Mt. Daniel, west to Pete Lake and the Dutch Miller Gap peaks, south to Mt. Rainier, and directly down to Cle Elum Lake.

Drive Interstate 90 east from Snoqualmie Pass about 27 miles and take the Salmon la Sac-Roslyn exit, following Highway 903 through Roslyn and Ronald, beside Lake Cle Elum, and at 16 miles from Roslyn reaching the community of Salmon la Sac. Turn right through the resort to the trailhead parking area by the Forest Service horse barn, elevation 2400 feet.

The first ¼ mile lies along a service road and pipeline to an unmarked junction. Take the left trail, which climbs steeply with many switchbacks to a difficult crossing (easier by late July) of Salmon la Sac Creek. Fill canteens, since this is the only certain water on the entire route. At 3½ miles is a junction with the Paris Creek trail; keep right. The way ascends the valley a bit farther and then starts a series of switchbacks up the hillside. At 4½ miles is a junction with the Sasse Mountain sheep driveway (to use this as an alternate approach, see below.) Keep left ¼ mile to a junction with the unmarked Jolly Creek trail. Go right, climbing steeply amid growing views for the final 1¼ miles to the 6443-foot summit, site of a fire lookout removed in 1968.

A jolly place to sop up panoramas. Carry a state road map to identify landmarks far out in Eastern Washington and a Forest Service map to name the innumerable peaks.

Though there may be snowfields to traverse then and the creek is difficult to cross, a magnificent time for the trip is June, when the way lies through fields of glacier lilies, spreading phlox, and lanceleaf spring beauty. Unfortunately, a band of sheep summers in the area and some of the meadows have been close-cropped.

An alternate approach saves about 1500 feet of climbing—at the cost of ½ mile or more of off-trail travel. Just .6 mile south of Salmon la Sac find two logging roads close together on the east side of the highway. Take the one nearest the resort (Little Salmon la Sac road No. 2216) and drive 4½ miles to an elevation of about 4000 feet. Park at a sharp switchback. The road goes on another ¾ mile but gets very rough; it is best to walk the road to the end and then climb straight up the hill to intersect the Sasse Mountain sheep driveway on the crest of Sasse Ridge. The forested slopes are steep but mostly brush-free. Be sure to mark the spot where the ridge is reached in order to retrace steps on the return. Follow the sheep trail north a little over a mile to the junction with the Salmon la Sac trail and proceed to the top of Jolly Mountain.

If transportation can be arranged, a good loop trip can be made by going up the Little Salmon la Sac road and down the Jolly Mountain trail.

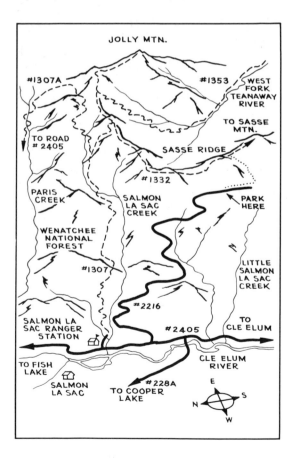

Mt. Stuart from Jolly Mountain

Round trip from Salmon la Sac 12 miles
Hiking time 7-8 hours
High point 6443 feet
Elevation gain 4043 feet
Best July through September
One day
USGS Kachess Lake

36 WAPTUS LAKE

The largest lake in the Alpine Lakes region, about 2 miles long and 3/8 mile wide, lying in a glacier-carved valley and reflecting the spectacular spire of 7197-foot Bears Breast Mountain and snowfields on Summit Chief Mountain. The approach is entirely through forest, mainly young trees growing up after some long-forgotten fire.

Though the trail makes a net gain of only 400 feet from road to lake, there are many ups and downs, and as is typical of routes heavily used by horses, the tread alternates between powdery dust and cobblestones and seldom is as soft and smooth as a hikers-only path.

Drive to Salmon la Sac (Hike 35) and cross the Cle Elum River bridge. Just beyond, at the edge of the campground, find the head of Waptus River trail No. 1310, elevation 2400 feet.

The route starts on a private road past a group of summer homes, then begins a gradual ascent, first on remnants of a road used years ago for selective logging, soon becoming genuine trail. At 2 miles, 3000 feet, top the low divide and drop to the Waptus valley floor at the easy ford of Hour Creek, about 3 miles. The camp here is rather horsey; hikers will be happier in any of the numerous small riverside sites up the valley.

The trail now climbs 300 feet, again drops a little, and at about 4 miles touches the bank of the Waptus River. Views here of 5295-foot Cone Mountain rising above the route ahead. The way henceforth remains close to the river, whose clear waters sometimes dance over boulders, other times flow so quiet and smooth they seem not to move at all.

At about 6 miles the trail rounds the base of Cone Mountain, opening views toward the head of the valley, and at 8½ miles reaches a junction. The left fork leads along the west shore of Waptus Lake and climbs Polallie Ridge (Hike 34) to Waptus Pass and Pete Lake (Hike 33).

The Waptus trail goes right, turning downvalley ¼ mile to a steel-and-wood bridge over the river, then heading upvalley again to cross Spinola Creek and join the Cascade Crest Trail coming from Deep Lake (Hike 39). At 9 miles the path arrives at Waptus Lake, 2963 feet, and a wonderful campsite with the best views of mountains reflected in water. However, this is also the most crowded camp; for other lakeside sites follow the Crest Trail 1½ miles along the shore.

The Crest Trail continues up the Waptus valley, ascending moderately for 3½ miles, then switchbacking 1400 feet in 2½ miles to Lake Ivanhoe at 4652 feet, 15 miles from the road. At 16 miles the trail reaches the 5000-foot summit of Dutch Miller Gap (Hike 19).

Round trip 18 miles
Allow 2 days
High point 2963 feet
**Elevation gain about 1000 feet, including ups and
  downs**
Best mid-June through November
USGS Kachess Lake and Mt. Daniel

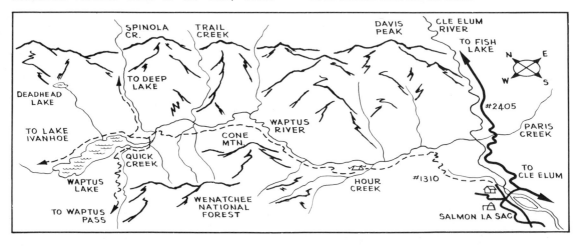

Waptus Lake and Summit Chief Mountain.

37 SPADE LAKE

A high and very beautiful alpine lake under the tall southern buttresses of Mt. Daniel. The deep blue waters, generally frozen until the middle of July, are surrounded by bare, rounded rock with striations that tell the story of the glacier that carved this cirque from the side of Mt. Daniel not so many thousand years ago.

The Spade Lake trail, originally a sheep driveway, is extremely steep and badly eroded; the horses the Forest Service mistakenly allows here aren't responsible for all erosion but they don't help. The way lies up a south-facing slope, which though largely shaded can be hot and dry; on sunny days set out from Waptus Lake no later than 7 a.m. The approximately 4-mile route takes from 3-5 hours up and 2-3 hours down—and to get to the beginning one must first hike 10 miles up the Waptus River.

Drive to Salmon la Sac and hike to Waptus Lake (Hike 36). From the east shore follow the Cascade Crest Trail around the north side a short mile and at 10 miles from the road find Spade Lake trail No. 1337, elevation 3000 feet.

The trail starts rough and steep, climbing straight up the hillside 1200 feet in about 1½ miles to 4200 feet, then alternating between short stretches of contouring, more steep climbing, and sometimes descents of 50-100 feet. The path remains difficult but the views improve, including an aerial perspective down on Waptus Lake. The first reliable water is at 2½ miles, 5200 feet. At 3 miles, 5400 feet, is a dramatic view of the summit spire of Bears Breast rising above great, smooth cliffs, and of glaciers on 7300-foot Summit Chief. The Crest Trail can be seen switchbacking up the opposite hillside toward Dutch Miller Gap. About now one can look ahead to glacier-polished rock at the outlet of Spade Lake and to the southern cliffs of Mt. Hinman, with a small piece of glacier showing. A last rugged mile of many little ups and downs leads to the lake at 5210 feet.

Campsites are located near the outlet, on a peninsula halfway around the south shore, and in heather meadows above the lake. The meadows are ribbed by outcrops of polished rock, making travel slow.

A worthwhile side-trip is Venus Lake, 5672 feet. Follow a fishermen's path ¾ mile along the east side of Spade Lake and climb the rocks just to the right of the waterfall another ¾ mile. Except for the narrow outlet (room for several campers) Venus Lake is surrounded by tall, naked cliffs.

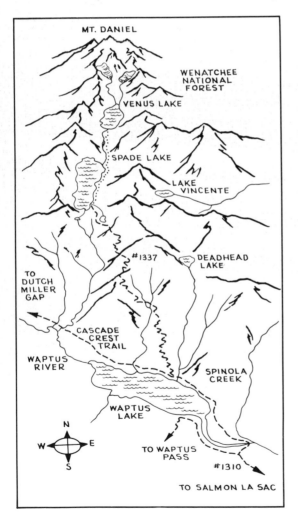

Round trip from the road 28 miles
Allow 3 days
High point 5400 feet
Elevation gain 3400 feet
Best mid-July through October
USGS Mt. Daniel

Glacier-carved rock at the outlet of Spade Lake

38   PADDY GO EASY PASS

A short, steep climb to a high pass with views out to great peaks and down to Fish Lake (Tucquala Lake) and the marshy valley of the Cle Elum River, and then an easy meadow-roaming walk to a lovely little lake. Flowers bloom here in mid-July but the lake is generally frozen until the end of the month. Thanks (no thanks) to the archaic 1872 Mining Laws, both the pass and lake are private land—one more reason to change the ridiculous old law.

Sprite Lake

Drive to Salmon la Sac (Hike 35). A few yards past the ranger station keep right on rough dirt road No. 2405 for 11 miles. About ¾ mile after passing Fish Lake Guard Station, find the trailhead, elevation 3400 feet, on the right side of the road behind a group of private cabins along a stream.

Paddy Go Easy Pass trail No. 1595 starts in woods and in ½ mile passes a creek, the last water for 2 miles. At 1 mile is a junction with an abandoned trail going to the guard station; keep left. The way now steepens, switchbacking up through dense timber to small meadows with views to the valley and to Cathedral Rock and Mt. Daniel. At about 2½ miles the trail forks (unmarked). The left fork switchbacks directly to the pass. The right fork detours by an old mine and a stream, rejoining the main trail ¼ mile below the pass. The final stretch traverses under red cliffs of a 6500-foot peak to Paddy Go Easy Pass, 3½ miles, 6100 feet.

The east slopes of the pass are mostly meadowland. Contour south along the ridge ¼ mile to a point directly above 5900-foot Sprite Lake and descend to the shores. Delightful campsites but no wood, so carry a stove. The tiny lake provides a striking foreground for The Cradle, the impressive 7467-foot peak across the valley.

Round trip to pass 6 miles
Hiking time 4 hours
High point 6100 feet
Elevation gain 2700 feet
Best mid-July through October
One day or backpack
USGS The Cradle

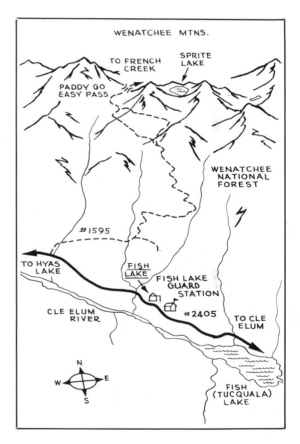

39   DEEP LAKE

Climb in forest to beautiful meadow country at the base of Cathedral Rock. Look in one direction down to the Cle Elum River and beyond to Mt. Stuart, second-highest non-volcanic summit in the Cascades and highest in the eastern section of the Alpine Lakes area, and in the other to 7899-foot Mt. Daniel, highest summit in King County and the western section of the Alpine Lakes. Look below to the green valley of Spinola Creek and, at its head, under the slopes of Daniel, the blue waters of Deep Lake.

Drive to Salmon la Sac (Hike 35). A few yards past the ranger station keep right on rough dirt road No. 2405, signed Fish Lake Guard Station. Drive 12½ miles (sign says 14), passing Fish Lake (Tucquala Lake) and the guard station, to a junction near the road-end. The right spur goes a few dozen yards to the Hyas Lake-Deception Pass trailhead. Take the left spur a similar distance to the Deep Lake trailhead, elevation 3350 feet.

The trail crosses the Cle Elum River on a bridge and ascends steadily but moderately in cool forest, at 1 mile passing a small creek and a junction with the old, abandoned trail to Deep Lake. At 2½ miles the new trail emerges into marshy meadows around the shores of little Squaw Lake, 4841 feet, a pleasant picnic spot and a good turnaround for an easy afternoon.

The way continues up in alpine forest and patches of flowers and growing views, traverses heather gardens along the ridge slopes, and at 4¼ miles, 5500 feet, reaches Cathedral Pass nearly at the foot of Cathedral Rock, at this point intersecting the new Cascade Crest Trail coming (when construction is complete) from Deception Pass.

To descend or not to descend—that is the question. The views from the saddle make it a satisfying destination, and parkland on the crest of the ridge invites wandering; in early summer, snowmelt ponds permit delightful camps.

If the lake is chosen, descend 1200 feet on the Crest Trail, which drops into forest in a long series of switchbacks, at 7¼ miles arriving on the east side of Deep Lake, 4382 feet. Campsites here and elsewhere along the shores. If time allows, explore to broad meadows at the lake

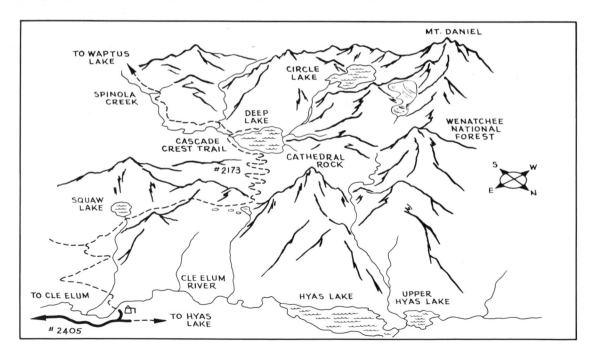

Deep Lake and shoulder of Mt. Daniel

outlet and to flowers and waterfalls at the inlet.

The Crest Trail proceeds down the lake to horse camps, the broad meadows, and onward along Spinola Creek to Waptus Lake.

Round trip 14½ miles
Hiking time 9 hours
High point 5500 feet
Elevation gain 2150 feet in, 1200 feet out
Best July through October
One day or backpack
USGS Mt. Daniel and The Cradle

Lower Robin Lake and Mt. Daniel

40 TUCK AND ROBIN LAKES

Wow! That's the only thing left to say by the time one reaches Robin Lakes. All other exclamations are used up on Tuck Lake and the dramatic views down to Hyas Lake and across the Cle Elum River valley to glaciers of 7899-foot Mt. Daniel. Surrounded by heather meadows and ice-carved granite, 6178-foot Robin Lakes surely must be ranked among the loveliest places in the Cascades.

This is a route, not a trail, and definitely not for hikers in tennis shoes. A path of sorts, very steep in spots and easy to lose, leads to Tuck Lake, beyond which every semblance of tread vanishes in boulder fields and huge slabs of granite.

Drive from Salmon la Sac to the Hyas Lake-Deception Pass trailhead, elevation 3350 feet (Hike 39). As many as 50-100 cars may be parked here on a good-weather weekend.

Hike north on the smooth and wide Cascade Crest Trail, with minor ups and downs, to Hyas Lake at 1½ miles, 3448 feet. The mile-long lake enclosed by mountains east and west, dominated by 6724-foot Cathedral Rock, is a popular destination for parties including short-legged beginning hikers.

Again with ups and downs, the trail proceeds by the lake and follows the river bottom, crossing several small streams. At approximately 3 miles it leaves the valley floor and starts a series of switchbacks up the right side of a small gully, and at about 4 miles crosses the gully (carrying a little creek) and begins switchbacking up the left side. The crossing is important to note, because about ⅓ mile beyond (about ⅔ mile short of Deception Pass) an "X" and an arrow chopped in a tree on the left side of the trail are the only clues to the start of the unmarked path to Tuck Lake.

The distance from the Crest Trail to Tuck Lake is about 2 miles, with an elevation gain of some 1000 feet. Allow 2 hours up, and on sunny days set out early enough to finish the ascent before noon; the west-facing slopes can be horribly hot.

The path, an old firemen's track, goes right, dropping a few feet and crossing two small creeks, and then heads up, alternating between spurts of climbing and stretches of level traversing. The way is easy to lose; be watchful and backtrack immediately if tread disappears.

At 5100 feet the route passes through an old burn close to bare rock outcrops; climb out on the rock for magnificent views down to Hyas Lake and across to Mt. Daniel. Amid ice-sculptured granite lies Tuck Lake at 5268 feet, 6 miles from the road; campsites where the trail first touches the lake and also at the outlet.

A mile farther and 900 feet higher are the two Robin Lakes. From the outlet of Tuck Lake, ascend the ridge dividing the lake from the valley. At 200 feet from the ridge top, drop slightly left and continue up a draw. From the top of the draw climb granite slabs, angling slightly south, to a 6400-foot high point above the Robin Lakes—which are merely the beginning of ecstatic high-country roaming.

Round trip to Tuck Lake about 12 miles
Allow 2-3 days
High point 5268 feet
Elevation gain 1900 feet
Best August through September
USGS Mt. Daniel and The Cradle

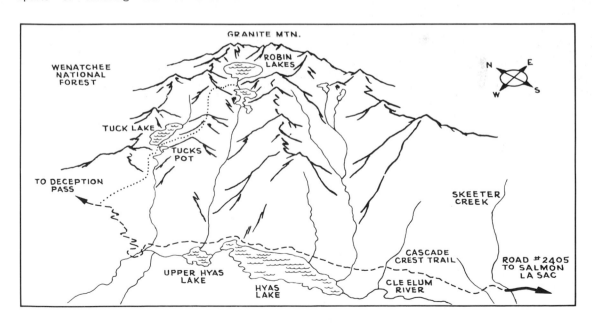

Air view of Marmot Lake. No Name and Jade Lakes on left below Mt. Daniel. Mt. Hinman on right.

41   MARMOT LAKE

Sample the variety of the Alpine Lakes: begin with a close-to-the-road and extremely-popular valley lake, climb to a cirque lake ringed by cliffs and talus parkland and fishermen, and wander on to a lonesome off-trail lake colored jade green by meltwater from a small glacier. Go from forests to heather meadows to moraines. Look up at the peaks from below, then out to the peaks from high viewpoints.

Drive from Salmon la Sac to the Hyas Lake-Deception Pass trailhead, elevation 3350 feet (Hike 39). Hike to Hyas Lake at 1½ miles, 3448 feet (Hike 40). The occupants of most of the scores of cars typically parked at the road-end stop here, content with the wading, swimming, fishing, camping, and scenery-watching.

Continue past the lake and along the river bottom, then up switchbacks to the Tuck Lake junction at about 4¼ miles (Hike 40), taking time to look back down to Hyas Lake and across the valley to Mt. Daniel and Mt. Hinman. At 5 miles the Cascade Crest Trail tops 4500-foot Deception Pass and turns north toward Deception Lakes. Turn left on trail No. 1066, signed Marmot Lake.

The path ascends gently to a 4700-foot rise, then descends moderately beside a small creek, and a short bit from the 2-mile marker (2 miles from Deception Pass) starts up again. At about 3 miles the constructed trail ends abruptly (the money ran out) and the route continues ½ mile on a steep fishermen's path to Marmot Lake, 4930 feet, 8½ miles from the road. Cliffs of Terrace Mountain and its ridges stand high above the water. The best camps lie ¼ mile south along the shore.

For fishermen and reflective campers Marmot Lake is sufficient, but for off-trail ramblers the best is yet to come. To visit 4330-foot Clarice Lake, contour from the outlet of Marmot Lake in open forest and meadows about 1 mile around the hogback to the north.

Jade Lake is a tougher and longer trip, recommended only for experienced wilderness travelers, but is more than worth the trouble—of which there is plenty. Follow the rough fishermen's track around Marmot Lake to the inlet and scramble up the steep and brushy gully to No Name Lake and on to Jade Lake, 5442 feet. The jade color comes from the rock milk supplied by a little glacier. Explore upward on ice-carved rocks to the ridge crest and stunning close views of much bigger glaciers on Mt. Daniel.

Deception Pass and Marmot Lake can also be approached from the north via the Deception Creek trail (Hike 6) or the Surprise Lakes (Hike 7).

Round trip 17 miles
Allow 2 days
High point 4900 feet
Elevation gain 1700 feet
Best July through October
USGS Mount Daniel and The Cradle

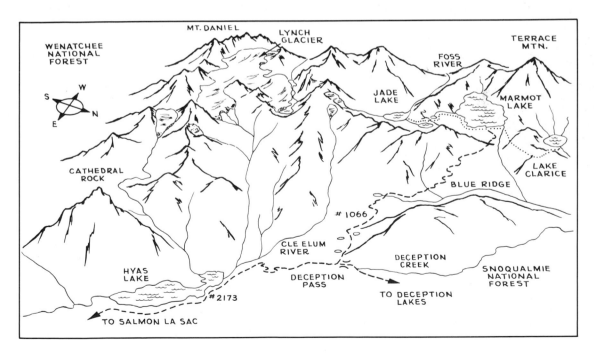

42   ESMERELDA BASIN

Walk between portal walls of Iron Mountain and Esmerelda Peaks into a peaceful basin of parkland and flower gardens and striking "serpentine barrens." Wander valley meadows and creeks to remnants of a mining settlement. Climb trails to broad views from Long's Pass or Fortune Creek Pass. Explore off the trail to secret nooks and high ridges.

Esmerelda Basin is splendid for day and weekend hikes, but also is an ideal area for families with small children to make a close-to-road basecamp for days of easy trips. Especially since this rainshadow country frequently is sunny while the Cascade Crest is drenched in mist and drizzle.

Drive US 97 north 5 miles from Interstate 90 and turn left on the Teanaway road. Follow "North Fork Teanaway" signs at all junctions, going 23 miles (the last 10 on gravel) to the road-end parking lot and trailhead, elevation 4243 feet. The hike starts on an old jeep road; however, the miners have gone and the entire basin is now closed to motorized vehicles and the roads are rapidly reverting to trails.

The way begins with a short ascent past a lovely waterfall at the basin lip, then flattens out in streamside greenery and rock gardens. At ½ mile is a junction. Good camps near here and at many other sites throughout the basin. (Though in late summer the only water may be near the junction.)

For Long's Pass. Turn right at the junction on the road signed "Ingalls Lake-Mount Stuart." In a steep ¼ mile is a junction with the trail left to Ingalls Lake (Hike 43). Go right, crossing a creek and switching back. Here a bulldozer track heads straight up, but stick with the footpath for pleasanter walking. The route switchbacks in alpine trees, flowers, and interesting screes. No water except early-summer snowmelt, so carry a loaded canteen. After again intersecting the mining road, at 2 miles the trail tops out at 6200-foot Long's Pass, with a magnificent view over Ingalls Creek to 9415-foot Mt. Stuart, second-highest non-volcanic peak in the state, and a panorama south to Mt. Adams and Mt. Rainier.

For Esmerelda and Fortune Creek Pass. Proceed up-valley from the junction at ½ mile, partly on the old jeep road and partly on new trail, at first in forest interspersed with marshy meadows, then increasingly in hillside gardens, gaining altitude moderately but steadily. At 2 miles the road goes left, crossing the creek, to the tumbledown log cabins and the diggings of Esmer-

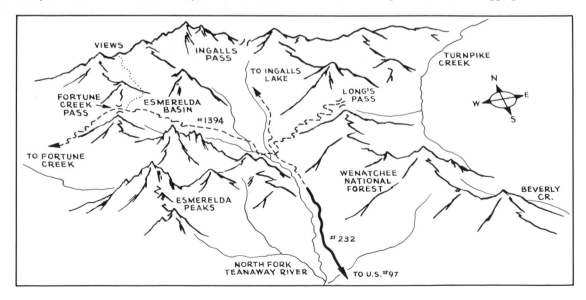

Mt. Stuart from Longs Pass

elda, 5200 feet. The trail now climbs more steeply along a rocky sidehill, in and out of trees, at 3 miles reaching the meadow saddle of Fortune Creek Pass, 6000 feet, and views over Fortune Creek to Hawkins Mountain, and back to Esmerelda Peaks. From just before the pass one can follow the sketchy County Line trail to a hidden basin and wander upward to a high saddle with the best views of all: down to a delightful little lake at the base of Ingalls Peak and across the Cle Elum River valley to Mt. Daniel and scores of peaks north and south.

Round trip to Long's Pass 4 miles
Hiking time 5 hours
High point 6200 feet
Elevation gain 2000 feet
Best mid-June through October
One day or backpack
USGS Mount Stuart

Round trip to Fortune Creek Pass 6 miles
Hiking time 5 hours
High point 6000 feet
Elevation gain 1800 feet
Best late June through October

43 INGALLS LAKE

A rock-basin lake at the foot of rugged Ingalls Peak, at the top of waterfalls plunging to Ingalls Creek, and directly across the valley from the massive south wall of 9415-foot Mt. Stuart, the highest peak between Glacier Peak and Rainier. The blend of blue lake, snowfields, ice-polished slabs of brown rock, lush green meadows, a glory of flowers, and groves of whitebark pine, larch, and alpine fir is magical. From a basecamp one can spend days of happy alpine wandering.

Drive to the end of the North Fork Teanaway road, elevation 4243 feet, and hike to Esmerelda Basin (Hike 42). At ½ mile turn right, and in ¼ mile more turn left on the old jeep road signed "Ingalls Lake-Mt. Stuart." Carry a loaded canteen; the climb can be hot and usually is waterless.

The road ascends steeply in forest, then levels out briefly and ends on a grassy flat. Now super-steep trail heads straight up, with scarcely a switchback, in fields of grass and blossoms, patches of small trees. Nearby ridges are a startling mixture of gray and brown and rusty-red rocks. South beyond Esmerelda Peaks appear Mt. Adams, the Goat Rocks, and Mt. Rainier. Higher up, the trail swings along the side of a narrow valley, winds through buttresses and flowers, and just below the pass comes to a small green bench with snowmelt (and camps) in early summer. The final stretch is a rough crawl up outcrops to Ingalls Pass, 6500 feet, about 2½ miles, and a grand view of Mt. Stuart. The way to here is mostly free of snow in late June, while slopes below to the north are still white. The ridge can be scrambled in either direction for higher views.

Drop abruptly into parkland with cold streams and delightful camps and traverse headwaters of a branch of Ingalls Creek, losing 300 feet or so. (Or better, but longer, leave the trail and contour beautiful little meadows.) Meager trail regains the 300 feet in climbing a low ridge of polished brown buttresses—and at last, below, is the lake. The way down to the 6463-foot shore is short and easy, but getting around the west side to the outlet requires a ticklish scramble up and down slabs and huge boulders. As reward, there is lonesomeness even when the rest of the area is crowded. And also the choicest arctic-alpine camps. And a view of Stuart that surely is unsurpassed.

From the outlet one can explore to Stuart Pass (Hike 14). From the trail one can roam to private meadow basins and wide-horizon ridges.

Round trip to Ingalls Lake 7 miles
Hiking time 8 hours
High point 6500 feet
Elevation gain 2600 feet in, 600 feet out
Best mid-July through October
One day or backpack
USGS Mount Stuart

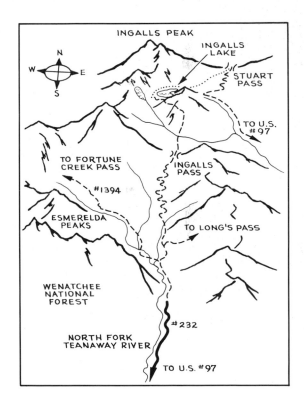

44   SUMMIT LAKE

An alpine lake, but don't be misled by the name—it isn't on the summit of anything. However, there are flower fields and a fabulous view of Mt. Rainier.

Drive US 410 to a complicated intersection at the southwest corner of Buckley, turn south on Highway No. 162-165 for 1½ miles, and turn left on Highway 165 and proceed 18 miles, passing Wilkeson and Carbonado, following signs to Ipsut Creek and Fairfax. Just before the entrance to Mount Rainier National Park, turn left on road No. 1811, cross the Carbon River on a wooden bridge, and drive about 6 miles uphill to a junction. Turn left a short bit to the end of the spur and find the trailhead, 4200 feet, to Twin Lake, Bearhead Mountain, and Summit Lake.

Going steadily east and constantly climbing, the trail starts up through a clearcut, makes a big switchback, and enters thick forest which cuts off sights and sound of the encroaching "civilization" of logging and automobiles. At 1 mile, 4800 feet, is wooded Twin Lake; keep left here at the junction with the Carbon trail.

The path rounds the lake and heads steeply uphill, passing subalpine ponds or marshes, depending on the season. Nearly at the top of the ridge the way turns west and traverses the slopes on a fairly level grade, at one point emerging from timber into a small meadow with a view of Rainier. At 2½ miles, 5400 feet, Summit Lake is attained. Bordering the shores are open fields covered with bear grass. On the west side is an old burn. The best camps are located on the east side where the trail first reaches the lake.

For the first and most essential side-trip, follow the trail around the lake, leave tread, find an easy route to the top of the 5737-foot hill, and look down at Coplay, Coundly, Lily, and Cedar Lakes. The view is grand of Mt. Rainier above—and equally broad but less grand of the network of logging operations below.

For another wandering, hike the trail past the lake a mile to the end, then climb Rooster Comb Ridge, and follow the crest down to boggy meadows; if ambitious, join the Clearwater trail and go ½ mile to 4700-foot Celery Meadows and a shelter cabin.

For an alternate trip, turn right at Twin Lake on the Carbon trail, keep right at all old trail junctions, and in 2½ miles from Twin Lake reach the 6089-foot summit, former site of a lookout, and a magnificent panorama of Rainier and the hinterland.

Round trip to Summit Lake 5 miles
Hiking time 3 hours
High point 5400 feet
Elevation gain 1200 feet
Best July through October
One day or backpack
USGS Enumclaw

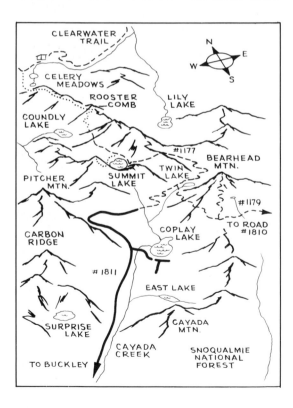

Summit Lake and north side of Mt. Rainier (John Spring photo)

Beargrass on Huckleberry Mountain (John Spring photo)

45   HUCKLEBERRY MOUNTAIN

Round trip 6½ miles
Hiking time 6 hours
High point 4764 feet
Elevation gain 3000 feet
Best late May to November
One day
USGS Greenwater

The sign at the trailhead accurately summarizes the trip: "Steep route to alpine meadows, panoramic vistas, and wildflowers 3 miles." The views of Mt. Rainier are fine indeed, and in early season the meadows are covered with flowers. The hike is especially pleasant in May and June, and offers a good opportunity to toughen soft muscles for harder hikes later in the summer.

Note: Take this trip soon. The Forest Service and Weyerhaeuser Company are building logging roads to the summit; before long Huckleberry no longer will be trail country.

Drive US 410 east from Enumclaw to 1 mile past the small town of Greenwater. Turn left on a road signed "Greenwater Campground-Weyerhaeuser Company" and go ½ mile to a junction. Take the left fork ½ mile to the camping and picnic area. Turn right and park near the Greenwater River, elevation 1740 feet.

Cross a footbridge at the downriver end of the campground and turn right to the trail sign. The first ½ mile through thick timber is nearly level but may be muddy. Note an old cabin which is missing large portions of its walls. Beyond a bubbling stream (fill canteens—the mountain is dry) the trail heads up the ridge, climbing steadily with few switchbacks. At 2½ miles is a spring—unfortunately not reliable. A bit farther is a clearing with a view of Mt. Rainier and rugged Willis Wall. The trail continues upward steeply, soon reaching alpine meadows of Indian paintbrush, lupine, and some years in mid-June, acres and acres of bear grass. Views of the White River and logging roads to the south.

At 3 miles is an unmarked junction with the trail leading to Mule Spring and westerly along the mostly-wooded ridge crest. Keep right ¼ mile to the top of Huckleberry Mountain at the 4764-foot site of long-abandoned Christoff Lookout. The trail follows the ridgetop east, passing above a small pond called Bone Lake, touching other summits of the mountain, and ending at high-elevation road No. 195 some 8 miles or more from the lookout.

An alternate trail from the highway, difficult to find and equally steep, starts behind the fish ponds at Slippery Creek.

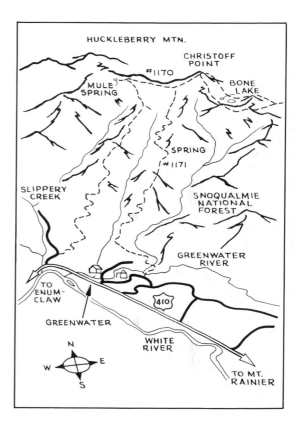

46 NACHES WAGON TRAIL

Walk the pioneer wagon route across Naches Pass and see blazes cut by emigrants, logs they rolled out of the way, dirt they shoveled, and trees they chopped. Unfortunately, you will see more tracks of vandals than pioneers, because the Forest Service permits motorbikes and jeeps on the route. These adventurers seeking a mechanical challenge have obliterated much of the pioneers' trail which should have been preserved for more respectful travelers with an appreciation of history. This may be the only pioneer trail left in the 48 states that hasn't been paved over or bulldozed. Yet the Forest Service not only allows jeeps and bikes, but has shortened the trail on the east side and—incredibly—cut it twice with logging roads near the famous "cliff."

Highlights can be enjoyed in a day hike to Government Meadows from the west side, but for a better appreciation of the trek of 1853, start from the east side, camp overnight at Government Meadows (where the pioneers spent months), and next morning descend the west side, over "The Cliff" where wagons were lowered on rawhide ropes. In either case, allow plenty of time for leisurely exploration.

For a day hike from the west, drive US 410 east from Enumclaw 20 miles to a log-trestle overpass, turn left on road No. 197, and go 8

Marker at Government Meadows

miles to the Greenwater River bridge. About ¼ mile beyond take the first spur road to the right and in ¼ mile more find the trailhead (a jeep track) at the foot of a ridge, elevation 2600 feet. Ascend the trail (track) 3½ miles through forest to Government Meadows, 4800 feet.

For an overnight hike, leave one car at the

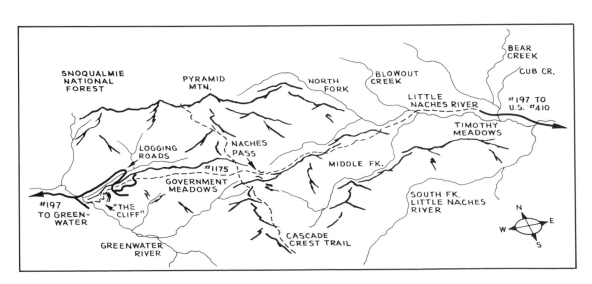

west trailhead and drive a second to Chinook Pass and 23.5 miles east from the summit. Turn left 12.5 miles on Little Naches road No. 197 to Timothy Meadows and the trailhead, elevation 3200 feet.

The first wagon train crossed Naches Pass in 1853. One or two others followed, but the route proved so difficult it was abandoned. In 1910 the Forest Service reopened the way for foot and horse travel. To "celebrate" the centennial of the first crossing, a group of jeepsters hacked and gouged over the pass in 1953, and since then the trail has been heavily used by motorbikes and four-wheel vehicles which have rutted the forest and churned meadows to gooey muck. Thanks to the vehicles, the trail is impossible to miss, but finding the remnants of the original wagon road requires imagination. Two clues are useful:

For one, the pioneers took the line of least resistance by detouring around big trees and logs; the jeepsters use chainsaws to make a more direct line, and thus in many places the old track is several hundred feet from the jeep ruts and relatively well-preserved. For a second clue, the wagons were top-heavy and to save shoveling on sidehills the pioneers frequently followed the ups and downs of a ridge crest; particularly on the west side, jeeps have contoured around some ridge tops.

In 5½ miles from the east trailhead, reach the wooded, 4900-foot summit of Naches Pass, and in another ½ mile the Cascade Crest Trail junction and campsites at Government Meadows. The next day, at ½ mile from the west trailhead, cross switchbacks of a logging road and descend "The Cliff," where pioneers lowered their wagons.

Round trip to Government Meadows from west side
  7 miles
Hiking time 5 hours
High point 4800 feet
Elevation gain 2200 feet
Best late June through November
One day or backpack
USGS Lester

One-way trip from east side 9½ miles
Hiking time 5 hours
High point 4900 feet
Elevation gain 1500 feet

Forest near Naches Pass

47   BIG CROW BASIN-NORSE PEAK

Lovely alpine meadows, one with a small lake, offering a wonderful weekend of wandering. However, the shortest way to the basin involves climbing nearly to the top of 6856-foot Norse Peak—an arduous backpack. Most hikers therefore settle for a day trip to the summit, an abandoned lookout site, and enjoy the views down to the inviting gardens and all around to panoramas extending from Snoqualmie Pass peaks to Mt. Adams, from golden hills of Eastern Washington to green lowlands of Puget Sound. The trail to Norse Peak usually is open for walking in late June; the meadow country remains under snow until mid-July.

Drive US 410 east 33 miles from Enumclaw to Silver Springs summer homes. A bit beyond, just before the Rainier National Park boundary, turn left toward the Crystal Mountain ski area. At 4 miles find the trailhead on the left side of the road. Parking is on the right, elevation 3900 feet.

The hike begins along an old logging road, passes a spring (fill canteens—this is the last sure water), and in ¼ mile enters onto true trail. The original path to the lookout was short and steep; the Forest Service recently improved the route, which now is somewhat gentler but considerably longer.

Very soon the tip of Mt. Rainier appears over the ridge to the west and every additional step reveals more of the mountain. By 2 miles the whole summit is in sight and the scene steadily expands as more elevation is gained. The route is confused here and there by crisscrossing of the old tread—take the path of least resistance, which generally is the new trail. At 4 miles, 6600 feet, the summit ridge is topped and a junction reached.

The right fork follows the ridge crest ¼ mile to Norse Peak. Look northeast into Big Crow Basin and east to Lake Basin and appealing Basin Lake. Look down to the Crystal Mountain ski area, one of the finest ski developments in the Northwest; unfortunately, winter doesn't last all year and the summer view is a hodgepodge of bulldozer tracks.

The left fork drops eastward 1 mile to join the Cascade Crest Trail, which descends ½ mile to Big Crow Basin; at about 5700 feet are a shelter cabin and good camping, though water may be scarce in late summer. Partway down find a side-trail leading over a low green ridge to Basin Lake, 6200 feet.

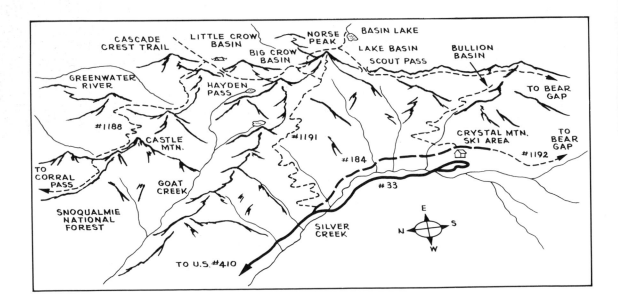

Mt. Rainier from Norse Peak

The meadows and peak also can be approached by intersecting the Crest Trail at Bullion Basin, or by taking the trail starting at Corral Pass, 5600 feet. The latter long and scenic route includes two descents and ascents of 800 feet each in 4 miles before joining the Crest Trail near Little Crow Basin (camps and water).

Round trip to Norse Peak 8½ miles
Hiking time 6 hours
High point 6856 feet
Elevation gain 2900 feet
Best late June through early November
One day
USGS Bumping Lake

Sheep Lake

48 SOURDOUGH GAP

A delightful bit of the Cascade Crest Trail (probably the easiest meadow walk in this entire book) through flower gardens and grassy fields to a high pass. A good overnight hike for beginners, except that camping space is limited and very crowded on weekends. Do the trip in early August when flowers are at their peak.

Drive US 410 east from Enumclaw to the summit of Chinook Pass, 5500 feet. Find the first available parking lot—which may be around the bend in the highway. The trailhead (Cascade Crest Trail No. 2000) is near the wooden overpass.

The trail goes north, paralleling the highway, dropping slightly in the first mile, at times on cliffs almost directly above the road. At about 1½ miles the way rounds a ridge, leaves the highway, and starts a gentle climb to Sheep Lake, 2½ miles, 5700 feet—a great place to camp if not crowded.

The moderate ascent continues through flowers, with a final long switchback leading to Sourdough Gap, 3 miles, 6400 feet. (About 500 feet below the gap the summit of Mt. Rainier can be seen briefly between two peaks to the west.)

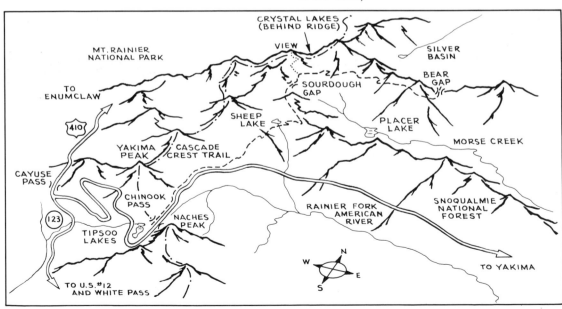

Sheep Lake and Naches Peak

Views from the gap are limited. For broader vistas, continue on the trail another ⅓ mile, descending a little to a small pass with looks down Morse Creek to Placer Lake, an artificial lake made by miners years ago.

For really wide horizons, ascend the 6734-foot peak west of the gap—not a difficult climb by mountaineering standards, but steep with a loose scree slope near the top. Drop a few feet north from the gap and start up along the base of cliffs, following a well-worn path. For the best footing stay off the scree. From the summit admire the vast white bulk of Mt. Rainier, peaks south to Mt. Adams, and north along the Cascade Crest. A vertical cliff falls to Crystal Lakes 900 feet below, seemingly only a swandive away.

Round trip 6 miles
Hiking time 4 hours
High point 6400 feet
Elevation gain 1100 feet in, 200 feet out
Best July through October
One day or backpack
USGS Mt. Rainier and Bumping Lake

115

49 AMERICAN RIDGE

As the crow flies, American Ridge is 17 miles long, but with twists, turns, and switchbacks, the trail takes 27 miles to complete the traverse. The way is mostly rough and sometimes steep, but the meadowlands are beautiful and lonesome. Flowers are in full bloom at the east end of the ridge about Memorial Day (the usual time that Chinook Pass opens) and at the west end in early August. The east end makes an excellent early-season trip when other high trails are still snowed in. Look for avalanche and glacier lilies and a rare pink-and-purple flower called steer's head.

The entire ridge is worth hiking, but only the east end is free of snow in June, and by August it is dry and hot. Therefore the recommendation is to hike from Goose Prairie to an intersection with the American Ridge trail and

Nelson Ridge from American Ridge

then go east (in June) or west (in August) along the ridge crest.

Drive US 410 east from Chinook pass 20 miles and turn right on the Bumping River road. In .6 miles is the eastern trailhead, elevation 2900 feet, signed Goat Peak trail No. 958; if a complete traverse of American Ridge is planned, start here.

At 9.3 miles from US 410 find Goose Prairie trail No. 972 on the right side of the road, elevation 3360 feet. Parking space in a small camp on the left.

The Goose Prairie trail is in woods all the way, beginning in fir and pine forest typical of the east slopes of the Cascades and ascending into Alaska cedars, alpine firs, and wind-bent pines. The route climbs steadily but never steeply. At 1½ miles the path crosses several small streams and begins a series of nine switchbacks, at 2 miles recrossing the same streams, the last

reliable water for a long stretch. At 4¾ miles is a spring which runs most of the summer; possible camping here. At 5 miles the ridge top is attained and the intersection with American Ridge trail No. 958, elevation 6200 feet.

Day hikers (any season) should follow the ridge west, climbing ½ mile to a point where the trail starts down into Kettle Creek drainage. Leave the trail and continue ¼ mile more up the ridge to a 6310-foot knoll with fine views of Mt. Rainier, Mt. Aix, and miles of ridges north and south.

Early-season overnight hikers should turn east, following the ridge through forest and meadows to Goat Peak at 11 miles, site of the former American Ridge Lookout, elevation 6473 feet, and a view of the spectacular cliffs of Fifes Peak. If transportation has been arranged, a party can continue 7½ miles down to the Bumping River road and the previously-mentioned Goat Peak trailhead, completing a one-way trip of 18½ miles with an elevation gain of about 3600 feet.

Midsummer and fall overnight hikers should turn west, climbing near the top of the 6310-foot knoll, then descending to campsites at shallow Kettle Lake, 6 miles, 5650 feet. (Below the lake is a small spring.) The trail contours around the head of Kettle Creek, climbing to the ridge crest at 10 miles, 6900 feet, dropping again to Big Basin at 11 miles, 6300 feet, a cirque with good campsites, bands of elk, and glorious scenery.

With some ups and more downs, the trail follows the ridge top from meadows back into alpine forest at a low point of 5500 feet, then up to meadowland at 6000 feet and a campsite near Mud Lake at 13½ miles. At 16½ miles is a junction with Swamp Lake trail No. 970, a popular route to Cougar Lakes in 1 mile and a steep way trail that joins the Crest Trail; No. 958 goes right, reaching American Lake at 18 miles and the Crest Trail at 19½ miles.

If transportation can be arranged, a one-way trip can be made via the Crest Trail to Chinook Pass, a total distance of 26.5 miles, or via the Swamp Lake trail to Upper Bumping road, a total of 21 miles.

Round trip from Goose Prairie to viewpoint 12 miles
Hiking time 7 hours
High point 6310 feet
Elevation gain 2900 feet
Best June through November
One day or backpack
USGS Bumping Lake

One-way trip from Goose Prairie to Cascade Crest Trail 19 miles
Allow 3 days
High point 6946 feet
Elevation gain 5500 feet
Best late July through October

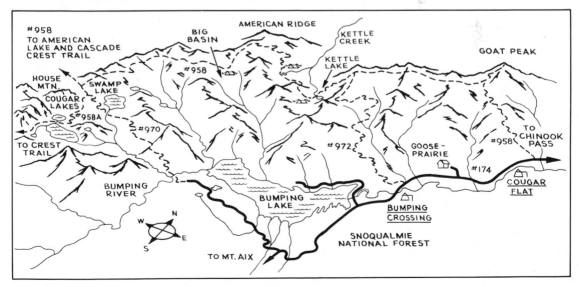

50 NELSON RIDGE-MOUNT AIX

High gardens in the blue sky of the rain-shadow, amid views east to the brown vastness of the heat-hazy Columbia Plateau, west to the shimmering white hugeness of Mt. Rainier, and south along the Cascade Crest to the Goat Rocks and Mt. Adams. Plus closer looks over meadows

and forests of the proposed Cougar Lakes Wilderness. This is not a beginners' trail—the way is steep, hot, and dry.

Drive US 410 east from Chinook Pass 20 miles and turn right on the Bumping Lake road 13½ miles to a junction. Take the left fork, signed road No. 162, 1½ miles and just before a bridge over Copper Creek turn left up a steep

Looking south along Nelson Ridge

road signed "Mt. Aix Trail." Park in a few yards, elevation 3700 feet. The rude road continues ¼ mile but this final stretch is best walked to the trailhead. Fill canteens at a creek not far from the beginning; the climb is long and can be thirsty.

The merciless trail attains highlands with minimum delay. For openers, the path ascends deep forest nearly to a branch of Copper Creek, but never gets to the water, instead switchbacking up a steep hillside. (Across the Bumping River, Rainier appears, and grows with every step.) At 2 miles the trail swings into subalpine meadows at the lip of a hanging valley but again never gets to the water. Switchbacks now trend out from the valley into open forest distinguished by superb specimens of whitebark pine.

At 4 miles, approximately 6000 feet, is a grassy promontory with views of Rainier, Adams, and the Goat Rocks. A nice campsite here in early summer, when snowmelt is available. This far makes a satisfying destination for a day hike, especially when slopes above are snowy or the party is pooped.

From the promontory the trail traverses parkland and scree 2 miles southward and upward to the wide-open crest of Nelson Ridge,

7100 feet, and a choice of wanderings. The up-and-down crest cries out for rambling in either or both directions. The trail contours and climbs a final rocky mile to the summit of 7766-foot Mt. Aix, one-time site of a fire lookout.

Because of their position on the east slope of the Cascades, and the mostly southwest exposures of the trail route, Nelson Ridge and Mt. Aix are free of snow weeks earlier than country a few miles distant. And if the tread at the hanging valley of Copper Creek is all white, as it may be through June, a short and simple detour up amid trees leads back to clear ground. Actually, the maximum flower display comes when patches of snow still linger. The locals consider this trail —whether to the promontory at 4 miles, to Nelson Ridge at 5 miles, or Mt. Aix at 6 miles—the best early-summer hike in the entire Bumping River area.

Round trip to Mt. Aix 12 miles
Hiking time 10 hours
High point 7766 feet
Elevation gain 4000 feet
Best mid-June through October
One day
USGS Bumping Lake

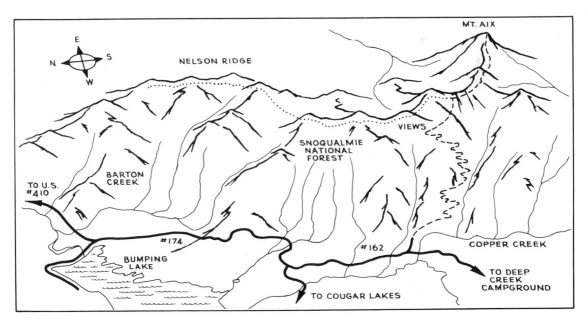

51   COUGAR LAKES

Two alpine lakes, a big one and a little one, surrounded by generous flower fields in late July and early August, blueberries in early September, and fall colors in October. From ridges above, wide views of Mt. Rainier and the Cascade Crest country.

Drive US 410 east from Chinook Pass 20 miles and turn right 10.8 miles on the Bumping River road to the end of pavement at Bumping Lake. Continue on road No. 174 to a junction at 2½ miles and turn right on the Upper Bumping road 3.6 miles to the road-end and trailhead, elevation 3600 feet.

The flat forest way leads in ½ mile to an easy ford of the broad and shallow Bumping River, which has exceptionally sharp rocks. A bit farther is a junction with the Bumping Lake trail. Go straight ahead, climbing moderately and steadily in woods and occasional openings to the outlet of Swamp Lake, 3.7 miles, 4800 feet; campsites at and near the shelter cabin.

The trail ascends several hundred feet in ¾ mile to an indistinct divide and a junction with the American Ridge trail (Hike 49). Go left ¼ mile to another junction. The righthand trail climbs past American Lake to the Cascade Crest; go left instead, rounding a ridge spur at 5300 feet and dropping into the lake basin, at 6 miles, 5015 feet, reaching the isthmus between the Cougar Lakes.

To the right is Little Cougar Lake, at the foot of the basalt cliffs of House Mountain. To the left is Big Cougar Lake. The shores offer numerous camps but the sites with the most privacy and largest views are in meadows along the inlet stream feeding Big Cougar Lake. (Be sure to camp a distance from lakeshore and streams.)

For extended horizons, climb a steep mile on the boulder-strewn path leading from the inlet of Big Cougar to the Cascade Crest at 6000 feet. Look for mountain goat, marmots, and rock conies (pikas). For maximum scenery and garden walking, wander north on the Cascade Crest Trail and in about 1½ miles turn right on the trail down to American Lake and back to Cougar Lakes, completing a 5-mile loop.

Round trip to Cougar Lakes 12 miles
Hiking time 8 hours
High point 5300 feet
Elevation gain 1700 feet in, 300 feet out
Best mid-July through October
One day or backpack
USGS Bumping Lake

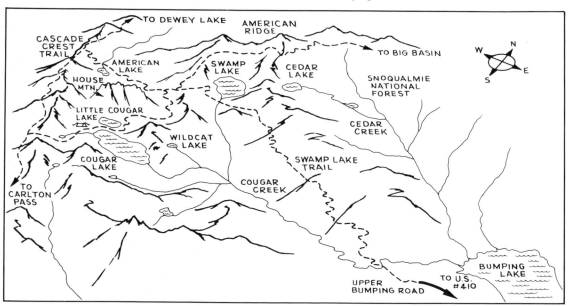

Little Cougar Lake and House Mountain

52 TUMAC MOUNTAIN

Hike through alpine meadows to an ancient volcanic cone and a colossal view of the White Pass lakes area. Do the climb in mid-July when upper slopes are covered with red and white heather plus a peppering of bright red paintbrush. The trip can be one day or overnight, camping at one of the lovely Twin Sister Lakes. Carry water; except for the lakes, the way can be quite dry.

Drive US 410 east from Chinook Pass 20 miles and turn right 10.8 miles on the Bumping River road to the end of pavement at Bumping Lake. Continue on road No. 174 to a junction at 2.5 miles and turn left on road No. 162, going 7 miles to the road end at Deep Creek Campground, elevation 4300 feet.

Find Twin Sister trail No. 980 on the south side of the campground. In a few hundred feet turn right at a junction and drop to a crossing of Deep Creek. On the far side the trail climbs steeply, with only a few short level spots, gaining 800 feet in a little over 1½ miles (all in woods) to Little Twin Sister Lake, 5100 feet. Just before the lake is an old mine tunnel filled with water.

The "little" lake (only a comparison, for both are quite large) has numerous bays and rocky points. To see it at its best, climb open slopes of the 5733-foot hill rising above the shores. To reach Big Twin Sister Lake, follow trail No. 980 westward ½ mile. Both lakes are outstanding and have beautiful campsites.

From Little Twin Sister Lake turn left on trail No. 1104, which in ½ mile turns toward Blankenship Meadows. Keep straight ahead on the Tumac Mountain trail, which aims at the peak. The way climbs steadily in open meadows 1 mile. Note how small trees are taking over the meadowland, a phenomenon which only recently has received attention. Are the trees just now growing after the Ice Age, or are they returning after catastrophic forest fires, insect invasion, or uncontrolled stock grazing of years ago? Whatever the reason, alpine meadows all over this portion of the Cascades are rapidly changing to forest, especially here and at Mt. Rainier.

The final mile is steep and badly chewed up by horses, but the views get steadily better and become downright exciting on the 6340-foot summit. The most striking is northeast, down to Blankenship Meadows and the three Blankenship Lakes (Hike 56). To the west are many tree-ringed lakes, a few of which can be seen, including Dumbbell Lake (Hike 54). Mt. Aix dominates the northeast horizon, the Goat Rocks and Mt. Adams the west, and Mt. Rainier the northwest.

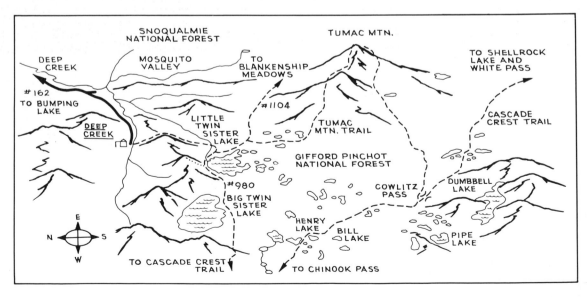

Beargrass on top of Tumac Muntain. Bismark Peak in distance.

Round trip 9 miles
Hiking time 5 hours
High point 6340 feet
Elevation gain 2100 feet
Best July through October
One day or backpack
USGS Bumping Lake and White Pass

53   HIGH ROCK

A short but steady climb to a lookout with a breathtaking view of Mt. Rainier. The cabin sits on a point of rock like the prow of a ship. Once this was a challenging hike, but now, in common with most Forest Service trails south of Rainier, is only an afternoon walk—or better, a morning walk, when the lighting is more striking. A good trip for small children, but hold their hands tight on the last bit to the summit.

Drive State Highway 706 east from Ashford 2.5 miles and turn right on Kernahan Road, signed "Big Creek Campground-Packwood." From this junction drive about 1 mile to a crossing of the Nisqually River on a steel bridge. At 1.5 miles turn left on road No. 152, signed "Packwood." In 3.5 miles pavement ends. At 4.3 miles turn right on Berry Creek road No. 149. Cross Big Creek and start climbing, passing junctions with Teeley Creek road No. 1454 at 5.7 miles, with Big Creek road No. 149C at 8.6 miles, and with road No. 1436 at 11.3 miles. At 12.5 miles is a view of the destination, High Rock, and at 14

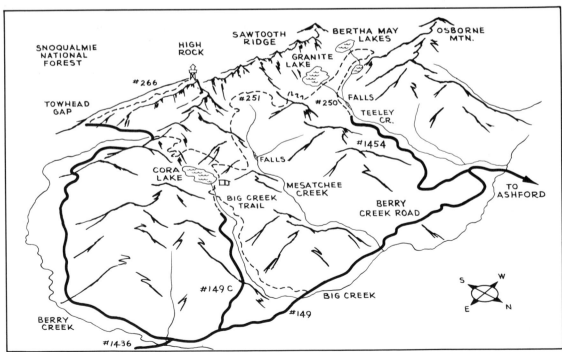

Air view of High Rock Lookout and Mt. Rainier

miles is the parking area and trailhead at Towhead Gap, elevation 4301 feet.

The trail starts on the north side of the gap, ascends a few hundred feet in a logged-off patch, and enters forest. The first mile is mostly through trees, gradually thinning. The final ½ mile to the lookout is fairly open, with views to Mt. Adams and Mt. St. Helens.

Climaxing all is the eye-popping panorama of Mt. Rainier. Nowhere in the National Park does one get this magnificent sweep from Columbia Crest down to the Nisqually Entrance. Observe the outwash from the catastrophic 1947 flood of Kautz Creek. Note hanging ice on the Kautz Glacier. Pick out peaks of the Tatoosh Range and Mt. Wow. See the green gardens of Indian Henry's Hunting Ground. When your eye shifts from The Mountain to your feet, hang on! Cora Lake is 1500 feet below, almost in spitting distance.

In mid-day Rainier is a big flat curtain of white. The best views are when the sun slants over the face of the mountain, the contrast of bright light and dark shadows delineating every

ridge and valley, even the trees in the parklands and crevasses on glaciers. Therefore plan to be at the lookout before 10 in the morning or after 4 in the afternoon.

To while away the heat and flat light of mid-day, before or after the summit climb, visit lovely Cora Lake, reached by a ½-mile trail from road No. 149C, a spur from Big Creek road No. 149, or Bertha May and Granite Lakes, reached by a 1-mile trail from Teeley Creek road No. 1454. A very nice 3-mile trail runs along under Sawtooth Ridge, connecting the lakes, but logging roads are so close, and trail-bikes so numerous, that the lakes are mobbed by noise-makers. A dirty shame. The Forest Service could have made it otherwise.

Round trip 3 miles
Hiking time 2 hours
High point 5685 feet
Elevation gain 1400 feet
Best June through October
One day
USGS Randle

54   DUMBBELL LAKE

If you like alpine lakes, this is certainly the trail— there are dozens of them, large and small. If you like tall, picturesque alpine trees, this is the trail—there are thousands of lovely specimens. And if you like fall hiking through the bright red leaves of huckleberry bushes, this is the trail—there are miles of color. The hike along a delightful section of the Cascade Crest Trail can be done as a day trip to Sand Lake or an overnight to Dumbbell Lake. The trail is a bit rough from heavy horse use and there are practically no distant views.

Drive US 12 east from White Pass .7 mile, turn left into White Pass Campground, and continue about ¼ mile to the trailhead near Leech Lake, elevation 4412 feet. This is Cascade Crest Trail No. 2000—except that in the local ranger district some signs call it No. 2034. A new and very confusing system of signing gives trail numbers rather than destinations. There is no problem so long as a party stays on the Crest Trail but any deviation requires a Forest Service map to decipher the signs.

The trail starts in forest, climbing 800 feet in 2½ miles to Deer Lake, 5206 feet, still in woods. Many people lose the trail here; while the most-used path heads for the lake, the Crest Trail turns sharply right and skirts a large, wet meadow.

At 3 miles is Sand Lake, 5295 feet, with numerous arms surrounded by meadows and alpine trees. Though the water is very clear, the shallow lake seems to have neither inlet nor outlet, so the water should be boiled before drinking. Sand Lake is an excellent turnaround for day hikers.

Now the trail wanders past numerous small lakes, climbing to 5600 feet at 4 miles. Several places offer glimpses southward of Mt. Adams and the Goat Rocks; Spiral Butte can be seen through the trees to the east.

At about 5 miles the trail switches from the east side of the crest to the west and descends in forest, losing 500 feet in ¾ mile. Now and then Mt. Rainier can be partly viewed through trees; for a better look walk off the trail 100 feet onto a low, rocky knoll located on the left side of the path soon after passing two small ponds.

At 6 miles the way skirts Buesch Lake, 5081 feet, and reaches a junction with Cramer Lake trail No. 1106. Follow this a short ¼ mile to

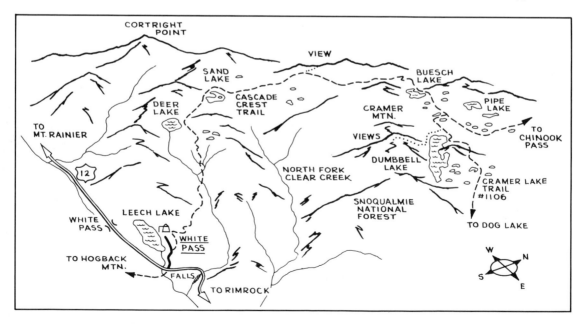

Dumbbell Lake, 5091 feet. Much of the lake is shallow; the rocky shoreline is very interesting. To appreciate its unusual shape, beat through a patch of brush and scramble to the bald summit of 5992-foot Cramer Mountain—and views much broader than merely the lake.

For an alternate return, follow Cramer Lake trail No. 1106 down to within ½ mile of Dog Lake, turn west on Dark Meadow trail No. 1107, and finish with a last mile on the Crest Trail. The distance is about the same but most of the way is in forest.

Round trip to Sand Lake 6 miles
Hiking time 4 hours
High point 5295 feet
Elevation gain 900 feet
Best mid-July through November
One day
USGS White Pass

Round trip to Dumbbell Lake 13 miles
Hiking time 7 hours
High point 5600 feet
Elevation gain 1200 feet in, 500 feet out
Best mid-July through November
One day or backpack

Fog blowing over Sand Lake

Phlox blooming on Hogback Ridge

55 SHOE LAKE

Meadows and parklands along the Cascade Crest, grand views of the Goat Rocks and Mt. Adams, and a beautiful lake in a green basin. All this on an easy day from the road.

Drive US 12 east from White Pass .7 mile to the parking lot and trailhead (Cascade Crest Trail) just opposite the road leading to White Pass Campground on Leech Lake, elevation 4400 feet. (Alternatively, for a shorter hike, park at White Pass ski area, 4400 feet, climb the ski hill 1½ miles, and take a short path which intersects the Cascade Crest Trail at a point 3 miles from the trailhead described above. For an even quicker trip, some hikers ride the chairlift to the top.)

From the formal trailhead east of White Pass, the way traverses and switchbacks open forest, touching a ski run at one point, and at 3 miles, 5900 feet, intersects the ridge crest and the path from the top of the chairlift.

Now the trail ascends into the gardens and scattered alpine trees on the slopes of Hogback Mountain and swings onto the west side of the crest, with a great view of Mt. Rainier. Attaining a 6400-foot saddle, the route contours steep, broad shale slopes on the east side of 6789-foot Hogback (an easy scramble from the trail to the summit) above the basin containing little Miriam

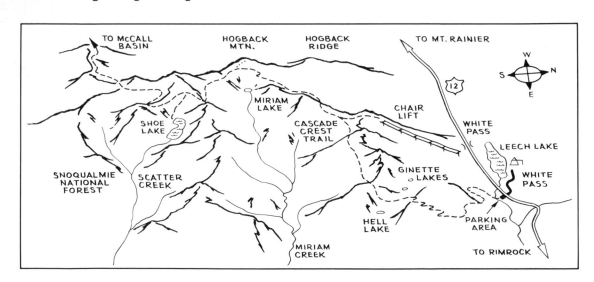

Shoe Lake and the Cascade Crest Trail

Lake, and climbs to a 6600-foot saddle, 6½ miles, in a spur ridge—and commanding views of the Goat Rocks and Mt. Adams. And below, the bright waters of Shoe Lake.

Drop ⅓ mile to the lake, 6200 feet, and fields of flowers. However, due to damage done by past overuse, camping has been banned that the meadows may have a chance to recover.

Round trip from trailhead east of White Pass 14 miles
Hiking time 7 hours
High point 6600 feet
Elevation gain 2200 feet in, 500 feet out
Best mid-July through October
One day
USGS White Pass

Round trip from top of White Pass Chairlift 8 miles
Hiking time 4 hours
Elevation gain 900 feet in, 600 feet out
Forest Service Wilderness Permit required

Blankenship Lake and Tumac Mountain

56 BLANKENSHIP LAKES

Small pocket-size meadows, vast grasslands, and beautiful mountain lakes make this country unique in the Cascades. The map calls the area "Mosquito Valley," and rightly so. Though the meadows are magnificent when bright green, the bugs are then numbered by the billions; the hike is much more enjoyable in late summer and fall.

Besides a USGS map, a party **must carry** a Forest Service map, because the local signing system gives only trail numbers instead of place names, guaranteed to confuse and lose anyone who forgets his map.

Drive US 12 east from White Pass 8.3 miles. A few hundred feet before Indian Creek Campground, turn left on road No. 1410, signed "Bootjack Summer Homes." Drive .8 mile to a junction and keep left, still on road No. 1410; at 3 miles from the highway is the parking lot by the trailhead sign, Indian Creek trail No. 1105, elevation 3400 feet.

The first 2 miles of "trail" lie along a very

rough mining road, perhaps partially passable to small cars and jeeps, but best walked. Just before the end of the road, find the start of true trail, which drops steeply 200 feet into a canyon, crosses Indian Creek, and climbs very steeply out of the canyon. At about 2½ miles listen for a waterfall; the canyon edge and a view of the lovely falls are just a few feet off the path, though one may have to try a couple spots before finding the only really good vantage point.

The trail crosses Indian Creek again at about 3 miles, recrosses at 4 miles, and at 4½ miles enters the large (⅓-mile long) Indian Meadows. The signing is very confusing here. Stay on trail No. 1105, passing trail No. 1148 to Pear Lake. The tread is faint as it traverses the meadow and heads west, but becomes distinct again beyond the grass. At 5 miles pass trail No. 1147 to Apple Lake, and at just under 6 miles take a short side-trail to the first of the three Blankenship Lakes, 5200 feet, a fair spot for a basecamp.

The first thing to do is explore the other two lakes, a stone's throw from each other. Next comes the ascent of 6340-foot Tumac Mountain, a small volcanic cone rising over the lakes and offering superb views; a trail leads to the top from the other side (Hike 52) but a path really isn't needed.

Another ½ mile along trail No. 1105 are Blankenship Meadows—many little clearings and one huge expanse. As is true of many other meadows in this portion of the Cascades, young trees are invading the grass. There are strangely few flowers in the meadows, but beargrass and lupine grow in the woods, and bog orchids and elephantheads in wet places. (Blankenship Meadows can also be reached by a 4-mile hike from road No. 162, near Bumping Lake.)

A 2-mile side-trip to Pear and Apple Lakes is a must. This can be done as a one-way walk, going first to shallow Apple Lake on trail No. 1147, then continuing on the same trail to deep Pear Lake, and returning to the main route on trail No. 1148.

Good camps at Indian Meadows, Blankenship Lakes, and Pear Lake.

Round trip to Blankenship Lakes 12 miles
Hiking time 6 hours
High point 5200 feet
Elevation gain 2000 feet in, 200 feet out
Best mid-July through October
One day or backpack
USGS White Pass

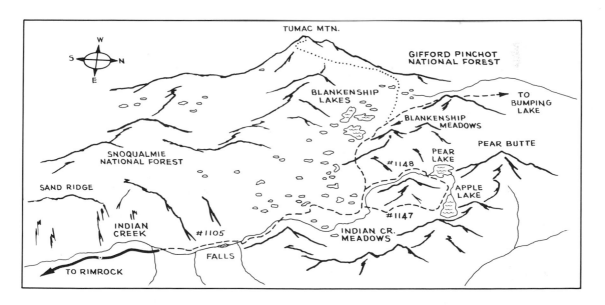

57 McCALL BASIN

Walk a valley floor carpeted with vanilla leaf growing under tall firs, hemlock, and cedar. Climb out of the valley, still in forest, join the Cascade Crest Trail, and traverse into meadows of McCall Basin. Then explore Glacier Basin, below the McCall Glacier and Old Snowy.

Drive US 12 east from White Pass 7.5 miles and turn right on the Clear Lake road. In 3 miles, just before crossing the Tieton River, keep left on road No. 134 and go 5 miles to the end of gravel surface. Park here rather than driving

the last few yards of ruts to the trailhead, elevation 3400 feet. Don't be confused by the Tieton Meadow trail, which starts at the same place; the correct route is North Fork Tieton trail No. 1118.

The first several miles follow the valley upward along the river, which in all this distance drops only some 200 feet. However, to bypass marshes and beaver ponds of Tieton Meadows, the trail is forced to take to the hillside and has many, many ups and downs. In about 1 mile are views of Bear Creek Mountain across the valley and tantalizing glimpses through the trees of

white peaks around Old Snowy. Actually, though, the scenery of the early part of the route is dominated by the logging activities of beavers.

At about 3 miles the trail abruptly leaves the valley bottom and starts a zigzag ascent to the ridge crest. Several times the path crosses a small creek. Occasionally the forest thins for views down the valley. At 7 miles, 4800 feet, is Tieton Pass and a junction with the Cascade Crest Trail.

Turn south on the Crest Trail, contouring the west side of a small, wooded knoll, climbing a bit to tiny Lutz Lake, 5000 feet, and then crossing to the east side of the crest and dropping slightly to McCall Basin, 9 miles, 4800 feet.

McCall Basin is a delicious green meadow, surrounded by forest, coursed by swift, milky waters of the Tieton River. Trees and low hills block the tremendous views a short wander away.

Climb the Crest Trail to a 5800-foot high point, or head up the meadows on the ridge to the south, or follow a foot-worn path along the river ½ mile to Glacier Basin. Each route leads to big views. McCall Glacier on the side of 7930-foot Old Snowy is the eye-catcher. Also impressive is 7768-foot Tieton Peak off to the east. Tiny McCall Lake is on the wooded knoll directly east of the basin.

A 3-day loop trip can be done by returning on the Crest Trail to Shoe Lake (Hike 55). Retrace the way as far as Tieton Pass, follow the Crest Trail northward, contour north around the west side of a knoll to a couple of small lakes, cross to the east side of the crest, and climb to a junction with trail No. 1117 at 6¾ miles. (This is the return leg of the loop.) Another mile leads to Shoe Lake, 6200 feet, at 7¾ miles from Mc-Call Basin, with an elevation gain of 1600 feet. To complete the loop, backtrack south 1 mile on the Crest Trail and take trail No. 1117 for 4 miles to North Fork Tieton trail No. 1118 and a final mile to the road.

Round trip to McCall Basin 18 miles
Allow 2-3 days
High point 5000 feet
Elevation gain 1600 feet plus ups and downs
Best July through November
USGS White Pass

McCall Basin-Shoe Lake loop trip 23 miles
Allow 3 days
High point 6200 feet
Elevation gain 3200 feet
Best July through November
Forest Service Wilderness Permit required

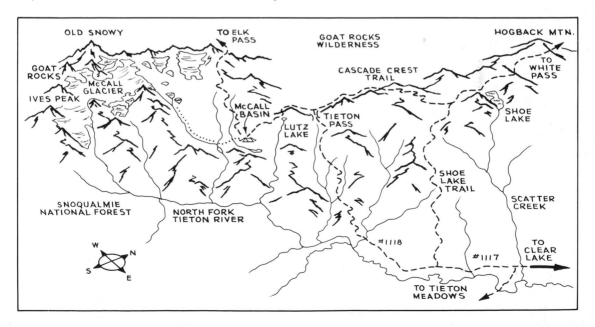

McCall Glacier and Old Snowy Mountain

58   DEVILS HORNS

Miles and miles of alpine rambling, on and off the trail, in the ultimate meadows of the Goat Rocks Wilderness. The entry through horse country is long, hot, and dusty, with 50-100 animals on the trail every weekend; the hoof-churned tread alternates between deep, choking powder and boot-sucking quagmire, and unless the wilderness ranger is on hand to control thoughtless riders, campsites often reek with horse droppings. Once above timberline, however, the horses are mostly left behind and quickly forgotten in the magnificence.

Drive US 12 east from White Pass 21 miles, considerably past Rimrock Lake, and turn right on the Tieton road heading back along the east side of the lake. Don't be confused by a camp-ground road; drive 4½ miles from the highway and turn left on road No. 123, signed "Graycreek Campground." At 11.5 miles (from the highway) is an unmarked junction—keep left. At 13.5 miles is another unmarked junction—keep right. At 17 miles the road is gated at the edge of private property. Park here and find the trailhead (No. 1120) beyond the gate, elevation 3900 feet.

The first 1½ miles traverse some of the prettiest subalpine meadows in the state. Unfortunately, this private land is being subdivided for the pleasure of a few rich people rather than being devoted to the recreational needs of everyman. Already an air strip is being developed.

At about 2 miles the way comes to the South Fork Tieton River, and a washed-out bridge and a horse ford. Usually a log jam can be found a few hundred feet upstream or downstream. If

A shoulder of Gilbert Peak

not, there is no alternative except to wade, since the river must be crossed at this point—trying to get over upstream just makes more problems, since most of the water comes from Conrad Creek, which shortly above emerges from a canyon.

At 3 miles enter the Goat Rocks Wilderness. At a little over 4 miles, 4200 feet, the trail for the last time crosses the Tieton River—now merely a jump wide—and starts climbing very steep and badly-eroded tread, gaining 700 feet in 3/4 mile. The way moderates and in the next 3/4 mile ascends 200 feet to Surprise Lake, 6 miles, 5100 feet.

The lake, surrounded by forest and with only a small view of snowy mountains, is the destination of most horsemen and all fishermen. Camping can be miserable if horses have been picketed in the few sites level enough for a tent. Nobody but a fanatic fisherman would walk so far on such poor trail simply to get to the lake.

The trail skirts the north shore and about 1/4 mile beyond enters small meadows; horses have churned the moist greenery into big gooey mud pies. The way climbs to the low point of a ridge at about 8 miles, 5800 feet. Here the horse trail and horses start down, while hikers take an old abandoned trail which heads left into a vast, park-like meadowland and the best alpine roaming in the Goat Rocks. For unexplained reasons, few horses enter these meadows.

The views! Amid a semicircle of high summits, to the west rises 8201-foot Gilbert Peak. The big one to the northwest is Tieton Peak. Devils Horns is the ragged peak with a topping of red rock. Farther northeast lies Bear Creek Mountain.

The abandoned trail strikes off toward Tieton Peak, going from one meadow to another and passing several small tarns. About 1 mile from the main trail is a somewhat difficult crossing of a fork of Conrad Creek. At 2 miles is the crossing of another fork, milky from rock flour milled by glaciers on Gilbert Peak. At 4 miles, approximately 5800 feet, the way ends under Devils Horns.

Explorations are unlimited. View the glaciers that feed Conrad Creek. Visit secluded basins on the east side of Gilbert Peak. Look for Warm Lake, which spends 11 months of the year buried under snow.

Round trip to the start of meadowlands 16 miles
Allow 3 days
High point 5800 feet
Elevation gain 1900 feet
Best mid-July through October
USGS White Pass (part only)

Round trip to trail's end under Devils Horns 24 miles
Allow 3 days minimum
High point 5800 feet
Elevation gain 1900 feet
Forest Service Wilderness Permit required

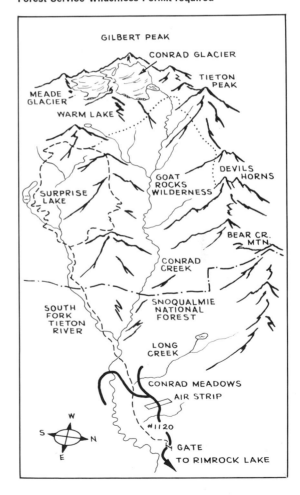

59 TRAILS END (PURCELL MOUNTAIN)

A forest basin topped by 5442-foot Purcell Mountain, once the location of Trails End Lookout. Nothing left now but a pile of rubble, two heliports, and a panoramic view. The basin and peak are surrounded by logging activities and the Forest Service plans eventually to build a permanent road and log this basin too. Due to hikers' complaints, unstable soil, and a Sierra Club lawsuit, the road has not yet been built. However, permanently saving this hike will require a lot more letters to the forest supervisor.

There are two approaches, the long Purcell Mountain trail which traverses the entire length of the basin, and the lookout trail climbing directly to the summit. Snow remains in the basin until the first of July, but the direct route can be hiked in mid-June with only a few snowpatches up high. The first 3½ miles of the Purcell Mountain trail, going along the south slopes of Prairie Mountain, are open to travel in early June.

Drive US 12 east from Randle toward Packwood. For the Purcell Mountain trail, at 5.6 miles turn left, then immediately right, and within 300 feet find the trailhead. For the lookout trail, continue .3 mile farther, turn left on an unmarked paved road (the old highway), and in 1 mile turn

Whalehead Ridge and Mt. St. Helens from Purcell Mountain

left on road No. 1303. In a mile look over the side of the Davis Creek bridge into a spectacular canyon. At 4½ miles from the paved road (11½ miles from Randle) turn left on road No. 1303C and in ½ mile park near Davis Creek.

The Purcell Mountain trail starts from the valley bottom at an elevation of 920 feet and switchbacks upward in a 160-year-old stand of timber, gaining 2500 feet in 3 miles. The trees provide shade but the slope faces south and has no dependable water, so carry loaded canteens. At 3 miles the trail passes "The Gate"—a local landmark though the gate has been gone a long time—and makes a big switchback. The way is still up, but the views improve. At 3½ miles is a junction with a path to springs and open meadows, 4400 feet, under Cockscomb Mountain. Now the trail levels off, still in timber, ascending slightly under 5065-foot Prairie Mountain. At approximately 5 miles is Little Paradise, 4800 feet, a small meadow surrounded by tall trees; water and camps can be found a bit below the meadow.

What to do now? One choice is to wander the short distance up Prairie Mountain; all but the summit and steep south side are wooded. The other choice is to continue 3 more miles to the top of Purcell Mountain and the panoramas.

The lookout trail starts from the road-end at Davis Creek, elevation 2800 feet, and follows an abandoned road. In 500 feet cross a collapsed bridge, turn right, recross the small creek on another collapsed bridge, and continue on the overgrown road about 500 feet to a trail sign. The trail, an abandoned skid road, zigzags almost to the top of the clearing and then enters forest with more zigzags. At 2½ miles the way reaches meadows and proceeds upward. At 3 miles, 5000 feet, just before the junction with the Purcell Mountain trail, is a possible camp. A final ½ mile climbs to the summit.

Round trip via Purcell Mountain trail 16 miles
Allow 2 days
High point 5442 feet
Elevation gain 4500 feet
Best July through November
USGS Randle

Round trip via lookout trail 7 miles
Hiking time 6 hours (unless maintained)
Elevation gain 2600 feet
Best mid-June through November
One day or backpack

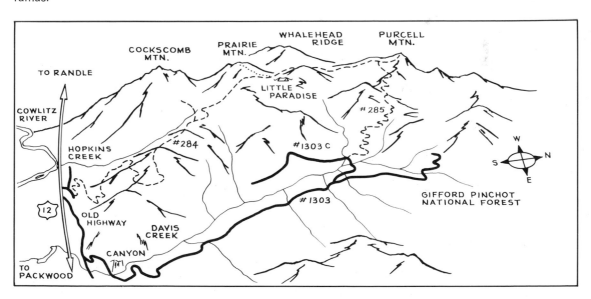

Smith Creek valley from Cispus Point

60 KLICKITAT TRAIL

Tradition says this is part of the trail followed by the Klickitats on trading excursions from their homes east of the Cascades, climbing from the Klickitat River to Cispus Pass (Hike 65), then descending to Puget Sound country. Though there may have been easier valley-bottom paths, the trail probably has been in use for many centuries, white settlers picking up where the Indians left off. Today, the route offers one of the most lonesome walks in the state, winding along ridge crests for 17 miles, mostly in forest with occasional tantalizing glimpses of mountains and valleys, but offering marvelous views from high points (and clearcuts). Tread often is so faint one must pay close attention to stay on the track; the

sense of remoteness is thus reinforced, and a feeling of kinship with the people who owned the land for thousands of years—or rather, in their ethic, were owned **by** the land.

But the white man has come, and though the trail is lonesome, seldom is it beyond sight or sound of logging. The way is paralleled by logging roads, cut once by a road (near Jackpot Lake), and hacked by several clearcuts. Only time will tell whether the Forest Service will adopt true multiple-use and preserve this rewarding trail, or strip off the trees and leave a wasteland of little interest to hikers.

To reach the west terminus of the trail, turn south in Randle, cross the Cowlitz River, and in 1 mile keep left on road No. 123. At 6 miles turn left on road No. 121 and in 15 miles (from Randle) find the trailhead on the left side of the road, elevation 3900 feet.

To reach the east terminus, drive State Highway 12 south from Packwood 2½ miles, turn east on Johnson Creek road No. 1302, and in 16 miles (from Packwood) find the trailhead opposite the junction of road No. 1302 and road No. 1104, elevation 4000 feet.

Signs at both ends call it "Klickitat Trail No. 7." By consulting a current Forest Service map, hikers can intersect the trail by climbing clearcuts from logging roads, but in doing so would lose a lot of the fun. The mileages and elevations given here are estimates; there are some mile markers along the route, but no indication where the counting starts.

From the west terminus, the trail climbs 500 feet, follows the ridge top, and in a bit more than a mile drops steeply to a clearcut. Once beyond this, the way passes under 5805-foot Twin Sisters and at about 4 miles, 5200 feet, comes to a junction with the Pompey Peak trail.

The next 1½ miles are a glorious combination of alpine meadows and forest groves. Castle Butte towers above. At Cispus Point, 5½ miles, are campsites and a rebuilt patrol cabin with a "Welcome" sign—and it surely is a welcome port in a storm. An absolute must is the ½-mile side-trip to the site of the old lookout and wide views of Rainier, Adams, St. Helens, Hood, and ridge upon forested ridge.

Now the trail descends into timber, dropping almost 1000 feet to Jackpot Lake, 6 miles, 4500 feet, and another logging mess. A traverse near the top of a 5500-foot butte offers more views. At 8 miles the route drops into headwaters of Deception Creek, crosses clearcuts, and at 9 miles contours under Horseshoe Point and gradually ascends to a saddle below 5733-foot Cold Springs Butte. Along here the tread is particularly faint and appears unwalked in years. The short side-trip to the summit of the butte is well worth the effort.

The path drops through forest to campsites at St. Michael Lake, 10½ miles, 4700 feet, contours past tiny St. John Lake, climbs nearly over the top of 5683-foot Mission Mountain, and goes downward in trees, passing a junction with the Elk Peak trail at 15¾ miles and at 17 miles reaching the east terminus on road No. 1302.

One-way trip 17 miles
Allow 2-3 days
High point 5400 feet
Elevation gain 4000 feet
Best mid-July through October
USGS Tower Rock, Steamboat Mountain

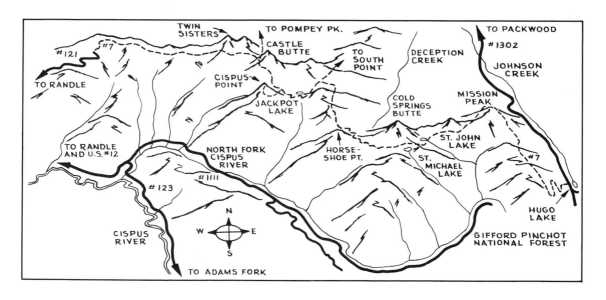

61 PACKWOOD LAKE

A tree-ringed lake on the edge of the Goat Rocks Wilderness. From the outlet, look up to 7487-foot Johnson Peak. From the inlet, look back to Mt. Rainier. A wooded island punctuates the picturesque waters.

Unfortunately, man has left his disastrous mark on this scenic treasure. Washington Public Power Supply System was allowed to dam the outlet to gain a small amount of "peaking" power and the Federal Power Commission mysteriously gave permission for the dam to be built 3 feet higher than specified in the agreement with the Forest Service. So far the power company has not been permitted to raise the lake above the natural level; if it ever is, the shore will be ruined.

Additionally, the trail was built so wide and flat and easy that every weekend the lake is overwhelmed by 200-300 people—little children, old folk, motorbikers, horsemen, all jumbled together. Near the outlet are a small resort and a few campsites—terribly overcrowded. To avoid standing room only, visit the lake on a weekday; otherwise, pause amid the crowds to enjoy the

Packwood Lake and Johnson Peak

view, then hike onward to Lost Lake.

There is no excuse for allowing horses and motorbikes on the trail, since the power company maintains a wide track along the pipeline. The motorbikers razz up and down both pipeline and trail, making a great noisy circle; many don't even stop at the lake.

From Packwood, next to the Packwood Ranger Station, drive east on road No. 1320, in 6 miles coming to a steel tower and, nearby, a large parking lot and the trailhead, elevation 2700 feet.

Trail No. 78 goes gently through big trees with occasional views over the Cowlitz valley toward Rainier, passing several springs in the first half—but the second half is dry, so carry water. Nearing the lake, the snowy, craggy Goat Rocks can be seen at the valley head. With ups and downs grossing 400 feet but netting a gain of only 100 feet, at 4¼ miles the trail reaches Packwood Lake, 2867 feet.

For less jammed-up camping, continue 4¾ miles to tiny Mosquito Lake, 4800 feet, or Lost Lake, 5165 feet, surrounded by alpine trees and flowery meadows.

Hikers seeking a special treat should try the Coyote Ridge trail, first climbing from Lost Lake, then contouring 7 airy miles along a 6700-foot ridge to the Cascade Crest Trail at Elk Pass (Hike 65). About half the distance is through steep mountain meadows high above timberline. The way is little traveled, very odd considering the superb scenery.

Round trip to Packwood Lake 9 miles
Hiking time 5 hours
High point 3100 feet
Elevation gain 400 feet, loss 300 feet
Best June through November
One day or backpack
USGS Packwood

Round trip to Lost Lake 18¼ miles
Allow 2 days
High point 5165 feet
Elevation gain 2300 feet
Best July through October

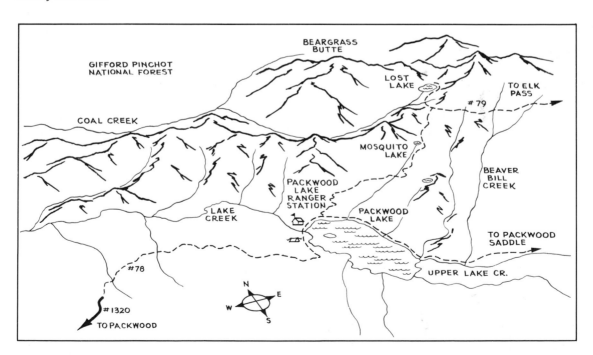

Old Snowy from Goat Ridge

62   GOAT LAKE

Take your choice: a long walk through the best flower gardens in the Goat Rocks, ending beside a high lake covered by ice until August; a shorter walk to panoramic views from the site of a former lookout; or a loop trip including Snowgrass Flat (Hike 63).

Maps of the area are very poor and mileages on signs seldom agree, so elevations and distances are mostly estimates.

Drive US 12 south from Packwood 2.5 miles and turn east on Johnson Creek road No. 1302. At 15.7 miles turn left on road No. 1104 and at 18.5 miles keep right on road No. 1118, in 19 miles from Packwood coming to Berry Patch and the trailhead, elevation 4600 feet.

Goat Ridge trail No. 95 starts off steep, gaining about 1100 feet in the first 2 miles through shady forest. In ½ mile pass a junction with the Snowgrass Flat trail. At 1½ miles is a junction with a spur trail going over the top of

6240-foot Goat Ridge, once a lookout point, and descending to rejoin the main trail. The summit detour adds approximately ¾ mile and 400 feet of climbing to the trip. The top affords the only really broad panoramas on the route and makes a good destination for day hikers.

From the spur junction the main trail swings around the east slope of the lookout summit, at 2 miles reaching a 5700-foot saddle and the other end of the lookout spur. The way now descends along the west side of the ridge, losing several hundred feet in ½ mile; here is the only view of Mt. Rainier except from the lookout. The trail passes an intersection with the Jordan Creek trail and ascends to Buckhorn Camp, 3 miles, 5700 feet. The next 1½ miles of minor ups and downs leave forest and traverse a hillside loaded with flowers in season—one of the finest displays in the South Cascades outside Mount Rainier National Park.

At 4½ miles, about 6100 feet, is a small basin and the last possible camping before Goat Lake. The route now climbs steeply to the Lily Basin trail at 5 miles, 6800 feet, and a magnificent view of Old Snowy; a sketchy side-trail leads to the summit of 7431-foot Hawkeye Point and a look straight down into Goat Lake. Follow the Lily Basin trail east, dropping 500 feet in a mile, swinging around the head of Goat Creek—along the path are striking views out the valley and off to Mt. Adams. At 6 miles is Goat Lake, 6500 feet, set in a grand alpine cirque walled on three sides by high peaks. Campsites at the outlet but no firewood.

To do the loop trip, continue 2½ miles on the Lily Basin trail to Snowgrass Flat and take trail No. 96 back to the cars, for a total distance of 13 miles.

Round trip to Goat Ridge 4½ miles
Hiking time 3 hours
High point 6240 feet
Elevation gain 1600 feet
Best late June through November
One day
USGS none

Round trip to Goat Lake 12 miles
Allow 2 days
High point 6800 feet
Elevation gain 2600 feet in, 700 feet out
Best August through October
Forest Service Wilderness Permit required

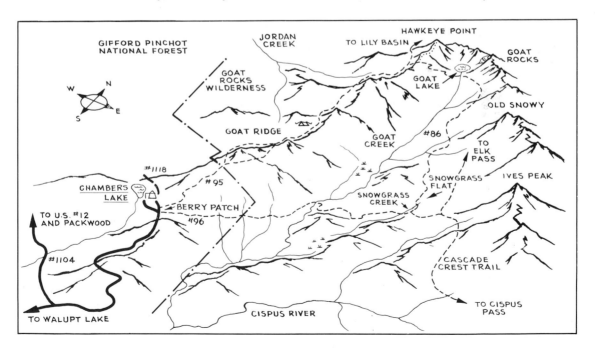

Mt. Adams and Cascade Crest Trail near Snowgrass Flat

63   SNOWGRASS FLAT

One of the most famous meadows in the Cascades, a riot of color during flower season. But when the flowers are gone the vast parklands higher up, with views of Adams, St. Helens, and of course, the Goat Rocks, still make the trip a genuine spectacular.

Drive from Packwood to Berry Patch (Hike 62) and the trailhead, elevation 4600 feet.

Set out in the woods on the new Snowgrass Flat trail No. 96, contouring the slopes of Goat Ridge to a junction with the old trail and then a crossing of Goat Creek, 4700 feet. Especially in early summer, stop at the bridge to apply insect repellent, lots of it, because from here the trail passes for ¼ mile through marshy forest where one may expect heavy attack by swarms of mosquitoes.

At 2 miles the trail begins climbing from the valley bottom, leaving behind the hordes of hungry bugs. At Bypass Camp, 3½ miles, cross Snowgrass Creek and continue up, emerging occasionally from trees into small meadows, and at 4 miles finally entering the open expanse of Snowgrass Flat, 5700 feet.

Because of overgrazing by horses and punishment by heavy foot traffic, and to give nature a chance to repair the damage, camping is no longer permitted in the Flat; however, Bypass Camp is only minutes below and makes a fine base for exploratory walks. From the Flat take either of two trails, northward or eastward (the latter unmarked), and hike another ½ mile and about 400 feet higher to join the Cascade Crest Trail. Campsites in the meadows here offer wide views, including all three southern volcanoes.

What to do now? For one choice, hike 2 miles south on the Crest Trail into the vast meadows of Cispus Basin and take the unmarked old path ¼ mile to Cispus Pass, 6473 feet, and superb views down the Klickitat River and out to 8201-foot Gilbert Peak.

Alternatively, hike the Crest Trail north to its 7600-foot high point on the side of Old Snowy (Hike 65). Or, for a loop trip back to Berry Patch, total distance 13 miles, traverse to 6500-foot Goat Lake and return by way of Goat Ridge (Hike 62).

Round trip to Snowgrass Flat 8 miles
Hiking time 5 hours
High point 5700 feet
Elevation gain 1100 feet
Best July through November
One day or backpack
USGS none
Forest Service Wilderness Permit required

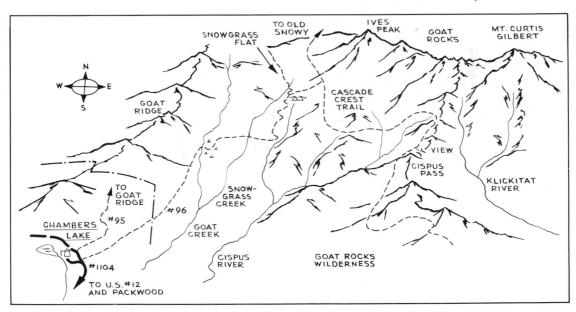

64   NANNIE RIDGE

A long hike through meadowland to a small lake, then on to views into the head of the Klickitat River and up to the rugged pinnacles of 8201-foot Gilbert Peak, highest in the Goat Rocks; or an easy day hike to Nannie Peak, overlooking meadows and summits of the Goat Rocks.

Drive US 12 south from Packwood 2.5 miles and turn east on Johnson Creek road No. 1302. At 18.5 miles (from Packwood) turn left on road No. 1114. At 20.5 miles the good logging road turns off and the very rough and dusty recreation road (still No. 1114) continues to Walupt Lake at 24 miles, elevation 3927 feet. Find the

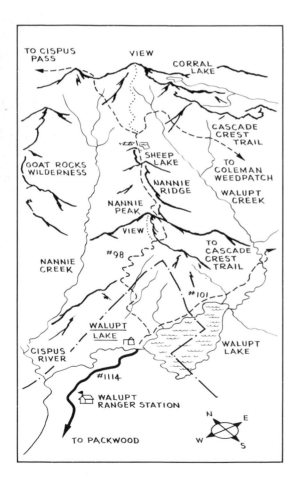

trailhead in the Walupt Lake Picnic Area.

Start on trail No. 101 and in a few yards turn left on Nannie Ridge trail No. 98 and begin to climb. The first 1½ miles are through timber, passing two small streams—the last water for 3 miles. At about 2 miles the trees thin out; the next mile is miserably rutted. At about 3 miles the way tops a 5600-foot ridge. On the very crest an unmarked, unmaintained but quite decent trail climbs in ½ mile to Nannie Peak, 5800 feet, site of a former lookout. The summit is a ¼-mile ridge of heather, grass, alpine trees, and rocks. Be sure to explore the full length— from the south end are views of Adams and St. Helens and from the north end views of Gilbert Peak and vast meadows.

Those who choose the longer trip now must lose a discouraging 300 feet as the main trail drops under cliffs. At 3½ miles is a pond (which may dry up in late summer) and another trail, also unmarked, switchbacking to the summit of Nannie Peak. A short bit beyond the pond look down on a small lake, about 500 feet below the trail, a tempting place to camp. After passing below more cliffs of Nannie, the way regains the ridge and meadow country and follows ups and downs of the crest to lovely little Sheep Lake, 5¾ miles, 5600 feet, surrounded by grass and flowers, an ideal camp. The best sites are on the ridge to the west beside a row of protecting trees. Walk around the shore for views of Adams and St. Helens.

A visit to a viewpoint above the Klickitat River is mandatory. There are two choices. For one, hike the ridge almost directly north a long mile to its summit at about 6200 feet. The other alternative is the pass at the head of Nannie Creek and Cispus Pass. For this follow the ridge trail a short ¼ mile to an intersection with the Cascade Crest Trail and go left and north on the Crest Trail, contouring around the 6200-foot ridge to where the Crest Trail crosses into the Klickitat drainage and the Yakima Indian Reservation; there are some steep ups and downs but the walking is pleasant.

Sheep Lake and Mt. Adams

Round trip to Nannie Peak 7 miles
Hiking time 4½ hours
High point 5800 feet
Elevation gain 1800 feet
Best July to October
One day
USGS none

Round trip to Sheep Lake 12 miles
Hiking time 8 hours
High point 5700 feet
Elevation gain 2300 feet
Best late July through September
One day or backback
USGS none
Forest Service Wilderness Permit required

147

65   GOAT ROCKS CREST

Walk between heaven and earth through a rock garden along a narrow, 7000-foot ridge dividing Eastern and Western Washington. This spectacular section of the Cascade Crest Trail is popular with horseriders, so try it in the first half of July, when the tread is free enough of snow for safe hiking but not yet passable to horses; tiny alpine flowers are then in bloom, too. The climax portion can be done as a round trip of about 8 miles from Snowgrass Flat (Hike 63), but the route is described here in its full length from White Pass to Walupt Lake.

Drive to White Pass, elevation 4400 feet, and hike 7 miles south on the Cascade Crest Trail to Shoe Lake (Hike 55).

From Shoe Lake the trail crosses a low ridge and drops 900 feet into timber offering an occasional view out, then ascends and contours to Tieton Pass, 12 miles, and a junction with the North Fork Tieton River trail (Hike 57). Going only slightly up and down, the way swings first along the west side of the crest, then the east, to McCall Basin, 14 miles, 5200 feet. (**Note:** In 1975 construction will begin on a new Cascade Crest Trail route from McCall Basin to Yelverton shelter. When complete, the present trail will be maintained for hikers only.) Now the route is up, some of it very steeply up, climbing 2 long miles to Elk Pass, 6600 feet One great compensation for the energy output is that the entire way is in open country with views of Mt. Rainier and miles of meadowland on the slopes of Coyote Ridge to the west. The last campsites for 3½ miles are in flat meadows before the final drag to the pass, at which is a junction with the Coyote Ridge trail (Hike 61).

Views broaden at the pass—down to Packwood Lake and across the immense depth of Lake Creek to rugged Johnson Peak. The trail follows the ridge several hundred feet higher and then descends. From here one senses the quality of the route ahead. The tread can be seen—blasted out of cliffs, gouged in scree slopes; in some places the crest of the ridge has actually been leveled off to give walking room.

The next 2 miles are mostly above 7000 feet, the highest section of the Cascade Crest Trail, and also the most dangerous. Meeting a horse party is bad business, because the horses cannot be turned around and thus hikers must backtrack to a safe turnout. Snowstorms can be expected in any month. Two parties of recent years have lost a member from hypothermia (exposure) and there have been several narrow escapes. Don't attempt this section in poor weather.

The trail first contours and climbs to a 7100-foot point with a view of weird-shaped towers and small glaciers on 8201-foot Gilbert Peak, highest in the Goat Rocks. There is also a fine view of Old Snowy, 7930 feet. Nooks and cran-

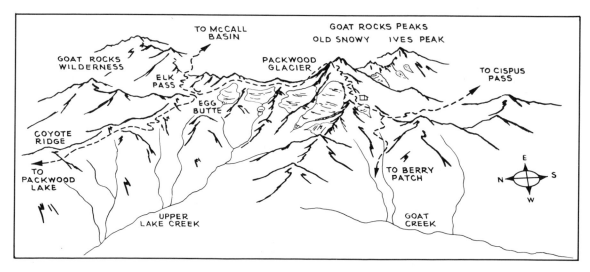

Gilbert Peak from the Cascade Crest Trail

nies hold the superb rock gardens, which are in full bloom during early July.

The way now follows ups and downs of the narrow crest, sometimes on the exact top and other times swinging around small knobs. From a spot a little beyond the lowest portion, it is possible to avoid a climb by contouring across the Packwood Glacier and rejoining the trail where several signs can be seen in a saddle on the skyline. The glacier crossing is easy in July, but by late August may involve hard ice; the best plan is to stay with the trail on its ascent to the highest elevation at 7600 feet on Old Snowy, a short side-trip away from the 7930-foot summit.

The trail now descends. At 6900 feet is a sturdy rock shelter built by the Bellevue Presbyterian Church in memory of Dana May Yelverton, who died of exposure on the crest August 4, 1962.

From the cabin the path drops into parkland, at 21 miles intersecting the Snowgrass Flat trail (Hike 63), then contouring into the glory of Cispus Basin. The route continues in meadows to the Nannie Ridge trail at 24 miles, and then by this trail 6 miles to Walupt Lake, as described in Hike 64.

One-way trip 30 miles
Allow 3-4 days
High point 7600 feet
Elevation gain 5300 feet
Best July through September
USGS White Pass
Forest Service Wilderness Permit required

66   ADAMS GLACIER MEADOWS

Parklands, meadows, waterfalls, and moraines, close views of lava cliffs, cinder cones, and glaciers, distant views of St. Helens and Rainier, all this and more in a paradise for wandering high on the slopes of Mt. Adams. The hike leads to a magnificent alpine camp used by summit climbers, a place variously called Mountaineer Camp, Adams Glacier Camp, or High Camp. Snow still covers some of the meadows in early July, but tiny alpine flowers are then blooming in the highest gardens and beargrass down lower. Later in the summer more of the meadows are open for roaming and the country is superb in every month on through autumn.

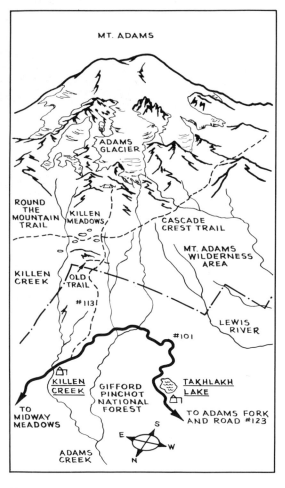

Drive south, then east from Randle 32 miles on road No. 123 and turn left on road No. 101, a narrow and dusty track that must be traveled with care. In 2 miles from the junction pass Taklakh Lake and at 5.7 miles (37.7 miles from Randle) find the parking area and trailhead, elevation 4600 feet.

Killen Creek trail No. 113 ascends toward the mountain in subalpine forest on a wide ridge. Occasionally the crest steepens and the path does likewise. At about 3 miles, 5800 feet, the way enters meadowland with the first dependable creek and remains of an old cabin. The camping here, just inside the Mt. Adams Wilderness, is wonderful, but there is better to come. In 3½ miles cross abandoned tread of the Cascade Crest Trail; a short bit farther is a reflecting pond and a junction with the new Crest Trail, elevation 6100 feet.

Beyond the junction the trail continues upward sometimes in alpine trees, sometimes in grassy meadows dotted in season by paintbrush, hellebore, and avalanche lilies, generally following slopes of a prominent ridge trending toward the peak. The tread soon becomes faint and in ½ mile one may be tempted by the wide-open terrain to forget the sketchy path and roam at will. Do so if desired, but be sure to take careful visual "fixes" on landmarks so the trail can be found again on the way out—from up high one ridge looks like the next and it's easy to get confused.

At 5½ miles the trail ends at High Camp, 6900 feet, near a saddle in the main ridge and not far above the green flats and meandering streams of Adams Glacier Meadows. The camp area lies along a snowmelt stream bubbling through gardens decorated with lava boulders and wind-sculpted clumps of trees. And the views! St. Helens, Rainier, and the Goat Rocks rise above forests and ridges of the Cispus River. Look north into the crater of Potato Hill, an old cinder cone, and out over ancient lava flows covered by scrubby trees. Especially look up to steep ice of the Adams Glacier cascading from the summit. Sunsets from this camp are beyond words—and also the dawns.

Spend a day or weekend or longer. Follow a waterfall down to the delights of Glacier Meadows. Follow the ridge up past lava cliffs,

Mt. Adams and Glacier Meadow

waterfalls, meadows, moraines to the edge of the
Adams Glacier. Climb higher onto the crest of
the northwest ridge of Adams and look down to
the Lava Glacier, and look up to the summit of
the great volcano and out to far horizons.

Much of the way back to the road the trail
points straight at Rainier, some compensation for
having to leave these heavenly meadows.

Round trip 11 miles
Hiking time 7 hours
High point 6900 feet
Elevation gain 2300 feet
Best mid-July through mid-October
One day or backpack
USGS Steamboat Mountain (30 minute)
Forest Service Wilderness Permit required

151

67 JUNIPER MOUNTAIN

Dramatic views up the Cispus River to Mt. Adams, out to Mt. Rainier and Mt. St. Helens, and over endless forested hills and valleys—all while walking a long ridge, sometimes on open hillsides covered with huckleberries, sometimes in second-growth timber just getting established after the tremendous Cispus fires of 1902 and 1929. The route provides a variety of trips: an easy afternoon stroll to a 4500-foot saddle (the trail this far generally is free of snow in early or mid-June); a day hike to Juniper Mountain; an overnight backpack; or a long approach to the Boundary Trail (Hike 68). Sorry to say, cattle graze the ridge, eating most of the flowers; also,

the east side is being logged all the way up to the 5000-foot timberline.

Turn south in Randle, cross the Cowlitz River, and drive 1 mile. Turn left on road No. 123 and in 9 miles (from Randle) turn right on road No. 112. At 10 miles leave pavement and keep straight ahead on road No. 111. In 14 miles turn left on road No. 1106 and at 18 miles find the trailhead, elevation about 3500 feet.

The trail goes a few hundred feet through a clearcut, enters second-growth forest, and climbs under two prominent knolls, ascending steadily, with frequent views, 2¼ miles to a 4500-foot saddle. The trail continues climbing, gaining 1100 feet to within a few feet of the top of 5593-foot Juniper Peak (4 miles, a good turnaround for day

Beargrass on Juniper Peak. Mt. Adams in distance.

hikers), then, dropping about 400 feet, goes under cliffs. At 5½ miles is a super-great huckleberry patch—outstanding even in an area famous for huckleberries. At 5¾ miles pass a tiny lake and campsites; the water is drinkable in early summer but later becomes murky.

At 7 miles is the Sunrise Peak trail, a ¼-mile side-trip up a steep stairway with handrails to the 5880-foot site of a former lookout; by the junction are a waterhole and a fair camp. At 7¾ miles, on a big saddle in the ridge, is Old Cow Camp with water and scenic camping. The trail again drops several hundred feet and passes under cliffs of 5788-foot Jumbo Peak, 9 miles, then descends to Dark Meadows, 12 miles, 4300 feet, offering plenty of water and campsites. From here a trail drops 3½ miles to road No. 123; a new logging road soon will shorten the distance to about 1½ miles.

From Dark Meadows the trail proceeds ¾ mile to good campsites in a large basin and in ¼ mile more reaches the Boundary Trail at a point 2 miles from the road at McCoy Pass.

Note the many sawn stumps along the ridge to Juniper. These are not from logging operations, but from the cutting of old snags, which make prominent targets for lightning strikes and then may flame like torches, sending sparks for long distances. Probably the snags were felled in the 1930s.

Round trip to Juniper Peak 8 miles
Hiking time 5 hours
High point 5593 feet
Elevation gain 2000 feet
Best mid-June through November
One day
USGS McCoy Peak

Round trip to Boundary Trail 26 miles
Allow 3 days
High point about 5788 feet
Elevation gain 2300 feet, plus ups and downs
Best July through October

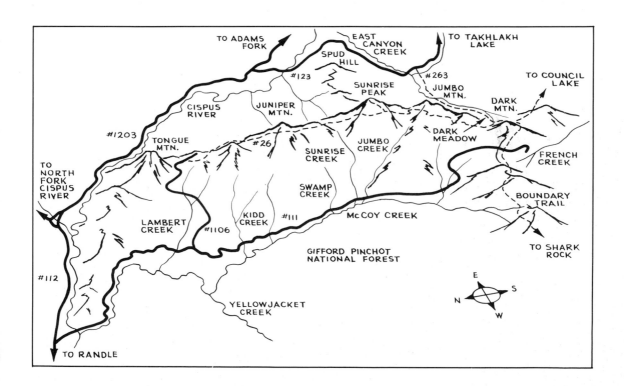

68 BOUNDARY TRAIL

A ridge trip that eventually will start at Mt. Adams, follow the crest of the Lewis River-Cispus River watershed (the boundary between the Lewis and Randle Ranger Districts, and thus the name), and finish at Mt. St. Helens. Currently, part of the way near Adams lies along roads, but 41 miles are complete. At six places roads cut the route, which therefore can be traveled in small sections if desired. For a good sample of the country, hike from McCoy Creek to Elk Pass.

The trail seldom drops below 4000 feet and just as seldom climbs above 5000 feet, mostly going through forest with frequent views. Parts are snow-free in mid-June but some steep north slopes hold dangerous snow patches several weeks later, so those intending to do the whole trip should wait until early July.

The hike can be taken in either direction, depending on whether one prefers to watch Adams or St. Helens grow larger and the other smaller. The east-to-west direction is described here.

Turn south in Randle, cross the Cowlitz River, and drive 1 mile. Turn left 33 miles on road No. 123 to Council Lake, 4200 feet, and find the head of trail No. 1. (Some trail, somewhere, had to be No. 1!)

The way starts with a steep climb up the abandoned Council Bluff road, then gradually drops to a stream crossing at 4½ miles and again goes up. At 6¾ miles round Table Mountain, at 8½ miles pass Prairie Mountain and a good camp, climb a few hundred feet, and drop to campsites at Dark Meadows. Climb again to a 4000-foot saddle at 12 miles and descend to McCoy Creek road No. 111, 14½ miles, 3800 feet. At 15½ miles are more camps in a basin south of the trail, which then rises steadily to 16½ miles. A bit beyond, keep left on new tread ascending to a 4800-foot viewpoint, 17 miles, then skirting below impressive cliffs of Hat Rock while dropping to 4000-foot Yellowjacket Pass; campsites here a few feet to the south.

At 21½ miles pass under 4800-foot Craggy Peak, next under Shark Rock, and with little change in elevation contour slopes of 5659-foot Badger Peak to Badger Lake, 25½ miles; numerous good camps. At 30½ miles cross Randle-Lewis River road No. 125 at Elk Pass, 3900 feet. The trail enters timber but soon emerges into a clearcut and follows a spur road ¼ mile before reverting to footpath and trees. At 33½ miles the route again strikes a road and goes along it almost 2 miles, partly on forest road and partly on a jeep track, crossing a stream at 34½ miles and at 35½ miles intersecting Spirit Lake road

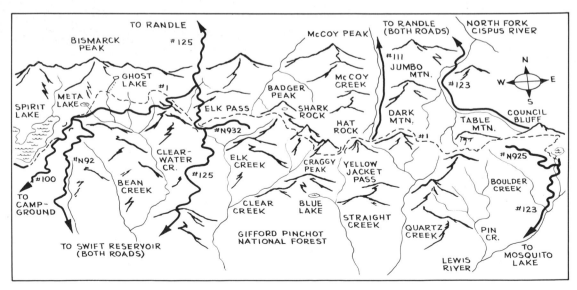

Mt. Adams from Boundary Trail on side of Hat Mountain

No. 100 and traversing a large clearcut. At 36½ miles re-enter forest; the tread here is cut into soft pumice—easy on the feet but slow walking, like mushy snow. At 37 miles pass three small streams (but no possible camps) and at 38 miles reach a ridge. There switchback up a slope burned in 1961, and at 39½ miles cross road No. 100 and pass an undeveloped path to Ghost Lake, a ½-mile side-trip. At 40 miles top the ridge and start down into Green River drainage, at 41½ miles reaching Meta Lake, 3600 feet, and campsites. At 42½ miles reach Independence Pass, 4000 feet, from which the trail drops to Spirit Lake, 3188 feet, 44½ miles. Walk the lakeshore trail 1 mile to Duck Bay boat launching area and the road.

One-way trip 45½ miles
Allow 4-6 days
High point 5000 feet
Elevation gain about 4700 feet
Best July through October
USGS Spirit Lake, French Butte, McCoy Peak, and
**   Steamboat Mountain**

69 BLUE LAKE

A lovely lake with a captivating charm, nestled in a basin, surrounded by forest. There are three routes to the truly-blue waters: Blue Lake Creek trail, 3 miles, in timber the whole way and crowded by people and machines; Bishop Ridge, a tough 10 miles with glorious views; and Mouse Lake trail, 9 miles, all in timber. Any two of the trails can be combined to make a loop trip; if the combination includes the view route, save that for the way home and avoid a grueling climb out of the valley.

Turn south in Randle, cross the Cowlitz River, and drive 1 mile. Turn left on road No. 123 for 13 miles (from Randle) and find the Bishop Ridge trail on the left side of the road. In 17 miles find the Blue Lake trail on the left side of the road. At 19 miles keep left on road No. 1302 and at 25 miles, just past the Adams Fork Campground sign, find the Mouse Lake trail, also on the left.

The shortest way is via Blue Lake trail No. 271, which starts from an elevation of 1900 feet and ascends steadily through tall fir trees, crossing Blue Lake Creek in sound of a waterfall and at 3 miles reaching the 4000-foot lake near the outlet. The best camps are here, but if crowded, poorer sites can be found at the upper end.

Bishop Ridge trail No. 272 starts at 1600 feet and switchbacks relentlessly upward 4 miles to the ridge top, about 4600 feet. The path offers considerable shade but can be hot, so carry water—there is none after the first ¾ mile. Going often up and occasionally down, the trail follows the crest, which at 5 miles becomes very narrow. Between 5½ and 6 miles is the location of a planned timber sale; the Forest Service intends to obliterate the logging road after the cutting is finished, in order not to interrupt the hiking route.

The trail stays on the ridge top as it gradually rises to a 5200-foot saddle, 7 miles, between Blue Lake and Yozoo Creek. Views here are magnificent, and on clear days Blue Lake really lives up to its name. On the Yozoo Creek side is a small pond about ⅓ mile and 500 feet below the trail; a possible campsite. Soak up the scenery and then continue several hundred feet—Mt. St. Helens comes in sight, and sharp Tongue Mountain across the Cispus; farther

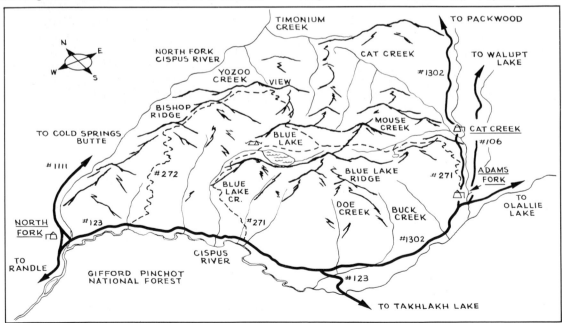

Blue Lake from Bishop Ridge

down-valley are Tower Rock, farms, and Mayfield Reservoir.

From this spot the trail ducks under a 5683-foot high point on the ridge and drops to a junction with Blue Lake trail No. 272 at 9½ miles, a short mile above the outlet.

To hike to Mouse Lake from Blue Lake, pass the Bishop Ridge trail and at 2 miles keep right on trail No. 271, reaching Mouse Lake and campsites at 5 miles, 4500 feet. Descend 4 miles to the road, 2500 feet.

Round trip via Blue Lake trail 6 miles
Hiking time 4 hours
High point 4000 feet
Elevation gain 2100 feet
Best mid-June through November
One day or backpack
USGS none

Round trip via Bishop Ridge trail 21 miles
Allow 2-3 days
High point 5200 feet
Elevation gain 3600 feet in, 1200 feet out
Best mid-June through November

70   INDIAN HEAVEN

A fascinating portion of the Cascade Crest Trail, with 17 lakes big enough to have names, 6 more on a short side-trail, and almost 100 smaller lakes, ponds, and tadpole pools, all in an area of around 5000 feet elevation, a mixture of forest, groves of alpine trees, and flat, grassy meadows, the foregrounds complemented by occasional glimpses of glaciered volcanoes. The Forest Service is contemplating designating the country from Red Mountain to the Berryfields as the Race Track Primitive Area.

The region can be sampled by taking a one-day, 10-mile loop hike, an overnight 18-mile loop, or by spending several days in order to include a visit to the Indian Race Track, where the rut made by racing horses still indents a meadow used for centuries as a tribal gathering place. The lakes melt free of snow early in July, but since Indian Heaven has been appropriately called "Mosquito Heaven," the trip is recommended for late August or September when the bugs are gone, and incidentally, the blueberries are ripe.

The starting point is Cultus Creek Campground, elevation 3988 feet. To get there from Trout Lake, drive north 16 miles on road No. 123. To get there from Randle, drive south 33 miles on road No. 123, turn left on road No. N84, to N85 to N852 to N88. Follow signs first

to Trout Lake, then Trout Lake Creek Camp, then Berryfields, and at 48 miles from Randle rejoin road No. 123, reaching the campground in 61 miles. (Mileages given here may not be accurate; the signs do not always agree.) The trailhead is in the back of a charge camp with no provision for hikers' cars, so park either at the guard station or the woodshed, making sure to leave the Forest Service access to its buildings.

Whatever the chosen trip, start on trail No. 33, thus avoiding a very steep and hot ascent of 1200 feet on trail No. 108, which is better used for the return leg of the loop.

Trail No. 33 begins in forest, climbing 600 feet in the first mile. At 1¾ mile make the short side-trip on trail 33A to Deep Lake with a view of Mt. Adams rising over tree tops, then on to Cultus Lake at 2 miles, 5050 feet, a body of water typical of many of the lakes, having trees around half the shore, meadows around the rest. To the southeast is 5925-foot Lemei Rock, and the northwest, 5706-foot Bird Mountain; one or the other of these peaks can be seen from a number of the lakes. The way climbs 100 more feet, then descends in ½ mile to meet Lemei Lake trail No. 179, signed but not shown on Forest Service maps.

For the short loop (see below), take the west fork at the junction. For the long loop, take the east fork, passing Lemei Lake in 3

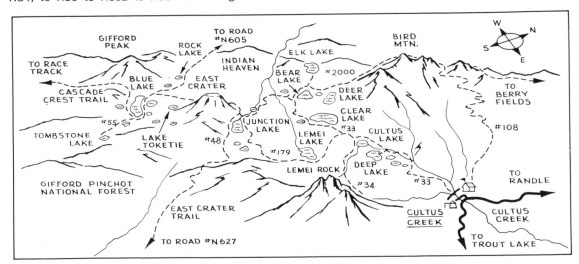

Bear Lake

miles and at about 6 miles reaching Junction Lake, 4370 feet, at the foot of wooded, 5500-foot East Crater, an old cinder cone; here is the junction with the Crest Trail.

To visit the Indian Race Track, go south from Junction Lake on the Crest Trail 2 miles to Blue Lake, one of the nicest of the Indian Heaven Lakes. From Blue Lake to the Race Track is a round trip of about 10½ miles. Follow the Crest Trail as it contours high on the side of Gifford Peak, climbs over 4987-foot Berry Mountain, and drops to meet trail No. 171A, which leads west ¾ mile to the Race Track.

To complete the long loop without a sidetrip to the Race Track, go north from Junction Lake on the Crest Trail, follow it 1½ miles to Bear Lake, 4800 feet, and return to the car as described for the short loop.

The short loop keeps right on trail No. 33 at the junction ½ mile past Cultus Lake, passes within a few yards of Clear Lake, and comes to Bear Lake at 4 miles. Cross the outlet (no problem) to join the Crest Trail on the far side; a ¼-mile side-trail leads from here to Elk Lake, 4685 feet. Head north on the Crest Trail, passing Deer Lake and numerous ponds. At about

7½ miles turn right on trail No. 108, climb 100 feet over a 5237-foot saddle in Bird Mountain, and drop steeply 1½ miles to Cultus Creek Campground.

Don't be fooled by the seemingly-flat terrain—the paths have many short ups and downs. Campsites are numerous, some by lakes and others by streams. The pumice soil is very fragile, so camp in the forest or in already established campsites. The lakes and streams have a very small flow of water so to avoid contamination keep camps far away from the water's edge.

Short loop trip 10 miles
Hiking time 6 hours
High point 5237 feet
Elevation gain about 1700 feet
Best July through October
One day or backpack
USGS Lone Butte

Long loop trip to Blue Lake 18 miles
Allow 2 days
High point 5237 feet
Elevation gain 2000 feet
Best July through October
USGS Lone Butte and Wind River

Klickitat Glacier on the east side of Mt. Adams, from Ridge of Wonders

71 MOUNT ADAMS HIGHLINE TRAIL

The classic trek of the Mt. Adams region, hiking a timberline route with ever-changing views of the huge, glacier-draped volcano, standing 12,326 feet high in the sky.

The missing link for a complete around-the-mountain loop is a 12- to 15-mile section in the Yakima Indian Reservation between Avalanche Camp and Ridge of Wonders. There is no trail and two glacier streams are serious problems, during July and August being raging torrents. Don't bother to look for logs—there aren't any. The only hope of crossing them is in early fall when melting has slackened and before heavy rains start. Hikers contemplating this section would do best to start at Bench Lake and learn the first day if the streams can be negotiated. Coming the other way, with time and food running short, one might be tempted to risk a dangerous ford on the last day of a hike.

From State Highway 141 at Trout Lake, drive north on the paved logging road No. FH17, signed "Mt. Adams Recreation Area." In 1½ miles keep right and follow road No. N700 signed "Bird Creek Meadows." At 5 miles pavement yields to gravel. At 11 miles the excellent logging road veers left; follow, instead, recreation road No. N80, which is extremely poor the rest of the way to Bird Creek Meadows, 17 miles, elevation 6500 feet.

The Mount Adams Highline Trail starts on trail No. 9, traverses 3 easy miles of glorious views and flower fields to the Timberline Camp road, 6300 feet, and contours on. At about 8¾ miles cross Salt Creek; the water tastes fine but crusted vegetation along with the banks testifies to the mineral content. The way climbs gently and at 9 miles, 6500 feet, joins the Cascade Crest Trail. To this point campsites, some with broad views, are numerous, but for the next 6 miles good drinking water may be hard to find—the streams flow from glaciers and tend to be excessively thick with rock milk; camping is possible, however, if one can tolerate the silt.

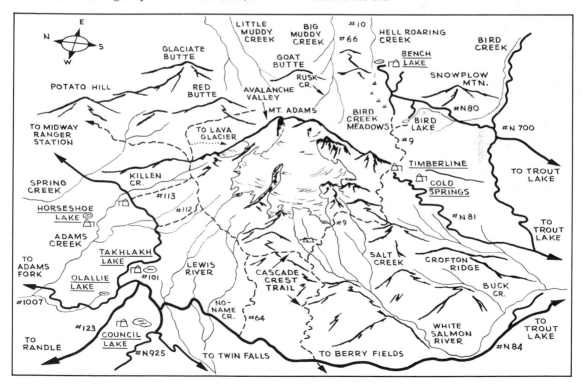

The Crest Trail swings under Pinnacle and Adams Glaciers. At 16 miles is a junction with trail No. 112, 3 miles distant from road No. 101. At about 18 miles, 6100 feet, is a junction with Killen Creek trail No. 113 (Hike 66), 3½ miles from road No. 101. At 18½ miles cross Killen Creek; campsites here.

At 1 mile from the junction with Killen Creek trail (¼ mile after crossing Killen Creek) turn right on trail No. 114, signed "Highline Trail." Follow 114 approximately 2 up and down miles to a foggy bottom, a lovely meadow traversed by a clear brook. The trail may be lost in the meadow in a confusion of paths leading to campsites.

The trail crosses the brook and from here on the way is up, first through forest to a boulder-

Mt. St. Helens from slopes of Mt. Adams

hopping crossing of a milky stream from Lava Glacier (the stream may be impossible during heavy melting periods). It then continues up— through an endless, shadeless moraine of pumice and lava, passing Red Butte to a 7000-foot saddle between Goat Butte and Mt. Adams. The trail is marked with huge cairns. The way is rough and made more difficult because one's eyes are more likely to be on the tremendous view of Adams than looking out for rocks in the trail.

From there the way drops to Avalanche Valley and the end of the trail at 25 miles. The valley is named for the ice which periodically drops from a mile-long hanging glacier onto the Rusk and Klickitat Glaciers.

For exploring, hike to the top of 7484-foot Goat Butte. For more exploring, go back to Foggy Bottom and follow the stream bed upward about 1 mile close to the toe of Lava Glacier. From here try to find wind caves and lava formations to the west. It is also possible to contour to Adams Glacier Meadows (Hike 66).

If Avalanche Valley alone is the goal, start on trail No. 113 for a hike of 10 miles each way.

One-way trip to trail-end 25 miles
Allow 3 days
High point 7000 feet
Elevation gain approximately 3000 feet
Best mid-July through September
USGS none

Camping on side of Mt. Adams. Mt. Rainier in distance.

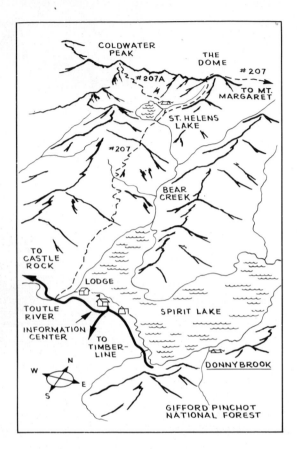

72 COLDWATER PEAK

A beautiful mountain lake, then a mountain-top site of a former lookout with views of peaks and lakes and the still-unlogged north slopes of Mt. St. Helens. Unfortunately this trail, like most others in the area, is overrun with motorbikes—after taking the hike, write to the Forest Service and complain about the mechanized abuse of the land. Also, though the walk is one of the most rewarding in the area, the Forest Service is logging within ½ mile of the peak.

From Castle Rock or Toledo on Interstate 5 drive Highway 504 about 45 miles to the Spirit Lake visitor information center—or actually, to ¾ mile short of the center, to the point where the highway bridge crosses the lake outlet. Find Mt. Margaret trail No. 207 on the north side of the road, elevation 3100 feet.

The first 3¼ miles to St. Helens Lake lie through a lovely stand of timber. At about 1 mile pass an acre of blowdown offering views to Spirit Lake. With some level sections, some downs, some steep ups, and numerous streams, the way climbs to 4567-foot St. Helens Lake, a popular family camping spot. The trail rounds the east shore; in high water of early summer the outlet may be difficult to cross.

At 3½ miles turn left on Coldwater Peak trail No. 207A. At 4½ miles the views start expanding and at 5 miles they literally explode as the 5727-foot summit of Coldwater Peak is attained. For the best look at Mt. Rainier, climb over a small rocky knoll.

A loop trip can be made by continuing to Mt. Margaret and going over the top and down the other side, as described in Hike 74. Better yet, camp at St. Helens Lake and climb both Coldwater and Margaret.

Round trip 10 miles
Hiking time 6 hours
High point 5727 feet
Elevation gain 2500 feet
Best July through October
One day or backpack
USGS Spirit Lake

Mt. St. Helens from Coldwater Peak.

73 MOUNT MARGARET BACK COUNTRY

A series of 10 alpine lakes, wildflowers, a ridge walk with views of four great volcanoes, and a chance to see a "calendar picture" of Mt. St. Helens rising above Spirit Lake—one of the three most famous mountain views in the United States. Take an easy overnight trip or spend a week-long vacation. The area is most colorful in early August when flowers are in maximum bloom, but much quieter in early July when snow keeps the motorbikes out.

This should be one of the most delightful hikes in the West, but thanks to the Forest Service interpretation of "multiple-use," the joy of peace and solitude is gone. Spirit Lake once was a quiet place for canoeing, fishing from a small boat, or just relaxing, but now high-speed motorboats churn the water and skiers aimlessly crisscross the lake. The trail is a speedway for motorbikes and is fertilized and odorized by an overwhelming number of horses. There is simply too much competition. Don't blame the mess on the local ranger—he doesn't make the rules. Only a lot of hikers writing letters to the Forest Supervisor, Gifford Pinchot National Forest, Vancouver, Washington 98660, and also letters to senators and congressmen, can bring about a change.

Campsite at Grizzly Lake

Drive east from Castle Rock or Toledo on Highway 504 about 45 miles to Spirit Lake. At the visitor information center make a sharp left turn, then a right, and continue a mile to Duck Bay parking lot. On the east side of the lot, elevation 3198 feet, is the start of Lakes trail No. 1, which changes to trail No. 211 in about a mile.

With minor ups and downs the trail follows the lakeshore, passing two campsites in the first 1½ miles. At 2 miles walk below Harmony Falls and at 2½ miles leave the shore and begin climbing. Be sure to look back at the famous calendar picture of lake and mountain.

The trail ascends in earnest, gaining 1300 feet to Norway Pass, 5¼ miles, 4508 feet. Now the way levels off, still in forest but with tree-framed views of Hood, Adams, and Rainier. At 5¾ miles pass a junction with Mt. Margaret trail No. 207 (Hike 74) and drop to Grizzly Lake at 7 miles, 4300 feet.

Descend a bit and climb to Obscurity Lake at 8 miles, 4337 feet, then onward to Boot Lake (and a beautiful early-August flower display) at 8½ miles, 4500 feet. The trail goes up and down, sometimes in flowers and sometimes not, and the lakes come fast—Panhandle, Shovel, Snow, Frog, and Heart. Other lakes can be reached by aid of map and compass. The farther one goes, the more solitude can be expected. At 12½ miles the trail passes Heart Lake, last of the series, and continues a very rough 2½ miles to Elk Prairie road No. 1002B—a good end-point for a one-way trip, but not a shortcut to the prettiest lakes.

Because of overuse, camping is restricted at some of the lakes. Many sites have been turned into barnyards by horsemen picketing animals right where hikers would otherwise sleep and eat. If the stench and the flies are too bad, look for private camps away from the lakes.

Mileages given on the signposts are very confusing and seldom agree with one another.

Round trip to Grizzly Lake 14 miles
Hiking time 7 hours
High point 4700 feet
Elevation gain 1500 feet in, 500 feet out
Best mid-July through October
One day or backpack
USGS Spirit Lake

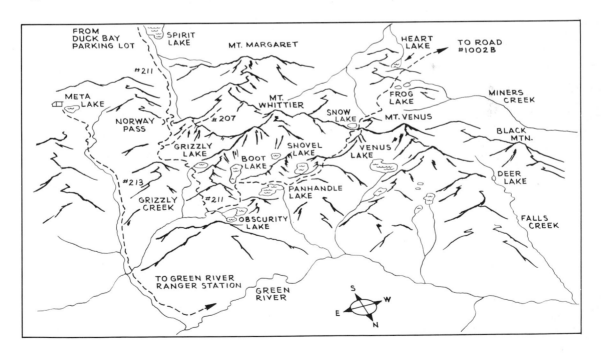

Spirit Lake and Mt. St. Helens from Mt. Margaret trail

74 MOUNT MARGARET

A high ridge of flower-filled alpine meadows with panoramic views down to Spirit Lake and across the waters to the symmetrical volcano of Mt. St. Helens and out over forested ridges to its companion "Guardians of the Columbia," Adams and Hood. Most of the way is on good trail, but there are several very steep stretches of soft pumice. The Forest Service has finally closed the trail to motorbikes, but violations of the closure are frequent, intensifying the serious erosion problem.

If a simple 15-mile round trip to the summit is planned, it is best to start near the outlet of Spirit Lake (see Hike 72). However, a loop trip is recommended and described here.

Drive to Duck Bay parking lot, elevation 3198 feet, and hike Lakes trail No. 1, which changes to trail No. 211 in about a mile, to Norway Pass, 5¼ miles, 4508 feet (Hike 73). Continue to a junction with the Grizzly Lake trail at 5¾ miles and turn left on Mt. Margaret trail No. 207. At 6 miles, just below 4900-foot Bear Pass, is a junction with an abandoned trail to Grizzly Lake.

From here the route ascends steeply over the top of a 5223-foot knoll, drops sharply into a saddle with views of Spirit Lake and St. Helens on one side and glimpses of Grizzly Lake on the other, and climbs steeply again. At about 7 miles the way tops one of the half-dozen summits of Mt. Margaret and enters a parkland of meadows and clumps of alpine trees. The second summit is the scene of a recent fire. The trail proceeds to the highest summit at about 7½ miles, 5858 feet. The grand vistas of forests and lakes and icy volcanoes make this a splendid turnaround point for round-trip hikers.

To complete the loop, follow the trail as it descends along the ridge, going over the tops of most of the small peaks, with more views of Spirit Lake and new views of St. Helens Lake and a look north to impressive Mt. Whittler. At 9 miles the path climbs up and down The Dome and drops through timber to a junction with Coldwater Creek trail No. 207 at 10 miles, and ¼ mile farther to St. Helens Lake, 4567 feet.

The rest of the route is described in Hike 72. At a bit more than 14 miles, elevation 3198 feet, the highway is reached. A 2-mile road walk (or ride) leads back to the start of the loop trip at Duck Bay.

Campsites are located along Spirit Lake and at St. Helens Lake. Meadow benches near the top of Mt. Margaret are glorious places to watch a sunset or sunrise, but the only water is from early-summer snowmelt.

Loop trip 14½ miles plus 2 miles of road
Hiking time 9 hours
High point 5858 feet
Elevation gain 2800 feet
Best mid-July through October
One day or backpack
USGS Spirit Lake

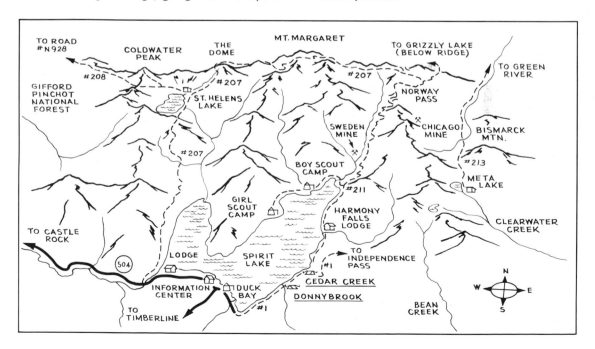

75 AROUND MOUNT ST. HELENS

Circle America's most graceful mountain, often called the Fujiyama of the West, a peak that in any other part of the country would be a national park. But the hike is not all fun because those who care little for the beauty have desecrated the splendors. As art treasures in the tombs of Egyptian pharaohs were stolen and melted down for the gold, loggers have cut merchantable trees right to timberline; not even the world-famous view from Spirit Lake is safe. Private firms are the major villains, but the Forest Service could have done much to save the natural magnificence.

Not only has the scenery been trampled half to death, but the round-the-mountain trail has been slashed to ribbons. The Spirit Lake road eliminated the route on the north side many years ago; more recently, logging has obliterated it on the south. Only on the east and west slopes is the trail intact—and the west side is in forest and thus may also be lost. There is some hope the Forest Service will re-establish the trail at timberline, creating a hiking route that would surely become as famous as the Ochudo Trail the Japanese have built around Mt. Fuji.

Though the complete circuit can still be hiked, the road-walking involved is little pleasure. The recommendation here is to make the loop by driving the roads and hiking the two sections of intact trail. The clockwise direction, which involves less elevation gain, is described here.

Begin the circle on the Spirit Lake road. Drive 40 miles east from Castle Rock on Highway 504, pass the county line (note spur road No. N903, the end of the round-the-mountain route) and continue 8 miles to the timberline parking

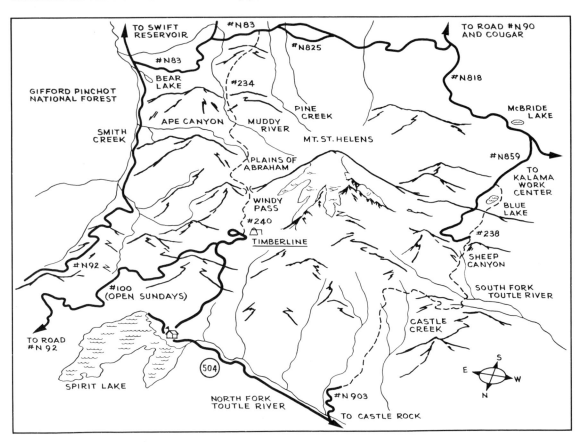

area, elevation 4300 feet.

Finding the official start of trail No. 240 may be difficult, in which case simply take any of the paths leading in ½ mile to 4900-foot Windy Pass, the notch in the left side of the mountain just at timberline. Descend to Pine Creek trail No. 234 at Smith Creek, 1 mile, 4200 feet; campsites here. Ascend the trail ½ mile to half-mile-wide and almost level Plains of Abraham, 4400 feet, swept clean of trees by massive winter avalanches from the summit of St. Helens. If time permits, scramble up one of the small cinder cones to the east. At 3¾ miles gape down into the narrow depths of Ape Canyon. Cross Muddy River and begin a descent close to Pine Creek. Camping here, and generally one of the two streams is clear enough for drinking. (Oddly, the meltwater from the Muddy Glacier frequently alternates between the creeks; usually one is dirty and the other clean.) The way drops steadily through small pines, entering solid forest at 5½ miles. At 6¼ miles is a shelter, but Pine Creek may be too loaded with rock milk for fastidious tastes. At 6½ miles reach road No. N83, 2900 feet, end of the first trail segment.

Drive (or hike if desired) west, crossing Pine Creek in less than ¼ mile. At 7.2 miles turn right on road No. N818, and at 12 miles turn right again on road N859. At 13.5 miles watch carefully for an intersection with road No. N847; turn right. At 14 miles is the Blue Lake trail and at 16 miles the road-end and trailhead, elevation 4000 feet. (These southern roads can be reached by driving Highway 503 to Cougar, or by crossing the mountains from Spirit Lake on roads No. N92, N83, and 100; the latter is open only on Sundays. Present logging on private land at either end of the trail may require detours; ask the ranger at Spirit Lake.)

Toutle trail No. 238 immediately descends into timber, crosses Sheep Canyon in about ¾ mile, climbs slightly, and in about 1 mile heads down in earnest. Cross the Toutle River at 1¾ miles, 2900 feet; the stream is wide but can be boulder-hopped. In a few hundred feet cross a second creek. Campsites at both. The trail now ascends to 4100 feet and at 3½ miles levels off. (For the only views possible from this segment of the circuit, leave the tread here, climb ¼ mile

Shoestring Glacier on Mt. St. Helens

through forest to the side of a gully, and look upward to St. Helens.) The trail remains level ¼ mile, then starts a long descent to the road. At 4½ miles enter a clearcut and follow a cat road along the border between private and National Forest land, which also is the boundary between Cowlitz and Skamania Counties, at 7 miles reaching road No. N903, 2900 feet, at a point of 1 mile from the Spirit Lake road. The Youth Conservation Corps is rebuilding the Toutle trail to bypass the logging area. When complete, the new route will provide interesting views of the mountain and lava flows.

Pine Creek trail:
One-way trip 6½ miles
Hiking time 4 hours
High point 4900 feet
Elevation gain 700 feet, loss 2100 feet
Best July through October
One day or backpack
USGS Spirit Lake

Toutle trail:
One-way trip 7 miles
Hiking time 4 hours
High point 4000 feet
Elevation gain 1400 feet, loss 2600 feet
Best July through October
One day or backpack

Craggy Peak and Meadow Basin Camp

76   SHARK ROCK

Follow a wooded ridge to a mountain lake, 2 miles of alpine meadows, and views, and views, and views. Nowhere else in the State of Wash- ington can one see so vast an expanse of solid virgin forest as in the vista over Straight Creek and Quartz Creek to Mt. Adams; only a few distant clearings far to the south break the solid green. Try this trip early in July; if conditions are right there may be miles of beargrass in bloom.

The trail is harassed by machines and jeopardized by logging, including a proposed timber sale 1/4 mile from Blue Lake. That the path has survived until now is due solely to a Sierra Club lawsuit. Logging at these high elevations is particularly shocking because the timber has relatively little commercial value—a quarter or more of the trees are left on the ground to rot after being cut.

From Lewis River Ranger Station on Swift Reservoir, drive 4.7 miles north on road No. 125 to a junction with road No. N92. Stay on No. 125 for 5.6 miles (from ranger station) and turn right on road No. N920. Watch all intersections carefully—some of the side-roads are used more than the main road. At 18 miles is a junction with road No. N923; keep left, still on N920. At 20 miles find an unmarked and undrivable side-road to the right, elevation 3400 feet. The trailhead is a few yards up the side-road and also unmarked as of 1970.

The trail starts as No. 80, in less than 1/4 mile coming to a junction marked with two pre-World War II signs calling this the Spirit Lake-Guler trail. Take the uphill path, signed Blue Lake trail No. 3. The path winds uphill, crossing several small streams and in 1 mile passing close to a clearcut which offers a possible shortcut. (To reach this alternate starting point, drive road No. N923 from its intersection with No. N920 some 2 miles to the second spur road after passing Wright Meadows. Turn left 1/2 mile to the logging area and find a footpath across the clearing.)

In the next 2 miles the trail climbs gently, eventually ascending a wide ridge. At a little over 3 miles the ridge becomes quite narrow and at times the route is steep. But the vista begins. At 5200 feet the way contours around a high point and drops to a view of Blue Lake at 3 1/2 miles. (To get to 4553-foot Blue Lake, hike the trail to the point where the lake comes clearly in sight and find an unmarked way trail down to the shore.)

The timber thins, the trail enters meadows, and at 4 miles, 5200 feet, is a short side-trail to a campsite—water is scarce after the snow melts. At 4 1/2 miles pass a side-trail leading 1/4 mile southeast to Basin Camp. After contouring slopes

of a knob, at 5 miles, 5200 feet, join trail No. 1, the Boundary Trail (Hike 68).

For the widest views along the route, wander up either of the grassy knolls at 3 1/2 or 4 miles. Shark Rock at the head of Clear Creek is the most impressive rocky peak on the Boundary Ridge.

Round trip to Boundary Trail 10 miles
Hiking time 5 hours
High point 5200 feet
Elevation gain 1800 feet
Best mid-July to early November
One day or backpack
USGS Spencer Butte, Quartz Creek, and McCoy Peak

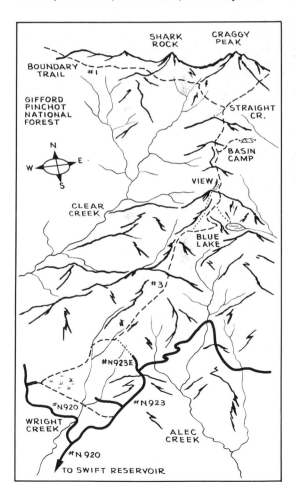

Bolt Camp on the Lewis River. In 1973 thieves made off with the rusty old saw.

77 LEWIS RIVER

A forest of huge firs, cedars, and maples serves as a canopy to a green and varied carpet of Oregon grape, vanilla leaf, moss dotted with oxalis, and shoulder-high brush. The Forest Service has promised to preserve in a natural condition a wide corridor along the Lewis River, keeping this trail, perhaps the last low-elevation valley path remaining in Gifford Pinchot National Forest, as a 9-mile sample and reminder of the many, many miles of such splendor that we inherited and have now mostly squandered. However, in 1973 the lower part of the trail was rebuilt to make it safe for motor bikes—a strange way to spend public funds when 90 percent of the travelers are on foot.

The trail can be hiked in either direction, and parties which can arrange transportation to allow a one-way trip would be well-advised to start at the top, which is 400 feet higher than the bottom. However, parties making a round-trip should start at the bottom and thus be sure to cover at least the lower 3 miles, where the best trees are; for this reason the bottom-to-top direction is described here.

From Lewis River Ranger Station on Swift Reservoir, drive .3 mile north and turn right on road No. N90. At 5.5 miles from the ranger sta-

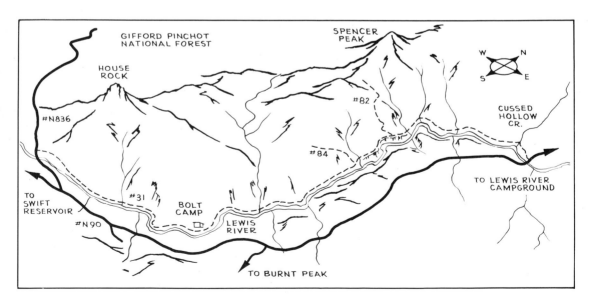

tion turn left on road No. N836, and at 6.2 miles cross the Lewis River bridge. At 6.6 miles turn right to the lower trailhead, elevation about 1100 feet.

To reach the upper trailhead, from the junction of roads Nos. N90 and 836 continue on No. N90 (avoiding side-roads that may be used more than the main one) to a concrete bridge over the Lewis River at 14.5 miles from the ranger station. A few yards from the west end of the bridge find the trailhead, elevation about 1400 feet.

From the lower beginning, trail No. 31 immediately drops to river level, about 1000 feet, and magnificent forest. The way winds along bottomland flats, climbs a small bank, and emerges into a clearcut at 1 mile. To somewhat beyond $1\frac{1}{2}$ miles the path follows the margin of the logging show before re-entering virgin trees. After a few steep ups and downs, at just under $2\frac{1}{2}$ miles is Bolt Camp; the shelter here is amazingly well-preserved considering it was built in the early 1930s. At 4 miles the valley narrows to a canyon, a good turnaround for round-trip hikers, since from this point the trail goes up and down a lot but never again reaches river level—though there are several spots where one can easily drop to the stream.

At 7 miles the trail climbs a 300-foot bluff. At $7\frac{1}{2}$ miles find a viewpoint a few feet off the tread and look down to the canyon sliced in columnar basalt. From here on the river is unseen and old forest yields to young forest dating from the Spencer Butte fire which swept the area in the 1920s; because snags are considered a major fire hazard, most were cut many years ago. At 9 miles cross Cussed Hollow and climb over the last bump to the upper trailhead at $9\frac{1}{2}$ miles, 1400 feet.

One-way trip 9½ miles
Hiking time 5 hours
High point 1600 feet
Elevation gain 1000 feet upstream, 600 feet downstream
Best March through November
One day or backpack
USGS Burnt Peak and Spencer Butte

Lewis River trail

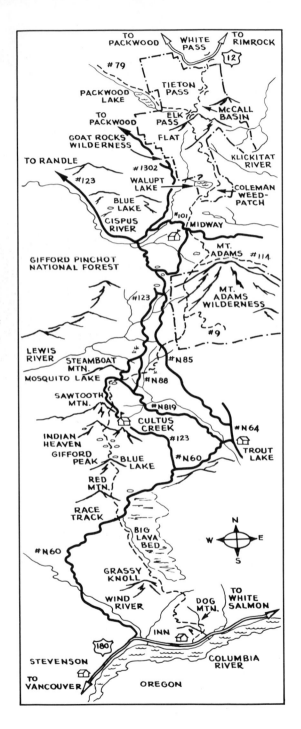

78 CASCADE CREST TRAIL

The Pacific Crest National Scenic Trail, which extends from Mexico to Canada, is most commonly called in the northernmost 470 miles by its older name, the Cascade Crest Trail. The 286-mile portion between the Columbia River and Stevens Pass traverses highlands past three grand volcanoes and penetrates the heart of two spectacular masses of high alpine peaks. The way isn't all pure fun because it also goes through lower, forested sections of the Cascade Range where logging roads and clearcuts have savaged the wilderness solitude. However, the feeling of accomplishment gained by traveling the full length of the crest cannot be spoiled even by the worst of the messed-up parts.

Few hikers complete the route in a single effort; most do the trail in short bits over a period of years. Those taking the whole trip at once can start at either end; the south-to-north direction is described here.

At many places the trail is being relocated for the sake of easier grades or better scenery. For example, to bring Crest hikers closer to a crossing of the Columbia River, the trail will be re-routed toward the Bridge of the Gods. In 1975 a temporary starting point may be established at Panther Creek on road No. 605 (near Wind River Ranger Station). For current information, contact Marvin Lindh, Engineer Department, U.S. Forest Service, Randle, WA.

The following brief summary is intended merely to provide a general impression of the route. For details of mileages and campsites, consult the Forest Service map and log of the Cascade Crest Trail, available free from any Forest Service office.

Columbia River to White Pass

Begin beside the legendary "River of the West," skirt the slopes of giant Mt. Adams, enjoy views to graceful Mt. St. Helens, and walk the airy crest of the Goat Rocks Wilderness—the most difficult, as well as one of the most dramatically beautiful, segments of the entire Crest Trail.

Drive US 180 east from Vancouver, Washington to the town of Stevenson and some 9 miles beyond to the parking lot and trailhead on the north side of the highway, elevation 186 feet.

Johnson Peak and Packwood Lake. Egg Butte in foreground. From Cascade Crest Trail.

At the west end of the parking area is a small cafe, the Crest Inn. (This trail route will be maintained. However, for the start in 1975, see paragraph above.)

Hike through forests, lava flows, and occasional views—the route interrupted by logging roads, clearcuts, powerlines, and pipelines. Go steeply up and down several times, passing Dog Mountain, Grassy Knoll, and Big Huckleberry Mountain to road No. N60 near Race Track Campground. **Distance from Columbia River to Race Track Campground about 27 miles; elevation gain about 5500 feet; hiking time 3 days.**

From road No. N60 climb miles of woods to Red Mountain and Blue Lake and the pond-dotted meadows and famous huckleberry fields of Indian Heaven (Hike 70). Pass near Bear Lake, go almost over the top of Sawtooth Mountain, cross road No. 123, and continue through Huckleberry Meadows to Mosquito Creek. Cross the road again and traverse the east side of Steamboat Mountain to a third crossing of road No. 123. **Distance from Race Track Campground to road No. 123 about 26 miles; elevation gain about 2900 feet; hiking time 3 days.**

The next stage is climaxed by the alpine gardens and glacial streams on the flanks of Mt. Adams. From road No. 123 cross road No. N88, Trout Lake Creek, and road No. N85, climb to Dry Meadows and Grand Meadows, cross road No. N84, traverse Swampy Meadows, and at 12 miles join the Mount Adams Highline Trail (Hike 71). At 22 miles leave the Highline Trail and at 23½ miles leave the Mt. Adams Wilderness at Spring Creek and proceed to road No. 101 at Midway Meadows. **Distance from road No. 123 to**

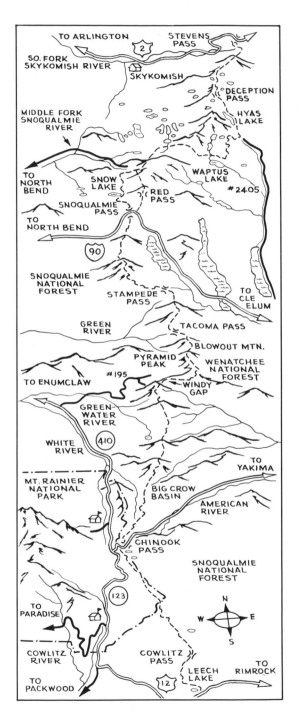

Midway Meadows about 29 miles; elevation gain about 3500 feet; hiking time 3 days.

Now starts the first long stretch of roadless country, most of it in the Goat Rocks Wilderness, including a couple miles which can be dangerous. From Midway Meadows go a short bit along a rough road, round a lava flow, and at 6 miles enter the Wilderness. Proceed past Coleman Weed Patch, intersect the Walupt Lake trail, and pass above Snowgrass Flat (Hike 63). Carefully, bewaring of hazards, climb the ridge above Packwood Glacier and traverse the shoulder of Old Snowy to Elk Pass (Hike 65), the route eases to McCall Basin (Hike 57), Tieton Pass, and Shoe Lake (Hike 55), at 34 miles leaving the Wilderness and descending to White Pass. **Distance from Midway Meadows to White Pass about 38 miles; elevation gain about 6100 feet; hiking time 4-5 days.**

One-way trip from Columbia River to White Pass about
   120 miles
Hiking time 13 days minimum
High point 7620 feet
Elevation gain about 18,000 feet
Best in May the first 27 miles, mid-July for the rest
USGS Hood River, Wind River, Willard, Steamboat Mtn.,
   Mt. Adams, and White Pass
Forest Service Wilderness permits required in Mt. Adams
   and Goat Rocks Wildernesses

White Pass to Stevens Pass

North from White Pass extend miles of marvelous meadows and lakes and large views of Mt. Rainier, then a lower and more wooded (and road-marred) section of the crest leading to Snoqualmie Pass, and finally the splendid assemblage of forests and cliffs and glaciers and flowers and waters constituting the Alpine Lakes Cascades. This scenic segment of the Crest Trail is close to population centers and extremely popular.

The first stage rarely leaves meadows and panoramas for long and passes numerous small lakes—too many to name here. From the White Pass Highway at Leech Lake (Hike 54) hike to Sand Lake, Cowlitz Pass, Fish Lake, and the Mt. Rainier National Park boundary at 15½ miles. Weave in and out of the Park, following the crest by Two Lakes, Dewey Lakes, and around the side of Naches Peak to Chinook Pass and US 410;

here leave the National Park. **Distance from White Pass to Chinook Pass about 25 miles; elevation gain about 2400 feet; hiking time 3 days.**

The opening third of the next part lies in alpine terrain as before, and the remainder in woods broken by roads. Climb from Chinook Pass to Sourdough Gap (Hike 48), traverse to Bear Gap and around Pickhandle Point and Crown Point, with views to the Crystal Mountain Ski Area, ascend the crest, contour below the summit of Norse Peak, and drop into Big Crow Basin (Hike 47). Proceed to Little Crow Basin, a junction with the Arch Rock trail, Arch Rock Camp, and Rod's Gap—where a Forest Service road is newly cutting the trail. Pass Government Meadows and cross the Naches Wagon Trail (Hike 46), contour under Pyramid Peak, and reach road No. 195 at Windy Gap. **Distance from Chinook Pass to Windy Gap about 27 miles; elevation gain about 2500 feet; hiking time 3 days.**

Now comes a portion with few views except in clearcuts. Go along the road a bit from Windy Gap, follow the crest nearly to the top of Blowout Mountain, descend in woods and clearcuts to Tacoma Pass and a logging road, and travel onward under Snowshoe Butte to Lizard Lake and the road at Stampede Pass. **Distance from Windy Gap to Stampede Pass about 27 miles; elevation gain about 1100 feet; hiking time 3 days.**

More forest travel—but much of the private land is being logged so the path is not always easy to find and not always pleasant, despite increasingly mountainous views northward. From Stampede Pass hike to Dandy Pass, Mirror Lake, contour Tinkham and Silver Peaks (Hike 26) to Olallie Meadow and Lodge Lake, climb to Beaver Lake, and drop down ski slopes to Snoqualmie Pass Ranger Station. **Distance from Stampede Pass to Snoqualmie Pass about 18 miles; elevation gain about 1400 feet; hiking time 2 days.**

From this point north through the superb wildlands of the Alpine Lakes Cascades the Crest Trail is in the process of being moved to a new line nearer the actual crest, but since the project will not be finished until the late 1970s, the 1974 trail is described here. The current "main" route crosses Red Mountain Pass (Hike 28), but because of the dangerous snow gully at

pass, usually is impassable until August and some years never does open for safe travel. The alternate route via Snow Lake is therefore recommended. From the Snoqualmie Pass Ranger Station walk the highway west, go under Interstate 90 to the Alpental road, and find the Snow Lake trail (Hike 27). Drop from Snow Lake to the Middle Fork Snoqualmie River and hike upstream passing around Goldmeyer Hot Springs to the Middle Fork road. **Distance from Snoqualmie Pass to Goldmeyer Hot Springs about 13 miles; elevation gain about 1600 feet; hiking time 2 days.**

Now, much hard work, rewarded by the magnificence of alpine lakes and rugged mountains. From near Goldmeyer Hot Springs walk the Middle Fork road past logging operations to the trailhead and climb to Dutch Miller Gap (Hike 19). Descend to Lake Ivanhoe and Waptus Lake (Hike 36), ascend to Deep Lake (Hike 39) and the ridge above, and drop to the Cle Elum River road. **Distance from Goldmeyer Hot Springs to Cle Elum River road about 30 miles; elevation gain about 4800 feet; hiking time 3 days.**

End the journey in mostly alpine country decorated with several outstanding lakes. From the Cle Elum River road pass Hyas Lake (Hike 41), climb to Deception Pass, go by Deception Lakes (Hike 6), cross Pieper Pass (Hike 7), and drop to Glacier Lake and Surprise Lake. Now switchback to a high pass, contour above Trapp Lake, descend to Hope Lake, pass Mig Lake, ascend to a pass above Swimming Deer Lake, proceed to a viewpoint above Lake Josephine (Hike 8), and drop to Stevens Pass. **Distance from Cle Elum River road to Stevens Pass about 26 miles; elevation gain about 6400 feet; hiking time 3 days.**

From Stevens Pass the Cascade Crest Trail continues 185 miles to Allison Pass in Canada. **See 101 Hikes in the North Cascades.**

One-way trip from White Pass to Stevens Pass about 166 miles
Hiking time 19 days
High point 6500 feet
Elevation gain about 20,400 feet
Best mid-July through October
USGS White Pass, Bumping Lake, Lester, Snoqualmie, Pass, Big Snow Mountain, Mt. Daniel, The Cradle, Scenic, and Stevens Pass

79 MOUNT ELLINOR

From 1853 to 1857 George Davidson surveyed Puget Sound, working from the brig **R. H. Fauntleroy,** named for his superior, the head of the U.S. Coast and Geodetic Survey. Needing names for the maps he was making, he drew upon the Fauntleroy family, calling the southernmost prominent peak on the Olympic skyline Ellinor, for the youngest daughter, the double-summited peak for her Brothers, and the highest point for her older sister Constance. Later, Davidson and Ellinor were married. However, subsequent mappers shifted Ellinor to a lower peak, replacing her with Mt. Washington.

A century and more later, hikers look from the summit of Ellinor over a panorama of the Cascades from Mt. St. Helens to Glacier Peak, and of the Olympics from neighboring Mt. Washington, whose profile can be imagined to resemble that of the general and president, to the distant white mass of Mt. Olympus.

Drive US 101 along Hood Canal to Hoodsport. Turn west 9 miles on the Lake Cushman road to a junction. Turn right 1.6 miles on road No. 245, then left 4.9 miles on Big Creek road No. 2419 to the trailhead, elevation about 3500 feet. Carry a full canteen; the slopes are dry.

The trail climbs rather gently in forest about 1 mile, then becomes steep and increasingly rough. Pause at a clearing for a look down through trees to Lake Cushman. At 2½ miles, about 5200 feet, is timberline and the trail-end, and for inexperienced hikers, the proper turn-around. The vistas of lowlands and Cascades are as good here as from the summit—and there is no danger of getting lost, as there may be on the final slopes.

If the party is experienced and the weather clear, ascend meadows, scramble a rock gully to its head, turn left over a spur ridge, and reach the top of the peak, 3 miles, 5944 feet. To previous views add others into the heart of the Olympics. The route above the trail is easy enough, and obvious in sunshine, but can be treacherous when fog blows in.

Round trip to summit 6 miles
Hiking time 7 hours
High point 5944 feet
Elevation gain 3000 feet
Best July through October
One day
USGS Mt. Steele and The Brothers

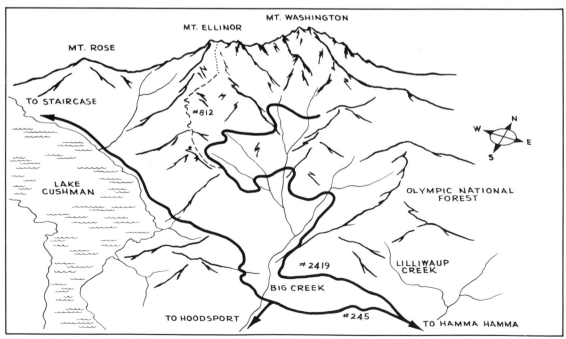

Hood Canal and Mt. Rainier from side of Mt. Ellinor.

80   FLAPJACK LAKES

Two subalpine lakes set side by side like flapjacks in a frying pan. Above the waters and the forests rise sharp summits of the Sawtooth Range, a group of peaks noted among climbers for the odd texture of the rock, which largely consists of "pillow lava" erupted under the surface of an ancient sea and now eroded into weird shapes.

Drive US 101 along Hood Canal to Hoodsport. Turn west to Lake Cushman and follow the North Fork Skokomish River road to Staircase Ranger Station and the trailhead, elevation 800 feet.

The trail follows an abandoned road the first 3.7 miles, then ascends moderately but steadily in cool forest to a junction at 7 miles. From here a faint way trail goes left to Black and White Lakes in 1¼ miles, Smith Lake in 1½ miles.

The right fork reaches Flapjack Lakes, 4000 feet, in a short mile. One lake, quite shallow, is well along toward becoming a marsh, while the other is deeper and ringed by rock buttresses; the two are separated by a narrow isthmus. Two shelters provide refuge in case of storm. The most striking Sawtooth summit from the lake is

The Horn—known to a party of hikers who saw it on an autumn night years ago with the full moon (made of green cheese, then) touching its yearning snout, as "The Mouse."

Actually, the trip only just begins at the lakes. For high and wide meadows and broad views, walk the Mt. Gladys trail 1½ more miles up a lovely valley of rocks and flowers and bubbling water to Gladys Pass, 5000 feet, between a rounded garden peak and a vicious finger of lava. Roam the gardens to the 5600-foot summit of Mt. Gladys. Stare at the frightening walls of 6104-foot Cruiser ("Bruiser") Peak, whose tower is visible from Seattle, standing like a boundary monument on the southeast corner of Olympic National Park.

Round trip to lakes 15.6 miles
Hiking time 10 hours
High point 4000 feet
Elevation gain 3100 feet
Best July through October
One day or backpack
USGS Mt. Steel
Park Service Camping Permit required

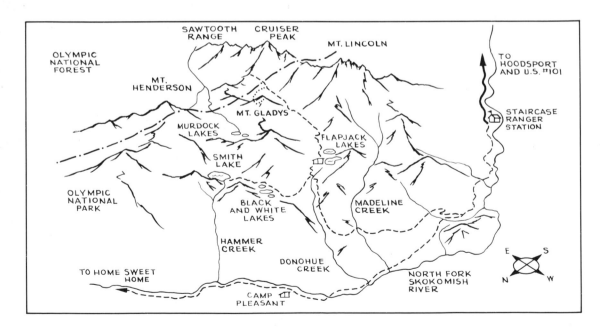

Upper Flapjack Lake and Mt. Lincoln.

81 HOME SWEET HOME

In early May, when a small elk herd is still in the Skokomish valley and trillium and calypso orchids are in bloom, walk the gentle trail to Nine Stream. In summer, climb from the valley to First Divide and broad views, then drop into Duckabush River drainage and the lupine meadows of Home Sweet Home.

Drive US 101 to Hoodsport and turn west to the end of the North Fork Skokomish River road (Hike 80), elevation 800 feet.

The North Fork Skokomish River trail follows an abandoned road 3.7 miles, then enters forest to

Mt. Steel from ridge above Home Sweet Home. Taken first of July when meadows are still covered with snow.

Big Log Camp, 5½ miles, a spacious area beside the stream. At 6 miles the way crosses the river on a bridge over a deep, quiet pool. Immediately beyond is a junction; go right. The trail climbs slightly to Camp Pleasant, 6½ miles, 1600 feet, on a large maple flat. This appropriately-named spot makes a good overnight stop for springtime backpackers; if the shelter is occupied, there are many excellent campsites nearby.

At 9½ miles, 2091 feet, is Nine Stream Shelter and the end of level walking. In the next mile the trail ascends at a comfortable rate through a big meadow, then forest. After that the way is continuously steep and often rough. Flower gardens become more frequent. Mt. Stone appears to the south.

At about 12 miles the trail reaches a meadow below Mt. Steel, turns sharply right, and climbs to the crest of 4688-foot First Divide, 12½ miles, and views across the Duckabush valley to Mt. LaCrosse, White Mountain, and the greenery of LaCrosse Pass.

The path descends ½ mile to Home Sweet Home, 4198 feet. Even from a bunk in the shelter one may enjoy the blossoms of avalanche lilies or lupine, depending on the season. The view is superb of 6233-foot Mt. Steel.

From First Divide a faint way trail goes around the south side of Mt. Hopper, but the route is rough and best left to very experienced travelers.

Many hikers continue from Home Sweet Home to Lake LaCrosse (Hike 98), 7 miles farther, with a loss of 2000 feet followed by a stiff gain of 2500 feet to the lake. From there they either proceed onward around O'Neil Pass to the Enchanted Valley trail or over Anderson Pass to the Dosewallips trail.

A few hikers drop from Home Sweet Home to the Duckabush River, hike 1½ miles downstream, and climb over 5566-foot LaCrosse Pass to Honeymoon Meadows on the Dosewallips (Hike 85). Only the vast meadows at the pass make this grueling 3000-foot ascent on a waterless, south-facing slope worth the effort.

Round trip to Camp Pleasant 13 miles
Hiking time 8 hours
High point 1600 feet
Elevation gain 800 feet
Best May through November
One day or backpack
USGS Mt. Steel

Round trip to Home Sweet Home 26 miles
Allow 2 days
High point 5688 feet
Elevation gain 4000 feet in, 500 feet out
Best mid-July through October
Park Service Camping Permit required

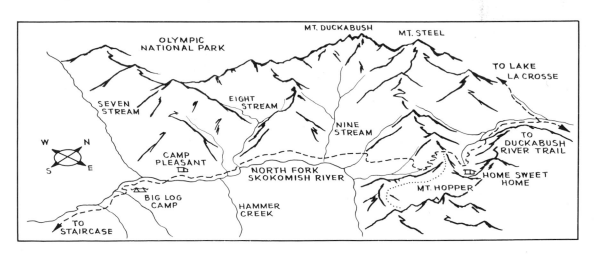

R LENA LAKE

asy trail, free of snow most of the year, through splendid forest to popular and often crowded Lower Lena Lake, surrounded by tall trees. Continue on steeper, rougher trail to the subalpine country of Upper Lena Lake.

Drive US 101 along Hood Canal to Eldon. Turn west on the Hamma Hamma River road about 9 miles to Phantom Creek and ½ mile beyond to the trailhead, elevation 685 feet.

The wide, motorbike-infested low-angle "super-trail" switchbacks gently and endlessly in forest shadows, crossing beautiful Lena Creek and soon thereafter reaching Lower Lena Lake at 2¾ miles, 1800 feet. The way passes a popular camp area and rounds the west shore ½ mile to other campsites near the head of the lake.

Shortly beyond the head of the lake is a junction. The path to the right follows East Fork Lena Creek into the Valley of Silent Men, crossing and recrossing the stream many times, to-

ward The Brothers, a principal summit of the Olympic horizon seen from Seattle. This boot-built track is mainly used by fishermen and climbers, but is well worth exploration by hikers who enjoy loitering beside cold water frothing and sparkling through rapids, swirling in green pools, all in the deep shade of old forest.

The left fork—no supertrail and with no motorbikes—follows West Fork Lena Creek, entering Olympic National Park at 4 miles. At approximately 5 miles, 2700 feet, the trail crosses a small creek, becomes steep and badly eroded. The present trail was built in the late 30s. It was steep then, but the tread was smooth and wide. Since then, a few windfalls have been cut. Otherwise, the trail has received no maintenance. Floods, slides, and fallen trees have taken their toll and only remnants of the original trail are left.

As the trail climbs, the vegetation changes from a fir forest to a subalpine. Heather and huckleberry appear along with Alaska cedar. There are occasional views down the valley towards The Brothers. The steepness ends abruptly at the edge of Upper Lena Lake, 4600 feet, 7 miles. A rough

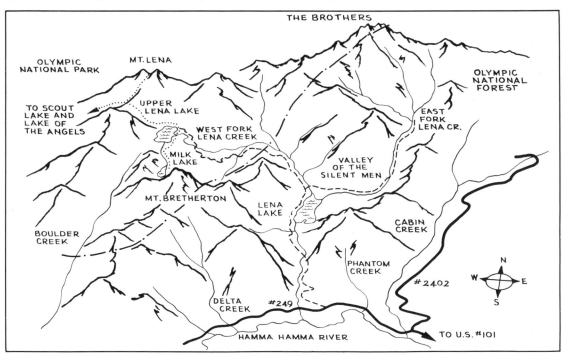

Upper Lena Lake and Mt. Bretherton

up and down way trail traverses the north side of the lake.

Camps are inviting, and the shore demands roaming, as do the meadows and screes ringing the cirque. For more ambitious explorations scramble to the summit of 5998-foot Mt. Lena, or ascend the creek falling from little Milk Lake, tucked in a quiet pocket and generally frozen until late summer, or follow a boot-worn track over a 5000-foot ridge near Mt. Lena to Scout Lake, or follow the ridge with its numerous tarns toward Mt. Stone and Lake of the Angels.

Round trip to upper lake 14 miles
Hiking time 12 hours
High point 4600 feet
Elevation gain 3900 feet
Best to lower lake April through November
Best to upper lake July through October
One day or backpack
USGS The Brothers
Park Service Camping Permit required

Cloud-filled Duckabush valley and The Brothers from Mt. Jupiter trail

83   MOUNT JUPITER

Look from Seattle across Puget Sound to the Olympic horizon, and right smack between The Brothers and Mt. Constance is Jupiter. Actually, the peak does not deserve inclusion in such distinguished company, but stands so far out in the front of the range as to seem bigger than it really is. And in fact, old Jupe offers unique combination views of lowlands and mountains. The summit ascent, however, is long and strenuous and usually dry and hot. Most hikers are content to climb the trail to the views and leave the summit to peakbaggers.

Drive US 101 along Hood Canal to a short mile north of the Duckabush River bridge. Turn west 3½ miles on Mt. Jupiter road No. 262 to a junction. Turn left on the fork signed "Mt. Jupiter Trail" and drive 3 steep and tortuous miles to the trailhead, elevation 2150 feet. (**Note:** Because of littering and debris dumping, on occasion the Forest Service is forced to close the road temporarily.)

The first mile switchbacks up south slopes of the ridge dividing the Duckabush and Dosewallips Rivers. At 1 mile, 2850 feet, the trail reaches the ridge crest, and here leaves state land and enters Olympic National Forest. The hike to this point, with splendid panoramas, can be done in late May and early June, when the trip is really the most pleasant, especially since rhododendrons are then in bloom along the lower trail.

However, the way goes on for those willing, following the ridge crest up and down, up and down, with more views, and finally climbs a very steep final mile to the summit, 7 miles, 5701 feet.

From the summit, or from the trail, the views are glorious—and thought-provoking. North beyond the Dosewallips is Mt. Constance, and south beyond the Duckabush are The Brothers. See the logging, steadily encroaching on state and Olympic National Forest lands. Westward is the protected grandeur of Olympic National Park. Eastward across Hood Canal and the Kitsap Peninsula are Seattle, the Space Needle, suburbia, smog, civilization.

Round trip 14 miles
Hiking time 10 hours
High point 5701 feet
Elevation gain 3600 feet
Best June through October
One day
USGS Point Misery and The Brothers

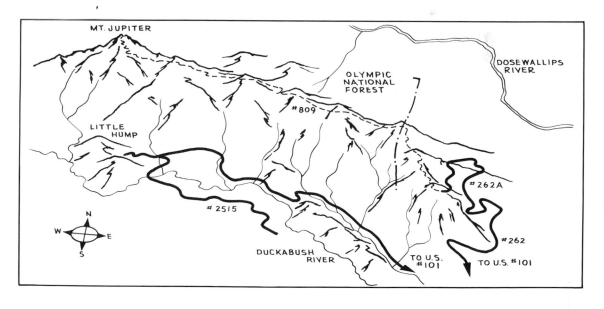

84   LAKE CONSTANCE

A classic tarn, the deep blue waters ringed by alpine trees and heather gardens and sheer cliffs of Mt. Constance. Mountain goats wander the precipices by day—and at night visit campfires to scavenge goodies. But hikers must earn their passage to the secluded cirque the hard way, climbing 3400 feet in only 2 miles. The trail is super-steep, somewhat dangerous in spots, and is not recommended for beginners or small children or the fainthearted.

Drive US 101 along Hood Canal to the Dosewallips River road just north of Brinnon. Turn west 14 miles to ½ mile inside the Park boundary and several wide spots that serve for the trailhead parking area at Constance Creek, elevation 1450 feet.

The first mile is brutal, virtually without switchbacks, gaining some 2000 feet to a short level stretch, and good forest camp, at the 1-mile marker. The second mile seems even steeper, though this is purely an optical illusion caused by the ladderways of tree roots and the short rock cliffs. Feet must be placed with care and hands used for balance. Caution is especially essential on the descent. At 2 miles, 4750 feet, the trail flattens into the cirque, and numerous fine—though badly overused and abused—camps around the lakeshore. Be sure to carry a stove; no wood is left for campfires.

Impressive as is the lake, the truly awesome scenery lies higher, beyond the portals of what oldtime Boy Scouts, feeling spooky, used to call "Dead Man's Gap." Follow a boot-beaten climbers' track above the lake, up talus, through the gap into Avalanche Canyon, a mile-long glacier trough between the east and west peaks of Constance. Solemn and spectacular it is, a place of crags, cliffs, and screes, snowfields and moraines. Hikers can walk safely to the canyon head at about 6000 feet. Those with ice axes and experience in snow travel can climb easily to Crystal Pass, and views down the glacier in Tunnel Creek.

The geology adds fascination. The weird, bumpy-looking walls of the canyon consist of "pillow lava" formed by molten rock erupting under the sea and cooling into these odd, rounded shapes. Heat and pressure metamorphosed limestone into pastel-colored rocks, often in variegated fault breccias of striking beauty. Hot mineralized solutions deposited green crystals of epidote intermixed with quartz and calcite.

The goats that tour the campsites by night and occasionally by day (such as on a Monday morning, after the weekenders have gone home) often can be spotted on cliffs, little kids gamboling about the airy rocks, older folks moving more deliberately.

Round trip to the lake 4 miles
Hiking time 7 hours
High point 4750 feet
Elevation gain 3300 feet
Best August through October
One day or backpack
USGS The Brothers and Tyler Peak
Park Service Camping Permit required

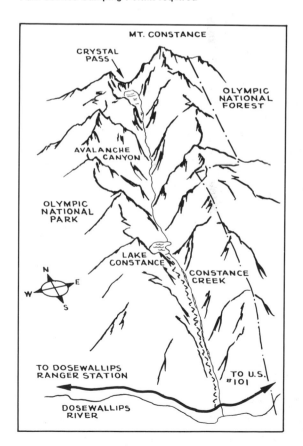

Lake Constance

85 ANDERSON GLACIER

Follow a long trail to the edge of one of the largest glaciers in the eastern Olympics. Enjoy glorious views down the Dosewallips River to Mt. Constance, over Anderson Pass to Mt. LaCrosse and White Mountain, down into the Enchanted Valley at the head of the Quinault River, and of course, across the Anderson Glacier to the summits of Mt. Anderson. In early August a wild array of flowers bloom, including small fields of

lupine and paintbrush that stand out dramatically against the rugged background.

Drive US 101 along Hood Canal to just north of Brinnon and turn west on the Dosewallips River road, coming to the end of pavement in 4¾ miles, Elkhorn Campground junction at 10¾ miles, Constance Creek at 13½ miles, and at 15 miles the road-end and trailhead, elevation 1540 feet.

The trail starts in deep forest with a showing of rhododendrons in late June, and after going up and down a bit reaches a junction at 1½

Anderson Glacier and Mt. Anderson

miles. Turn left to Dose Forks Camp and cross the river. At about 2½ miles the way again crosses the river, now the West Fork Dosewallips, this time on a bridge perched spectacularly some 100 feet above the water. The trail climbs steeply to dry forests high above the stream, which flows in so deep a gorge that often it cannot be heard.

The trail descends a bit to a welcome drink of water and abused campsites at 5 miles, then climbs high again and with minor ups and downs reaches the small opening of Diamond Meadow at 6¾ miles, 2692 feet. A shelter here and pleasant campsites by the stream. At 7¼ miles the trail once more crosses the river and begins a steady ascent, at about 8 miles climbing steeply beside the raging torrent as it tumbles through a narrow gorge. At 8¾ miles, 3627 feet, the valley opens into the broad, flat expanse and good camps of Honeymoon Meadows, named years ago by a Seattle couple who long since have celebrated their golden wedding anniversary. One final time the trail crosses the river, here only a jump wide (a big jump), and ascends a rough path to Anderson Pass Shelter

("Camp Siberia") at 10 miles and Anderson Pass at 10½ miles, 4464 feet.

The Anderson Glacier trail climbs steeply from the north side of the wooded pass, emerging from trees and in ¾ mile ending at a small tarn amid boulders and meadows. A few feet farther lead to the 5200-foot edge of an old moraine and the views.

The West Fork Dosewallips trail to Anderson Pass often is included in longer trips: a 27-mile one-way hike down Enchanted Valley (Hike 97); a 49-mile one-way hike to O'Neil Pass and out the Duckabush River (Hike 98); a 36½-mile one-way hike out the North Fork Skokomish River; and a 41-mile loop trip via O'Neil Pass and the upper Duckabush, returning to the Dosewallips with a grueling 3000-foot climb to LaCrosse Pass.

Round trip to Anderson Glacier 22½ miles
Allow 3 days
High point 5200 feet
Elevation gain 4000 feet
Best mid-July through October
USGS The Brothers and Mt. Steel
Park Service Camping Permit required

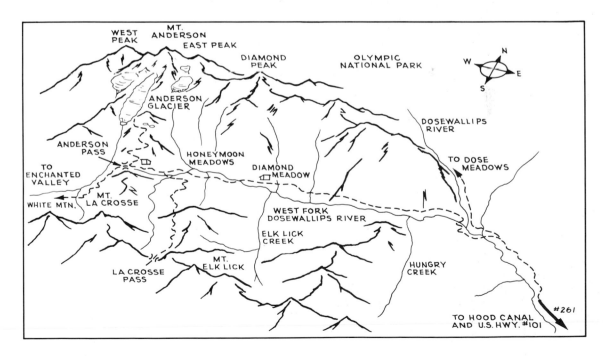

86   HAYDEN PASS

Miles of marvelous forest, then alpine meadows waist-deep in flowers, where fragrance makes the head swim on warm days, where a quiet hiker may see deer, elk, marmots, bear, and perhaps a goat on a high ridge. All this and impressive views too, plus numerous fine campsites at short intervals along the trail. The pass makes a superb round-trip destination, or can be included in an across-the-Olympics journey to the Elwha River, or in a 10-day giant loop over Low Divide and returning via Anderson Pass.

Drive US 101 along Hood Canal to the Dosewallips River road just north of Brinnon. Turn west 15½ miles (the final 2 miles in the National Park are steep and rough) to the road-end campground and trailhead, elevation 1540 feet.

A gentle 1½ miles through open forest with a dense groundcover of salal and rhododendron (the latter blooms in early July) lead to Dose Forks Shelter. A bit beyond is a junction with the trail to Anderson Pass (Hike 85); take the right fork and start climbing. At 2 miles note animal prints at a soda spring. Cross many little streams, nice spots for resting and drinking. At 2½ miles a side-trail heads up to supremely-scenic but far-above Constance Pass.

As the path ascends, Diamond Mountain appears across the river; from a well-marked point, see Hatana Falls. At about 8 miles the valley widens and the trail crosses a series of meadows. At 9 miles pass the Graywolf side-trail and continue in steadily more open terrain, with wider views, to Dose Meadows at 13 miles, 4450 feet.

Beyond the meadows is a small canyon, crossed on a bridge; the creek-size river has a lion-size roar. At 13½ miles, 4600 feet, the way enters the vast garden basin of the headwaters, surrounded by high peaks. The trail crosses the river one last time and switchbacks to Hayden Pass, 15½ miles, 5847 feet. In early summer a large, steep snowbank blocks the tread; be cautious.

Hayden Pass is the low point on the narrow ridge connecting Mt. Fromme and Sentinel Peak. North is Mt. Claywood, east are Wellesley Peak and the Dosewallips valley, south is glacier-covered Mt. Anderson, and west are the Bailey Range and distant Mt. Olympus.

Down from the pass 1 mile on the Elwha

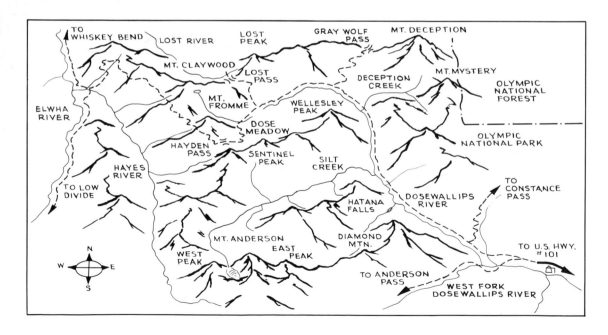

Avalanche lilies on Hayden Pass (John Spring photo)

River side, just before the trail enters forest, find a delightful campsite by a bubbling creek.

For the across-the-Olympics hike, continue 9 miles and 4200 feet down from the pass to the Elwha River trail and then 17 miles more to the Whiskey Bend road-end (Hike 92).

Round trip to Hayden Pass 31 miles
Allow 3-4 days
High point 5847 feet
Elevation gain 4250 feet
Best July through October
USGS Tyler Peak, The Brothers, and Mt. Angeles
Park Service Camping Permit required

195

87 MARMOT PASS

Before World War II, in an era when Boy Scouts were perhaps the principal wanderers of the Olympic wilderness, the "Three Rivers Hike" was among the most popular trips from old Camp Parsons. Thousands of Scouts now middle-aged vividly recall their introduction to highlands on the grueling "Poop Out Drag," climbing steeply and endlessly upward along a sun-baked south slope, arriving in late afternoon at Camp Mystery, then taking an after-dinner walk through flower gardens and broad meadows to Marmot Pass and thrilling evening views down to shadowed forests of the Dungeness River, 3000 feet below, and beyond to Mt. Mystery, Mt. Deception, second-highest in the Olympics, and the jagged line of The Needles, all etched in a sunset-colored sky.

Drive US 101 along Hood Canal to ½ mile north of the Quilcene River bridge, 1.5 miles south of the town of Quilcene, and turn west on the Quilcene River road, a paved but unmarked county road. At 1.4 miles pavement ends at a Forest Service junction. Go left on road No. 2812 and at 10.7 miles from the highway turn left on road No. 272. Signs are confused at several

places so watch carefully for road numbers. At 15.3 miles, just beyond 10 Mile Shelter and Wet Weather Creek, find the start of Big Quilcene trail No. 831, elevation 2500 feet.

The trail follows the river bottom through cool forest, crossing numerous step-across creeks, passing many close-up looks at the lovely river. At 3 miles is Shelter Rock Camp, 3600 feet, and the last water for more than 2 miles.

Now the way turns steeply upward into the hot, dry scree, alternating with flowers, of the famous (or infamous) Poop Out Drag, so named because on these slopes in years past many a little 12-year-old Scout tottering under a big pack beneath the brutal sun abruptly fell on his face and thought he could never rise again.

At a bit past 5 miles the suffering ends as the trail abruptly turns into Camp Mystery, 5400 feet, with a delightful spring and campsites in alpine trees. Except for snowmelt there is no water above, so this is the spot to camp.

The trail continues upward, passing under a cliff and opening into a wide, flat meadow—which, sad to say, has become a race track for the motorbikes the Forest Service allows here. At 6 miles, 6000 feet, the way attains Marmot

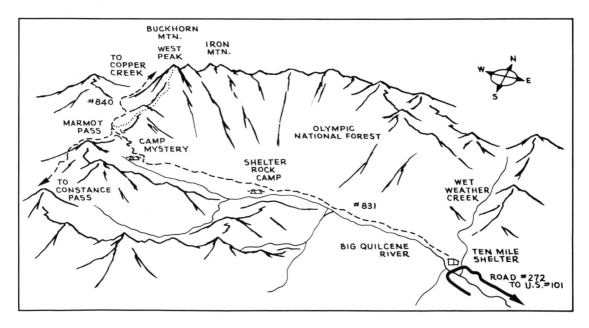

Warrior Peak and Mt. Constance from hill on south side of Marmot Pass

Pass and panoramas westward.

The legendary Three Rivers Hike descended the trail 1½ miles to Boulder Shelter, followed Dungeness trail No. 833 to Home Lake and Constance Pass in Olympic National Park, climbed Del Monte Ridge, and plunged down the interminable short switchbacks of the Sunnybrook trail to the Dosewallips River trail, and thence to the road.

Fine as the views are from Marmot Pass, nearby are even better ones. For a quick sample, scramble up the 6300-foot knoll directly south of the pass. For the full display, turn north of the pass on trail No. 840, leading to Copper Creek, and in ¼ mile leave tread and wander easy slopes to the 6950-foot west summit of Buckhorn Mountain. Especially striking are the dramatic crags of 7300-foot Warrior Peak and 7743-foot Mt. Constance.

Round trip to Marmot Pass 12 miles
Hiking time 9 hours
High point 6000 feet
Elevation gain 3400 feet
Best July through mid-November
One day or backpack
USGS Tyler Peak

Headwaters of Silver Creek from side of Mt. Townsend

88   MOUNT TOWNSEND

Climb to a northern outpost of the highlands. Look down to the Strait of Juan de Fuca, Puget Sound, Hood Canal, and across the water to Mt. Baker, Glacier Peak, and faraway Mt. Rainier. In the other direction, of course, see the Olympic Mountains. The steep southeast slopes of the trail route melt free of snow in early June, and usually only a few easy patches are encountered then. Mid-June is best, though, when the entire forest road is lined with rhododendron blossoms, spring flowers are blooming in the lowlands, and summer flowers on the south-facing rock gardens higher up.

Two popular trails lead to the summit of Mt. Townsend. The one from Townsend Creek, ascending the southeast side, is described here. The other, the Little Quilcene trail from Last Water Camp, is slightly longer but perhaps cooler walking in midsummer.

Drive US 101 south from the town center of Quilcene 1.5 miles nearly to the fish hatchery. Turn west on a paved road 1.4 miles to a junction, where pavement ends. Go left on road No. 2812 (taking care at subsequent forks to avoid side-roads which may be more heavily traveled) 13.6 miles and turn left on road No. 2764. In 1.4 cliff-hanging miles is the road-end and trailhead, elevation about 3600 feet.

For the alternate trail, drive road No. 2812 another 5 miles and turn left on road No. 2909 for 2 miles, then left on Road 2909J for 3 miles to the Little Quilcene River trailhead, elevation 4000 feet.

The Townsend Creek trail ascends steadily in timber 1½ miles, then opens out and steepens somewhat to Windy Camp, 2½ miles, about 5000 feet. Pleasant camping around little Windy Lake.

The way continues upward in parkland with a scattering of small flower gardens. At just under 3 miles is an unmarked junction. The left fork climbs over a saddle, drops into Silver Creek, and climbs again to campsites at Silver Lakes, approximately 5 miles; one small lake is on the trail and the other is hidden. The right fork heads up the mountain, topping the ridge at 4 miles, 6000 feet, then following the crest, pass-

ing 100 feet below the first summit at 4½ miles, and running to the most northerly part of the ridge and the second summit, connecting there with the Little Quilcene trail and a trail down to Silver Creek.

Which summit is the higher? They are so evenly matched—with only 50 feet difference—you must try both to know. Wander to the summit of your choice and soak up the view over the waters to the Cascades, and over the rolling meadow ridges of the Olympics. The rugged peaks to the south are Mt. Constance and its neighbors, and farther away, The Brothers.

Round trip 9 miles
Hiking time 5 hours
High point 6280 feet
Elevation gain 2700 feet
Best June through November
One day or backpack
USGS Tyler Peak

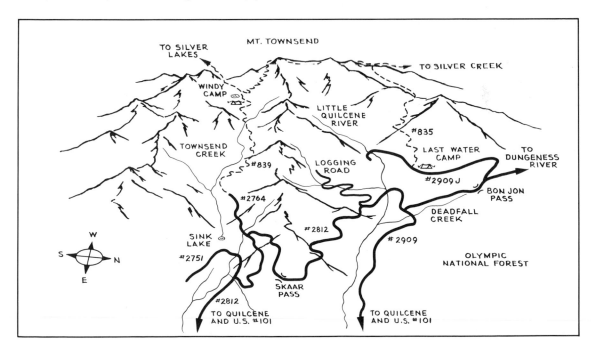

Royal Lake and Graywolf Ridge

89 ROYAL BASIN

Splendid forests and streams, an alpine lake and fields of flowers, all surrounded by some of the highest and craggiest peaks in the Olympics. Allow plenty of time for the entry hike because the last several miles are rough and in places quite steep. Plan at least an extra day for roaming.

Drive US 101 westward towards Sequim. A few hundred feet before Sequim Bay State Park, turn left on a gravel road 1 mile to the paved Palo Alto county road. (Alternatively, continue 1½ miles on the highway and turn left on Palo Alto road; the gravel shortcut saves about 2 miles.) Turn left on the paved road, at 4 miles from the highway reaching the end of pavement and at 6½ miles the end of the county road at a Forest Service junction. Turn left on road No. 2909, at 7.5 miles turn right on road No. 295, and at 17 miles go left on road No. 2825. At 18.5 miles, beside the bridge over the river, find Dungeness River trail No. 833, elevation 2500 feet.

The trail follows the water—always within sound and often in sight. At 1 mile, 2700 feet, is a junction of streams and trails; take the right fork, Roy Creek trail No. 832 (the creek is called

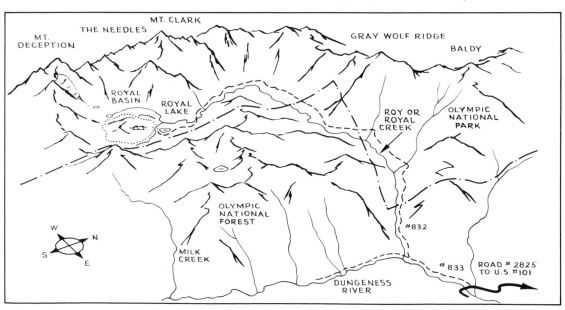

Royal on some maps). In 2 miles enter a corner of Olympic National Park and at 3 miles (illogically!) re-enter Olympic National Forest. This far the way is entirely through forest, including beautiful specimens of fir, with a floor sometimes a soft mattress of moss and other times a broad green carpet of vanilla leaf. At around 4 miles the trail begins traversing small flower meadows, each one larger than the last. The path also steepens and becomes rougher and at 4½ miles re-enters the Park. Ahead are glimpses of Graywolf Ridge and crags of The Needles.

The valley bends sharply southward and narrows and at about 6 miles, 4700 feet, the trail climbs a little cliff and enters the lower part of Royal Basin, covered with alpine trees and small meadows thick with scrub willow. The trail crosses Roy Creek and several tributaries on flimsy poles; note the milkiness of the main creek, which carries glacier-milled rock-flour. A final steep climb leads to Royal Lake, 7 miles,

5100 feet. On the far shores are a few campsites in the woods. Near the sound of a waterfall directly west is a large camp under a huge overhanging rock; to find it, follow a path around the upper end of the lake, then over a small knoll.

Several boot-beaten tracks lead to high gardens. Any will do, but take care to skirt certain green, flat meadows which in fact are marshes. Make a grand tour to the very top of the basin. Below huge piles of moraine, find a tiny milk-blue lake fed by the small glacier on the side of 7788-foot Mt. Deception. Continue to the ridge crest and look down to the fairyland of Deception Basin.

Round trip to Royal Lake 14 miles
Allow 2 days minimum
High point 5100 feet
Elevation gain 2600 feet
Best mid-July through October
USGS Tyler Peak
Park Service Camping Permit required

Goats on Mt. Angeles

90   MOUNT ANGELES

Once upon a time this was a challenging hike from lowland forests to alpine meadows, then along a craggy peak to some of the most glorious views of Olympic National Park. Forests, meadows, and views remain, but the challenge accepted by those who start at the bottom is like a big balloon, punctured, when greeted on top by people in street shoes walking paved trails. Most hikers, therefore, prefer to forget the challenge— they begin at the top and work down to the tall timber. (Such a plan, of course, requires either two cars or a pickup below by a non-hiking friend.)

The trail, which does not go to the actual summit of Mt. Angeles, is rough in spots. For an alternate trip with almost the same views and better tread, take the Lake Angeles trail. Both routes have the same start and finish and are approximately the same length, but the lake trail has more people.

Drive 18 miles from Port Angeles to Hurricane Ridge and find the Lake Angeles-Klahhane Ridge trail at the east end of the Big Meadow parking lot, elevation 5225 feet.

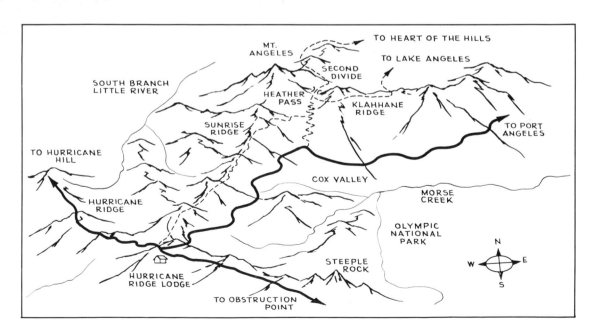

The first few hundred feet of paved pathway lead east around a low green hill. Soon the trail becomes gravel and in ½ mile narrows to normal mountain tread winding 2 miles along Sunrise Ridge, sometimes on the crest and sometimes contouring small knolls. Just before crossing the south slope of Mt. Angeles, pass a meager boot-beaten path leading upward, the climbers' route to the summit. At 2½ miles is a junction with the Switchback Trail, a steep ½-mile shortcut from the highway which saves the "bother" of hiking 2 of the best alpine miles of the whole trip. From the junction the main trail switchbacks up 900 feet to 5900-foot Heather Pass at 3½ miles and the junction of the Lake Angeles and Mt. Angeles trails.

The views here are superb, with Mt. Olympus in one direction, and in the other, Port Angeles, the Strait of Juan de Fuca, the San Juan Islands, Vancouver Island, and Mt. Baker. If mountain goats have not been seen before, look around carefully; there are many in the vicinity, as evidenced by their wool on trees, rocks, and thistles and by their numerous paths crossing shale slopes. This side of Mt. Angeles is geologically unusual, having vertical erosion lines in tilted sedimentary strata.

From the junction the Lake Angeles trail follows along Klahhane Ridge about another 1½ miles and then descends meadows into woods, reaching Lake Angeles at 6½ miles, 4196 feet, and continuing down in timber to the trailhead behind the ranger's quarters at Heart of the Hills, 10 miles, 1817 feet.

From the junction the Mt. Angeles trail drops 300 feet into the head of Ennis Creek, traverses shale slides, and climbs over Second Divide at 4½ miles, about 5800 feet. The way through the shale is hard to follow; don't be misled by certain goat trails which look better than the people trail.

From Second Divide the path descends rapidly, traversing more shale and crossing a spur ridge to Heather Park at 6 miles, 5500 feet, featuring a meadow at the foot of an avalanche slope, some flowers, lots of heather, and great gobs of views. The remaining 4 miles are in trees, passing Halfway Rock at 8 miles, and finishing at the Heart of the Hills trailhead in 10 miles.

One-way trip 10 miles
Hiking time 5 hours
High point 5900 feet
Elevation gain 1200 feet
Best mid-July through October
One day
USGS Mt. Angeles and Port Angeles
Park Service Camping Permit required

Moose Lake and meadowlands of Grand Valley

91 GRAND VALLEY

A grand valley it surely is, with a string of lakes in glacier-scooped basins, meadows to roam and waterfalls to rest by, high ridges to ramble and broad views to admire. Popular though the lakes are with fishermen, the valley has plenty of room and alpine hideaways for getting away from crowds.

Drive US 101 to Port Angeles and turn south 17 miles on the Olympic National Park highway to Hurricane Ridge. Just before the lodge turn left on a narrow and scenic dirt road through parklands along the ridge crest. In 8½ miles, on the side of Obstruction Peak, is the road-end, elevation 6200 feet.

The drive is beautiful and so is the trail going south along the meadow crest of Lillian Ridge a mile, with views over Elwha River forests to Mt. Olympus, then swinging around rocky slopes of a small peak to a notch in the ridge, 6450 feet. Now the way drops steeply down slate screes and lush flowers to open forest on the floor of Grand Valley, and a junction at 3½ miles, 5000 feet.

The left fork leads in ¼ mile to a shelter beside Grand Lake, 4750 feet, then descends Grand Creek to 4000 feet and climbs through Badger Valley to Obstruction Peak, reached in 5 miles from the junction. (The "badgers" actually are marmots; listen for their whistles.) This route makes an excellent loop-trip return to the road.

The right fork ascends ½ mile to Moose Lake, 5100 feet, and another ½ mile to little Gladys Lake. Good camps at all the lakes and elsewhere in the valley; no need to stick close to the throngs of fishermen.

The supreme wandering lies above the lakes. The trail climbs to Grand Pass, 5½ miles, 6400 feet, and drops to Cameron Creek. But an even better exploring direction is off the trail to the valley head, loitering amid flowers, cold streams, meltwater ponds, and snowfields, then scrambling easily to a 6701-foot peak with views west to the Bailey Range and Mt. Olympus, south to Mt. Anderson, east to Mt. Deception, The Needles, and Graywolf Ridge, and infinitely more wildland peaks of Olympic National Park.

Round trip to Moose Lake 8 miles
Hiking time 6 hours
High point 6450 feet
Elevation gain 300 feet in, 1000 feet out
Best July through October
One day or backpack
USGS Mt. Angeles
Park Service Camping Permit required

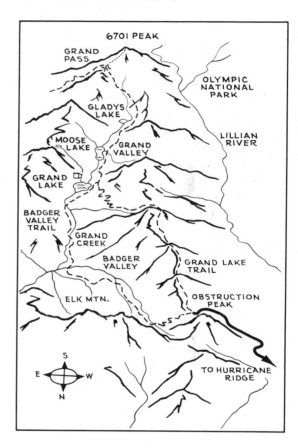

Student Conservation Program volunteers at work rebuilding the Hayes River Patrol Cabin (John Spring photo)

92 WHISKEY BEND TO LOW DIVIDE

No whiskey, but a lot of waterfalls and forest scenery, can be found on the 28-mile Elwha River trail from Whiskey Bend to Low Divide. The valley is very heavily traveled in summer, especially below Elkhorn, by hikers and horses, including large groups of Boy Scouts, but the natural beauty and historical interest more than compensate for crowds. Spend a day or weekend on the lower trail—or spend a week hiking the complete trail, loitering at lovely spots, taking side-trips. Before setting out, be sure to read Bob Wood's delightful book about the 1889-90 Press Expedition into this country.

Drive US 101 west from Port Angeles 8 miles and turn left on the paved Elwha River road 2 miles to the National Park boundary. At 2.1 miles from the boundary, just past the Elwha Ranger Station, turn left on the Whiskey Bend road and drive 5 miles (sometimes rough and steep) to the road-end parking area, elevation 1100 feet.

The trail is wide and relatively level, with occasional glimpses of the river far below, to Cougar Mike's Cabin at 1½ miles. Here a ½-mile side-trail descends to the old homestead of

Humes Ranch, where elk may sometimes be seen, mainly from late fall to spring.

At 4½ miles, 1273 feet, is Lillian Shelter beside the Lillian River. Pause for refreshment, because the next stretch is the toughest of the trip, climbing 700 feet from the hot, dry Lillian Grade through an old burn, then dropping for the first time to the Elwha River at about 8 miles, 1242 feet. The trail goes up and down, never near the river very long, to Mary Falls Shelter, 8¾ miles, and a nice view of the falls. Now the way climbs again, passing a ¼-mile side-trip to secluded Canyon Camp shelter, and at 11½ miles, 1400 feet, reaches Elkhorn Guard Station and Shelter. (About ¼ mile beyond is another small shelter at Stony Point.)

The trail crosses an alder bottom where elk or deer may be seen and passes two old summer-home cabins of pre-park days—Drum's Cabin (12 miles) and Remanns' Cabin (13 miles, 1450 feet) and climbs again and drops again into Press Valley. At the upper end of the valley, 16¾ miles, 1685 feet, is an old shelter at Hayes River Camp and Hayes River Patrol Cabin built in 1969 by 40 volunteer boys enrolled in the Student Conservation Program. Here is a junction with the Hayden Pass trail (Hike 86).

At 21 miles, 1900 feet, is a shelter at Camp Wilder. Easily cross a washed-out section of the trail at Buckinghorse Creek and at 26 miles

reach Chicago Camp, 2099 feet, a jumping-off point for Mt. Olympus climbers. The trail now leaves the valley bottom and switchbacks in forest to the meadows of Low Divide, 28¾ miles, 3602 feet, and there meets the North Fork Quinault River trail (Hike 96).

Round trip to Low Divide 57 miles
Allow a week or more
High point 3602 feet
Elevation gain about 2500 feet plus many ups and
**   downs**
Best June through October
USGS Mt. Angeles; Mt. Steel and Mt. Christie
Park Service Camping Permit required

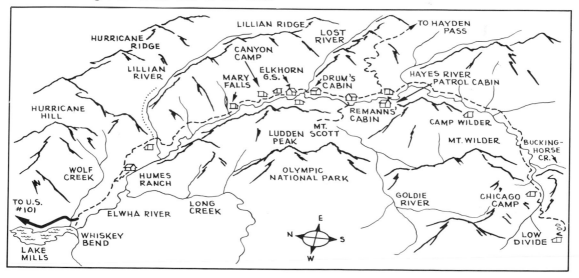

93   HIGH DIVIDE

Soleduck forests, tarns and gardens of Seven Lakes Basin, meadows of the High Divide, and views across the green gulf of the Hoh River to glaciers of Mt. Olympus and far west to the Pacific Ocean. The trail is busy and the lakes crowded—sad to say, some are actually polluted —but the country is big and beautiful and offers a variety of wanderings short and long. By planning only to **look** at lakes and not to camp by them—alternative sites are numerous—hikers can enjoy solitude even now, when the fame of the area draws thousands of visitors annually. A loop trip is recommended as a sampler of the riches. (Actually, the bio-welfare of Seven Lakes Basin and the High Divide demands that the amount of camping in the fragile terrain be reduced, with more emphasis on day visits from camps in the valley forests.)

Drive US 101 west from Lake Crescent (Fairholm) 2 miles to the Soleduck River road. Turn left 14.2 miles to the end and trailhead, elevation 2000 feet.

The trail ascends gently in splendid old forest 1 mile to the misty and mossy gorge of Soleduck Falls. Close by is the junction, 1950 feet, with the Deer Lake trail—see the concluding segment of the clockwise loop described here.

The Soleduck trail continues up the valley of gorgeous trees, passes the Appleton Pass trail at 5 miles, 3000 feet, and soon thereafter crosses the river and climbs steeply to grasslands and silver forest of Soleduck Park and Heart Lake, 7 miles, 4800 feet.

Shortly above, at 8½ miles, the way attains the 5100-foot crest of the High Divide, and a junction. The left fork runs the ridge 3 miles to a dead-end on the side of Cat Peak, offering close looks at the Bailey and Olympus Ranges.

Turn west on the right fork into a steady ridge-top succession of views and flowers. At 10½ miles a side-trail descends 1½ miles left to 4500-foot Hoh Lake, and from there to the Hoh River (Hike 95). Here, too, a path climbs a bit to the 5474-foot summit of Bogachiel Peak and the climax panoramas. Plan to spend a lot of time gazing the full round of the compass.

The route swings along the side of the peak, at 11½ miles passing the side-trail to Seven Lakes Basin, and traverses Bogachiel Ridge above the greenery (and often, a band of elk) in Boga-

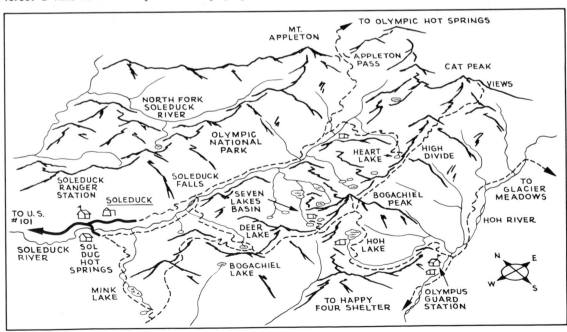

Bluebells on High Divide. Mt. Olympus and Mt. Tom in distance.

chiel Basin. Snowfields linger late on this stretch, and may be troublesome or dangerous for inexperienced hikers who try the trip too early in the summer.

The trail contours the ridge above the Bogachiel River almost 2 miles, then in subalpine trees drops to Deer Lake at 3500 feet and a junction with the Bogachiel River trail (Hike 94) at 15½ miles. Past the lake, the trail descends in lush forest to Soleduck Falls at 19 miles and in another mile to the road.

Loop trip 20 miles
Allow 3 days
High point 5474 feet
Elevation gain 4000 feet
Best August through October
USGS Bogachiel Peak and Mt. Carrie
Park Service Camping Permit required

94   BOGACHIEL RIVER

A beautiful hike through large old trees, rain forest foliage, and luxuriant mosses. In autumn, the vine maple, alder, and big leaf maple stage a glorious color show. Elk, deer, cougar, bear, and other animals may be seen by quiet and lucky hikers. A late-fall or winter visitor usually has the forest all to himself, the only footprints on the trail those of elk.

The valley offers a superb day trip for virtually any time of year, or a weekend for more extended enjoyment of wilderness greenery and streams, or a long, magnificent approach to alpine climaxes of the High Divide.

Drive US 101 to Bogachiel State Park. Turn east on the Bogachiel River road, passing several side-roads to homesteads; keep left at each intersection. After the last homestead, at 3.6 miles the road abruptly becomes very rough and crosses a small creek. Many people prefer to park here, but adventurous drivers can continue 1.4 miles to the Bogachiel River, elevation 300 feet. At this point hikers may follow the old trail to the left (unmarked) through cut-over land for ¼ mile to an old logging road or follow the road to the right. (Two fordings of side creeks are required on the latter road to reach the Park boundary at about 2 miles.)

The first 1½ miles of the old and often-muddy trail follow vestiges of a logging road dating from logging operations during the early years of World War II. Amid second-growth forest, look for giant stumps with springboard holes in both sides. Then virgin forest begins.

Bogachiel Shelter and the old guard station, recently rebuilt by the Student Conservation Program, are 4 miles from the Park boundary and make a good lunch stop and turnaround point for day hikers.

Near the shelter a branch trail climbs north over 1041-foot Indian Pass and drops to the Calawah River; at 6¼ miles another side-trail climbs over the ridge south to the Hoh River road.

The valley path continues gently in lovely forest, never far from the river and sometimes beside it, to Flapjack Shelter at 8¼ miles. At about 12 miles the river forks. While the trail follows the North Fork, the narrow but pristine main river valley can be explored on a side-trip for 6 miles if you don't mind wading creeks and scrambling over high banks and fallen trees.

At 14¾ miles are Fifteen Mile Shelter and a bridge crossing the stream. At 15½ miles is Hyak Shelter, where the valley narrows into a slot, and at 18½ miles Twenty-One Mile Shelter, 2214 feet. At around 21 miles the trail abandons gentility, steeply ascending a dry hillside above the North Fork headwaters to 4300-foot Little Divide, then dropping to Deer Lake at 24 miles, and climbing in parklands to the meadow crest of the High Divide. For alternative exits to Sol Duc Hot Springs, see Hike 93.

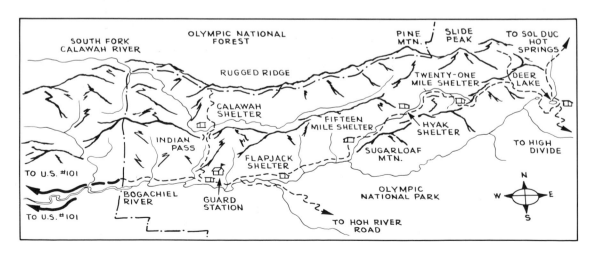

Bogachiel River (John Spring photo)

Round trip from Park boundary to Bogachiel Shelter
 8 miles
Hiking time 5 hours
High point 560 feet
Elevation gain 260 feet
Best March through November
One day or backpack
USGS Olympic National Park or Spruce Mountain

One-way trip to Sol Duc Hot Springs via Deer Lake
 30½ miles
Allow 2-3 days
High point 4304 feet
Elevation gain 4000 feet
Best July through October
Park Service Camping Permit required

Rain forest along Hoh River trail

95   HOH RIVER

From around the world, travelers are drawn to the Hoh River by the fame of the Olympic rain forest. Most of the 100,000 annual visitors are richly satisfied by the self-guiding nature walks at the road-end, but more ambitious hikers can continue for miles on the nearly flat trail through huge trees draped with moss, and then climb to alpine meadows and the edge of the Blue Glacier.

Drive US 101 to the Hoh River road and turn east 19 miles to the Hoh Ranger Station and Campground, elevation 578 feet. The hike begins on the nature trail starting at the visitor center; before setting out, study the museum displays explaining the geology, climate, flora, and fauna.

The way lies amid superb, large specimens of Douglas-fir, western hemlock, Sitka spruce, and western red-cedar, groves of bigleaf maple swollen with moss, and shrubs and ferns. Gravel bars and cold rapids of the river are never far away, inviting side-trips. Here and there are glimpses upward to snows of Mt. Tom and Mt. Carrie. In winter one may often see bands of Roosevelt elk; were it not for their constant grazing, the relatively open forest floor would be a dense jungle.

At 2½ miles a way trail departs right,

fording the river and ascending Tom Creek 1¼ miles to a dead-end far from crowds. Beside the Hoh River at 3½ miles is the Park's largest known Sitka spruce, 51½ feet in circumference.

Any distance can make a full day, what with long, lingering pauses. Happy Four Shelter, at 5½ miles, elevation 800 feet, is a logical turnaround for a day hike, and also a good campsite for backpackers.

The trail remains level to the next camp at Olympus Guard Station, 9 miles, 948 feet. At 9½ miles is a junction with the trail to High Divide. The valley trail then climbs a bit to the bridge over the spectacular canyon of the Hoh at 12 miles, 1400 feet, leaves the Hoh valley, and climbs more to the shelters at forest-surrounded Elk Lake, 14¼ miles, 2500 feet.

Now the grade becomes steep, ascending through steadily smaller trees, with views across Glacier Creek of snows and cliffs, to the twin shelters (which may soon be removed) at Glacier Meadows, 16½ miles, 4200 feet. Wander a short way in flowers and parkland to a viewpoint near the foot of the Blue Glacier, where torrents pour down ice-polished slabs to the forest below. Or follow the trail ½ mile to the end on the bouldery crest of a lateral moraine. Admire crevasses and icefalls of the glacier, and the summit tower of 7965-foot Mt. Olympus.

Elk feeding near Olympic Guard Station

Round trip to Happy Four Shelter 11 miles
Hiking time 6 hours
High point 800 feet
Elevation gain 225 feet
Best March through November
One day or backpack

Round trip to Glacier Meadows 34 miles
Allow 3 days
High point 4200 feet
Elevation gain 3700 feet
Best mid-July through October
USGS Olympic National Park or Mt. Tom and Mt. Olympus
Park Service Camping Permit required

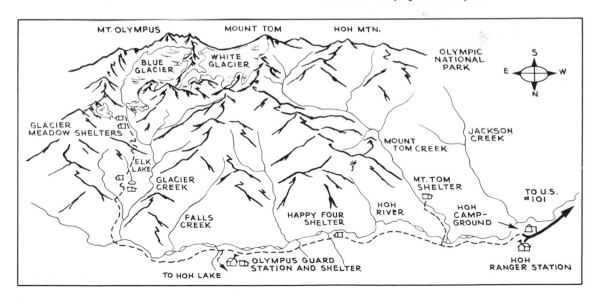

96 NORTH FORK QUINAULT RIVER

Hike a short way through magnificent rain forest in a low valley, open to travel almost the entire year. With a little luck, see the elk herd which winters here. No luck is needed to see the festoons of moss hanging from trees and feel underfoot the soft moss carpet covered by acres of oxalis.

Or, hike a long way to Low Divide and perhaps continue down the Elwha River (Hike 92) to complete the classic, 46-mile cross-Olympic route. Low Divide is often used, also, in connection with the Hayden Pass trail (Hike 86) for a Boy Scout 50-mile hike.

Drive US 101 from Aberdeen to the town of Amanda Park on the Quinault River. Continue 2 miles and turn right on the North Shore Road 14 miles (pavement ends in 8 miles) to the Quinault River bridge. Turn left 3½ miles to the road-end at the North Fork Ranger Station, elevation 519 feet.

The unmarked trail starts on sometimes-visible ruts of a road abandoned for so many years the ranger has no idea what it was for. The old roadbed is covered with moss, making walking a pleasure on the narrow path along the center. In ½ mile is a good view up-river toward Mt. Lawson. With minor ups and downs the way follows the flat river bottom, passing Wolf Bar Camp at 2½ miles. Now the trail climbs 300 feet and henceforth traverses the hillside, well above the river, crossing a number of tributary creeks on high bridges. At 4½ miles, just past Wild Rose Creek, is the site of Halfway House, elevation 800 feet, where a cabin was built to service a hunting lodge at Low Divide. During winter months snow may be encountered beyond here. At 7 miles, about 1100 feet, is Francis Creek Shelter, and in another mile, Trapper Shelter.

The trail passes the site of a pioneer cabin at Kimta Creek, about 10 miles, and the valley narrows to Twelve Mile Shelter at 12 miles, 1800 feet. At 12½ miles the trail crosses the Quinault River at 16 Mile Camp, 2005 feet. (No doubt 16 miles from the junction of the North Fork and East Fork.)

From the river crossing the way steepens, with a noticeable change in vegetation, and ascends to meadowland near 3602-foot Low Divide, the broad pass between the Quinault and Elwha Rivers, 18 miles from the road. Here begins the Elwha River trail (Hike 92). Once, on a bet, a Port Angeles man made the 46-mile over-the-Olympics route via Low Divide in a single day.

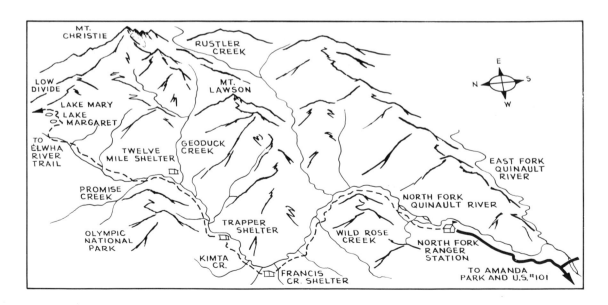

Oxalis along the North Fork Quinault River

Round trip to Low Divide 36 miles
Hiking time 18 hours
High point 3602 feet
Good to Halfway House all year
Best to Low Divide June through October
One day or backpack
USGS Mt. Christie
Park Service Camping Permit required

97   ENCHANTED VALLEY

Walk beside the river in open alder and maple forest, and miles through cathedral-like fir forest where future generations of loggers will come to see what their grandfathers meant when they boasted of big trees. The climax is Enchanted Valley, a large alpine cirque ringed by 3000-foot cliffs. The trail has many ups and downs and during rainy spells is a muddy mess, but in such country, who can complain?

Drive US 101 to the south-side Lake Quinault road. Turn easterly, skirting the lake and winding up the valley. Pavement ends at 12 miles. In 13 miles pass the North Fork bridge and at 21 miles Graves Creek Campground. Continue on the final narrow road to the trailhead 18½ miles from US 101, elevation 907 feet.

The trail crosses Pony Bridge over the Quinault River at 3 miles; the lovely canyon under the bridge is worth a trip in itself. In another ½ mile climb around the canyon and drop back to the river. For the next 10 miles the way alternates, up and down, between flat bottoms (alders and maples) and terraces several hundred feet above the river (groves of tall fir and cedar). With any luck a hiker should see elk. At 7 miles pass a junction to O'Neil Creek Camp, ¼ mile off the main track.

All along are tantalizing glimpses of peaks above, but at about 10½ miles the change from lowlands to alpine is dramatic. Suddenly one leaves heavy timber and bursts into the mountain world of rock and ice. To the left are cliffs of 6911-foot Chimney Peak. To the right is 6400-foot White Mountain. Both are dominated by the twin peaks of Mt. Anderson, divided by a small glacier: the sharp pyramid is 7366-foot West Peak, the highest point; the more massive peak in the middle is 7321 feet.

Coming down to earth, the valley has widened out. The lower part is floored with dense brush but farther up are flower fields. At 13½ miles cross the Quinault River, now a small creek (except in meltwater floods of spring, when the torrent may be impassable). Walk a short bit through meadows to the three-story Enchanted Valley Chalet, built in 1930 as a commercial hotel and now maintained by the Park Service as a public shelter. The structure will hold 50-60 people but often is full to overflowing, so be prepared to camp out. Be sure to carry a stove; cooking facilities are limited in the chalet and wood may be wet outside. Those unable to do the full 11 miles in a single day can stop overnight at any of a number of campsites along the way.

Beyond the chalet the trail climbs 2500 feet in 5 miles to 4500-foot Anderson Pass and descends the West Fork Dosewallips River 10 miles to the road (Hike 85). Another trail leads to O'Neil Pass and Hart, Marmot, and La Crosse Lakes (Hike 98).

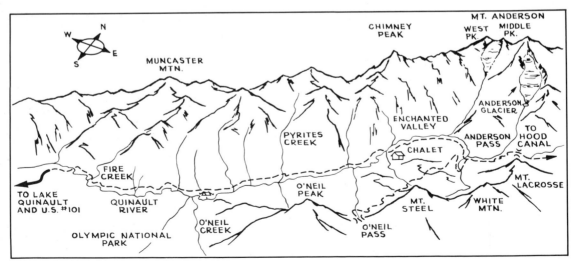

What's the best season for the trip? Well, some winters there is little snow in the lower valley, which thus can be walked in December or March when hardly any other country is open. Early spring is wonderful, when birds are singing and shrubs and maples are exploding with new leaves, and yellow violet and oxalis are blooming, and waterfalls and avalanches tumble and slide down cliffs. So is summer, when alders and maples canopy the valley bottoms in cool green. But fall is also glorious, with big leaf maples yellowing and the trail lost in fallen leaves. Better try it in all four seasons.

Round trip 27 miles
Allow 2-3 days
High point 1957 feet
Elevation gain 1050 feet plus ups and downs
Best March through December
USGS Olympic National Park or Mt. Christie and
Mt. Steele
Park Service Camping Permit required

Chimney Peak, left, and Mt. Anderson, right, above Enchanted Valley

Lake LaCrosse. Mt. Duckabush on left.

98   LAKE LACROSSE-O'NEIL PASS

In the heart of the Olympic wilderness, 16 miles from the nearest road, a group of beautiful alpine lakes sparkle amid a wonderland of heather and huckleberries. Quicker ways of reaching the lakes are mentioned in the last paragraph, but the one described here is the classic approach, via O'Neil Pass, on one of the most spectacular trails in the National Park, traversing ridges high above the Enchanted Valley of the Quinault, with many and magnificent views and flower fields.

To reach the O'Neil Pass Trail, hike 17 miles and gain 2400 feet up the Enchanted Valley (Hike 97) to the beginning at about 3400 feet (incorrectly shown as 3100 feet on the USGS map).

The O'Neil Pass trail starts from the Enchanted Valley trail beside a small torrent and heads westward and up, in a few yards going by a small camp. The way alternates between forest and wide-view meadows. At 1 mile are campsites and a crossing of White Creek; a hillside beyond gives the best look at Mt. Anderson.

At 1½ miles is a mountain hemlock with a sign saying it is 6 feet, 3 inches in diameter and 136 feet tall—a midget compared to the lowland variety but huge at this elevation. At 2 miles is an Alaska cedar identified as 7 feet, 6 inches in diameter and 114 feet tall.

The trail climbs to 4500 feet and then contours for miles, mainly in grass and blossoms. Directly across the valley is Chimney Peak, an impressive 6911 feet high. Views are breathtaking down the Quinault River to Lake Quinault and, if lucky, the ocean. The trail drops a bit, rounds a shoulder of the ridge, and ascends to O'Neil Pass, 7½ miles (25 miles from the road), 4900 feet, and close-ups of Mt. Duckabush. Still in meadows, the way descends to Marmot Lake, 8½ miles, 4400 feet. The O'Neil Pass trail ends here in a junction with the Duckabush River trail.

Scattered through higher gardens are Hart Lake, Lake LaCrosse, and Buck Lake. To get there, find the trail behind Marmot Lake Shelter and switchback upward ¾ mile to a junction. The left fork contours ½ mile to Hart Lake, enclosed on three sides by vertical cliffs; a shelter and good campsites. The right fork continues ¾ mile uphill to Lake LaCrosse, 4800 feet, perhaps the most splendid alpine lake in the Olympics, with views across the water to massive 6233-foot Mt. Duckabush and more graceful 6300-foot Mt. Steel. Another mile farther is Buck Lake, too small for fish and thus more private; there is no trail, but an experienced hiker can find the way from Lake LaCrosse west over a 5500-foot saddle and down to the 5000-foot shores. Camping is great at all the lakes.

The lakes can be approached in various other ways. For one, hike the Dosewallips trail (Hike 85) and drop over Anderson Pass 1½ miles, losing 1100 feet, to the start of the O'Neil Pass trail. Or, hike directly to the lakes by way of the Duckabush River trail 20 miles to Marmot Lake, gaining 4500 feet including some major ups and downs. For another, hike the North Fork Skokomish River trail (Hike 81) 19½ miles to Marmot Lake, gaining 5200 feet counting ups and downs. The lakes can also be included in imaginative one-way and loop trips.

One-way trip to Lake LaCrosse:

Via Quinault River and O'Neill Pass 26½ miles
  Elevation gain 4000
Via Anderson Pass and O'Neil Pass 22 miles
  Elevation gain 5200
Via Duckabush River 20 miles
  Elevation gain 4500 feet
Via North Fork Skokomish River 26½ miles
  Elevation gain 5200 feet
By any route, allow 5 days minimum
Best mid-July through September
USGS Mt. Steel
Park Service Camping Permit required

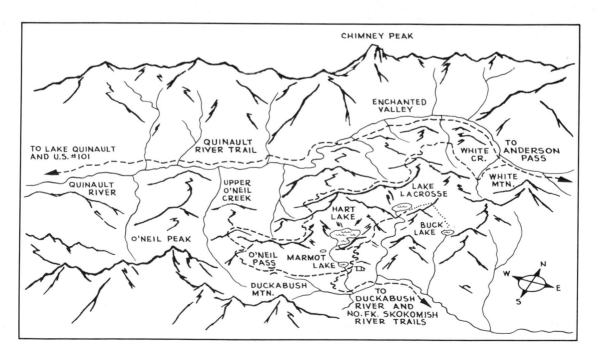

Portage Head at north end of Shi-Shi Beach

99   POINT OF THE ARCHES

Here, perhaps, is the most scenic single segment of the Washington ocean coast, with needle-like sea stacks, caves, and arches to explore, tidal pools, and miles of sand beaches. But visit the area soon; land developers are starting to sell lots and unless they can be stopped a proposed road eventually will convert the beach from wilderness into a runway crowded with people. Incredibly, Point of the Arches itself, which should belong to all of us, is privately owned (and not by the Makahs, from whom it was stolen generations ago). To prevent disaster, Congress must add the Point and Shi-Shi Beach to Olympic National Park.

Drive from Port Angeles on narrow, tortuous State Highway 112 to the Makah village of Neah Bay. At the west end of town turn left and follow signs to "Air Force Base and Ocean Beaches," crossing and recrossing a private logging road— stay on the public road. In 3 miles turn left over the Waatch River on a concrete bridge, again avoid the private road in favor of the public road, in about 6 miles cross the Soos River, and pass a cluster of Indian homes on Mukkow Bay at 6½ miles. Beyond the settlement the road climbs into woods above the beach and in 1 mile deteriorates rapidly. Park either near the houses or where the road gets sloppy. Overnight hikers do best to ask at one of the houses for parking space, for a fee; car-looting is a problem here.

The parking area and road are on the Makah Indian Reservation. The ocean beach and all adjacent land belong to the Makahs so private property rules apply. Camping on Mukkow Beach is also subject to restriction, though generally allowed; clam digging is prohibited.

The virtually undrivable road over Portage Head is pleasant walking under a canopy of trees. During wet weather be prepared for much mud. In about 1 mile push through the roadside brush for dramatic looks down to the surf. At 1½ miles, where the road comes to the edge of the bluff for the first unobstructed views of the ocean, are two "trails," side by side. The first drops like a shot to the north end of Shi-Shi Beach and is slippery and even scary. The other, several yards away, is steep enough but descends amid trees that provide handholds and a feeling of security. (If the tide is high, follow the road, which dwindles to a jeep track and in a mile nearly touches the beach.)

A short distance from the foot of the trail is the south end of Portage Head, with spectacular sea stacks, tidal pools, and a shipwreck. Hike about 2 miles south on the beach, leaving the reservation, passing a number of good campsites (the most reliable source of water in summer is Petroleum Creek), to the fabled Point of the Arches. The long string of stacks and islands can be reached and explored at very low tide; the going is rough over sharp and slippery rocks and involves some wading.

Travel south of the Point can be difficult, since there are several heads with no trails over the tops, requiring a very low tide to get around the bases or considerable bushwhacking to go over the tops. Before going over look for the thinnest salal and on top of the heads stay in the forest where there is little brush. About 6 miles from Point of the Arches is the Ozette River; a bit north of the river a private vacation-home road

(another threat to the wilderness beach!) leads inland 4½ miles to Ozette Lake.

At low tide, in dry spells, it may be possible for sturdy hikers to wade the knee-deep Ozette River and continue to Cape Alava (Hike 100).

Round trip to Point of the Arches 7 miles
Hiking time 4 hours
High point 150 feet
Good all year
One day or backpack
USGS Cape Flattery and Ozette Lake

100 CAPE ALAVA- SAND POINT LOOP

Two trails from Ozette Lake to the ocean, plus the connecting stretch of Olympic National Park wilderness beach, make a magnificent loop hike for one day or several, for winter as well as summer, passing a deserted homestead, the site of an Indian village, and miles of wild surf.

Drive from Port Angeles on State Highway 112 past Sekiu and turn left on the Ozette Lake road to the road-end ranger station, campground, and parking lot where the Ozette River empties from the lake, elevation 36 feet. Both trails depart from the same point and the loop is equally good in either direction. Begin by crossing the

bridge over the river; on the far side the trails diverge.

If the counterclockwise loop is chosen, take the Cape Alava trail, which goes a short bit on abandoned road and plunges into dense greenery of salal, hemlock, and other shrubs and trees. The path is sometimes flat, sometimes up and down a little, much of the way on planks—which may puzzle and irritate summertime hikers, but not those who do the trip in fall or spring when all the bare ground is black muck, or in winter when every depression is feet deep in water. Walk with caution—the planks can be slippery and the memories of the average hiker include a pratfall or two.

At 2 miles the route opens out magically

Beach camp at Cape Alava

into a broad bog—Ahlstroms Prairie, partly a one-time lake filled in by natural processes, partly a pasture cleared early in the century by a homesteader, Lars Ahlstrom. At the far side of the bog are remnants of a cabin and outbuildings. There are ghosts here. Pause a while to meet them.

Again the trail enters greenery, and now a far-off roar can be heard, and now the way tops a forested crest—and below are the loud breakers and beyond is the vast Pacific horizon. The trail quickly drops to the beach of Cape Alava, 3½ miles.

Camping space for scores of people (but often overcrowded in summer by hundreds of people) is available on a grassy wave-cut bench, the site of an Indian village occupied for centuries. There are many, many ghosts here, plus archaeologists excavating houses buried in a mudslide 500 years ago; other buried houses, dating back at least 2500 years, are awaiting excavation. For side-trips, explore at low tide out onto Ozette Island and Cannonball Beach, covered with large, round concretions, or hike 1½ miles north to the Ozette River and a far look toward Point of Arches (Hike 99).

The beach south 3 miles to Sand Point is easy walking at anything less than high tide, and offers an assortment of sands and rocks and tidal pools; camps and dependable water at several places. Halfway is Wedding Rock, inscribed with Indian petroglyphs. A few yards of boot-beaten track allow high-tide passage around the rock.

South ¼ mile from Sand Point are two shelters, and ½ mile farther south is a third; in trees along the beach are countless good (and in summer, crowded) camping areas. For side-trips south, see Hike 101.

To complete the loop, find the trail in the woods at Sand Point and hike 3 miles to Ozette Lake, again on planks in lush brush and forest.

Loop trip 9½ miles
Hiking time 6 hours
High point 170 feet
Elevation gain (ups and downs) about 500 feet
Good all year
One day or backpack
USGS Ozette Lake
Park Service Camping Permit required

Indian pictographs at Wedding Rock, south of Cape Alava

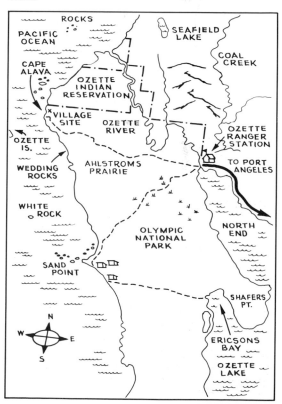

Quillayute Needles south of Cedar Creek

101   RIALTO BEACH TO CAPE ALAVA

Olympic National Park first became famous for rain forests and glaciers set within a magnificently large area of mountain wilderness. Now, though, it is known far and wide for still another glory—the last long stretch of wilderness ocean beach remaining in the conterminous United States. North and south from the Quillayute River extend miles and miles of coastline that are now almost exactly as they were before Columbus—except that in 1492 Indians had permanent homes and temporary camps at many places along the coast now deserted.

Winter and early spring months often offer the best hiking weather of the year, but storms can be hazardous. Facing a cold rain with miles of beach to hike is miserable and can lead to hypothermia (exposure).

The north section, from Rialto Beach to Cape Alava, makes a longer but easier walk than the south section described in Hike 102. There are no really difficult creek crossings, only one

headland that cannot be rounded at low tide, and most of the way is simple sand and shingles, interrupted occasionally by short stretches of rough rock.

Be sure to obtain a tide chart beforehand and use it to plan each day's schedule. Much of the route can be traveled at high tide, but at the cost of scrambling over driftwood and slippery rocks, plodding wearily through steep, loose gravel, and climbing up and down points. Moreover, some headlands cannot be climbed over and the beach at low tide provides the only passage. Be prepared to hike early in the morning or late in the evening, with layovers during the day, if the tides so dictate.

Drive US 101 to 2 miles north of Forks. Turn west on the La Push road 8 miles, then turn right on the Mora Campground-Rialto Beach road 5 miles to the parking lot at the beach.

In ½ mile is Ellen Creek, the first possible campsite. Here and elsewhere the "brown water," colored by organic solutes, looks like tea, but is perfectly pure and delicious. At 1½ miles, just beyond the sea stack with the Hole in the Wall, are meager camps and the first headland, which has several small points, one requiring

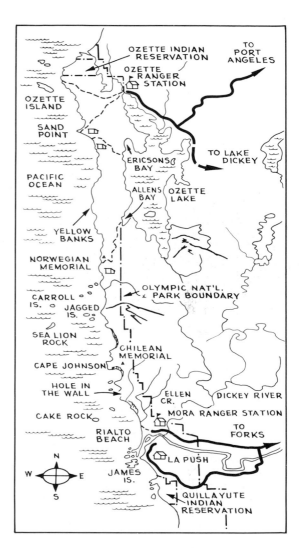

low tide to get around. At 2½ miles are camps near the Chilean Memorial, which commemorates one of the countless ships wrecked on this rugged coast, and at 3 miles begins the long, rough rounding of Cape Johnson, which has no trail over the top and can be passed at low tide only, as is true of another rough point immediately following. A point at 5 miles must be climbed over on a short trail and one at 6 miles rounded at low tide. At 6½ miles is Cedar Creek (campsites) and immediately beyond is a point that can be rounded at low tide or crossed on a steep, short path.

At the Norwegian Memorial (another ship-wreck and more camps), 7½ miles, a trail leads inland 2¼ miles to Allen's Bay on Ozette Lake. (There is no trail along the lake, so unless a boat pickup by the resort has been arranged, this is not a shortcut to civilization). Passing campsites every so often and at 10 miles a low-tide-only point, at 13½ miles the way comes to Yellow Banks, the point at the north end of which must be rounded at low tide.

At 15 miles is a shelter and a trail going 2 miles to Ericsons Bay on Ozette Lake. At Sand Point, 15½ miles, are two more shelters, innumerable campsites in the woods, and a trail leading 3 miles to the Ozette Lake road (Hike 100).

The wilderness beach continues north to Cape Alava, 18½ miles, and a second trail to the Ozette road, 22 miles (Hike 100).

One-way trip 22 miles
Allow 3 days
High point 100 feet
Good all year
USGS Olympic National Park or La Push and Ozette Lake
Park Service Camping Permit required

102 THIRD BEACH TO HOH RIVER

Wild forest and wild ocean, woods animals and sea birds, tidal pools and wave-carved stacks, the constant thunder of surf, and always the vast mysterious horizon of the Pacific. This south section of the Olympic National Park wilderness ocean strip is shorter but more complicated than the northern one described in Hike 101, requiring detours inland to cross headlands and creeks

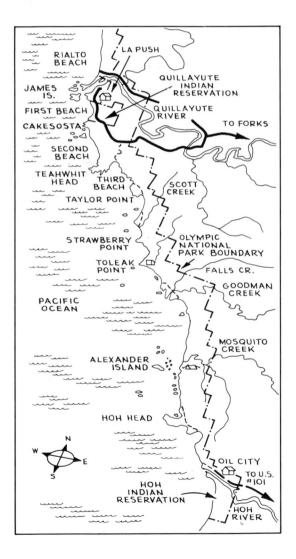

and demanding even closer attention to the tide chart.

Warning: Goodman, Falls, and Mosquito Creeks are high all winter, and after a period of heavy rain or melting snow are virtually unfordable.

Drive US 101 to 2 miles north of Forks. Turn west on the La Push road 12 miles to the parking lot at the Third Beach trail, elevation 240 feet.

Hike the forest trail, descending abruptly to the beach and campsites at ¾ mile. Head south along the sand and in ½ mile look for a prominent marker on a tree above the beach, the start of the trail over Taylor Point—which cannot be rounded at the base. The trail climbs into lovely woods, dropping to the beach at 3 miles and a small head which can be rounded at any time except high tide.

At 3½ miles is a point which can be rounded at low tide or climbed over by a short trail to reach Scott Creek, with campsites in the woods; another very small point immediately south can be rounded in medium tide. At 4½ miles is Strawberry Point, low and forested and simple, and at 5½ miles, Toleak Point, ditto. Shortly beyond is Jackson Creek (camps).

At 6½ miles a trail ascends a steep bluff and proceeds inland through beautiful forest to crossings of Falls and Goodman Creeks (cliffs make a shore passage impassable), returning to the surf at 7¾ miles. The beach is then easy to Mosquito Creek, 10 miles; ford the stream at low tide. (Camps here.) Climb small points at 10½ and 10.9 miles, and at 11.1 miles round another at low tide (the way over the top is strenuous). Two more points in the next mile can be crossed on rough paths but are better passed at low tide.

At 12 miles a trail climbs the large promontory of Hoh Head, which cannot be rounded in any tide, and regains the beach at 12¾ miles. Going by a campsite or two, at 13½ miles the way comes to the last point, a heap of big rocks which must be rounded at low tide. From here a narrow, low-tide-only strip of beach leads to the mouth of the Hoh River, 14¾ miles. A trail follows the river inland to the Oil City road-end, 15½ miles.

The Oil City road reaches US 101 in 12 miles, at a point about ½ mile north of the Hoh river bridge.

Air view of the Graveyard of the Giants, Taylor Head in foreground, Scott Bluff in center.

Warning: Cars at the Third Beach parking area have been frequently broken into. Do not leave any belongings visible inside the car.

One-way trip 16 miles
Allow 3 days
High point 250 feet
Good all year
USGS Olympic National Park or La Push and Forks
Park Service Camping Permit required

227

TIME OF YEAR TRAILS ARE PASSABLE

The following list shows when trails are generally free enough of snow to be passable. The time varies every year by a week or two depending on the depth of the winter snow and warmth of the spring. Even when considered passable, trails may have snow patches for another 2 weeks, or maybe all summer. Expect occasional snowstorms at high elevations even in the middle of summer. This new snow will generally melt in a few hours.

If alpine flower fields are one of the trail's attractions, plan the hike between mid-July and early August. For blueberries, try late August and fall, and for fall color, go in mid-September to early October. High mountain lakes generally don't open up until mid-July.

If you want to be alone on the trail, try early in the season or after Labor Day, but avoid the high country hunting season except in National Parks.

ALL YEAR

99 Point of the Arches
100 Cape Alava
101 Rialto Beach
102 Third Beach

MARCH

77 Lewis River
94 Bogachiel River
95 Happy Four Shelter
96 Halfway House
97 Enchanted Valley

APRIL

16 Mount Si
82 Lower Lena Lake
92 Elwha River

MAY

5 Trout Lake
14 Lower Ingalls Creek
21 Bandera Mountain
45 Huckleberry Mountain
81 Camp Pleasant

EARLY JUNE

1 Mount Persis
2 Lake Serene
32 Little Lake Kachess
49 American Ridge (lower part)
53 High Rock
59 Prairie Mountain
61 Packwood Lake
78 Cascade Crest Trail (southern section)

83 Mount Jupiter
88 Mount Townsend
96 Low Divide (Quinault River)

MID TO LATE JUNE

23 Granite Mountain
25 Annette Lake
30 Mount Margaret
34 Polallie Ridge viewpoint
36 Waptus Lake
42 Esmerelda Basin
46 Naches Wagon Trail
47 Norse Peak
50 Nelson Ridge-Mount Aix
62 Goat Ridge
67 Juniper Mountain
69 Blue Lake

EARLY JULY

3 Tonga Ridge-Mount Sawyer
5 Foss Lakes
6 Deception Creek
10 Snow Lakes (Icicle Creek)
14 Ingalls Creek
15 Lennox Creek
16 Snoqualmie Lake
17 Hester Lake-Myrtle Lake
20 McClellan Butte
22 Pratt Lake
26 Silver Peak
27 Snow Lake (Snoqualmie Pass)
30 Lake Lillian
32 Mineral Creek Park
34 Polallie Ridge
35 Jolly Mountain

39 Deep Lake
40 Hyas Lake
41 Marmot Lake
44 Summit Lake
47 Big Crow Basin
48 Sourdough Gap
52 Tumac Mountain
57 McCall Basin
59 Trails End (Purcell Mountain)
61 Lost Lake
63 Snowgrass Flat
64 Nannie Peak
65 Goat Rocks Crest
67 Juniper Ridge
68 Boundary Trail
70 Indian Heaven
72 Coldwater Peak
75 Around Mount St. Helens
78 Cascade Crest Trail
79 Mount Ellinor
80 Flapjack Lakes
82 Upper Lena Lake
86 Hayden Pass
91 Grand Valley
92 Low Divide

MID-JULY

7 Surprise Lake
8 Lake Josephine
9 Larch Lake
11 Lake Caroline
12 Lake Stuart-Colchuck Lake
13 Lake Mary
19 Dutch Miller Gap
24 Melakwa Lake
28 Commonwealth Basin
29 Gold Creek
31 Rampart Ridge
37 Spade Lake
38 Paddy-Go-Easy Pass
43 Ingalls Lake
51 Cougar Lakes
54 Dumbbell Lake
55 Shoe Lake
56 Blankenship Lakes
58 Devils Horns
60 Klickitat Trail
66 Adams Glacier Meadows
71 Mount Adams Highline Trail

73 Mount Margaret Back Country
74 Mount Margaret
76 Shark Rock
81 Home Sweet Home
85 Anderson Glacier
87 Marmot Pass
89 Royal Basin
90 Mount Angeles
95 Glacier Meadows (Mount Olympus)
96 Lake LaCrosse

LATE JULY

4 Necklace Valley
7 Surprise Mountain
10 Enchantment Lakes
19 LaBohn Gap
49 American Ridge (upper part)
64 Nannie Ridge

EARLY AUGUST

33 Spectacle Lake
40 Tuck and Robin Lakes
62 Goat Lake
84 Lake Constance
93 High Divide

STILL MORE HIKES IN THE ALPINE LAKES, SOUTH CASCADES, AND OLYMPICS

The 102 hikes represent all provinces of the Cascades from Stevens Pass to the Columbia River, and of the Olympics. Heaviest emphasis has been placed on areas close to major population centers. There are other great walks in the two ranges; many are described in the books noted below, which may be obtained from bookstores, shops specializing in mountain equipment, or in many cases by mail order directly from The Mountaineers. (See listing of Mountaineer Books at the end of this volume.)

PHOTO BOOKS AND GENERAL

The Alpine Lakes

Approximately 100 color photos by Ed Cooper and Bob Gunning. Text by Brock Evans, foreword by Dave Brower. Published by The Mountaineers.

Cool, Clear Water

175 photos by Bob and Ira Spring, 31 in color, showing the varied manifestations of Northwest water from glaciers to the ocean. Text by Harvey Manning. Published by Superior Publishing Co.

The Cascade Range

About 40 of the color photos by Ray Atkeson are in the Cascades from Stevens Pass to the Columbia River. Published by Belding.

Wildflowers of Mount Rainier and the Cascades

96 color pages of flowers one often sees while hiking. Emphasis is on appreciation of the flowers. Photos by Bob and Ira Spring. Authoritative and interesting text by Mary Fries. Published by The Mountaineers.

The Challenge of Mount Rainier

Detailed history of climbing on the mountain by Dee Molenaar. Many sketches by the author showing the climbing routes. Published by The Mountaineers.

Across the Olympic Mountains: The 1889-90 Press Expedition

The story of the first party to cross the range, by Robert L. Wood. Published by the University of Washington Press and The Mountaineers.

The Olympic Rain Forest

102 photos, 15 in color, by Johsel Namkung and Ruth Kirk. Text by Ruth Kirk. Published by University of Washington Press.

WINTER GUIDE BOOKS

Snowshoe Hikes in the Cascades and Olympics

Texts, maps, and photos by Gene Prater include 65 trips in the Alpine Lakes and South Cascades and Olympics. Published by The Mountaineers.

HIKING GUIDES

Trips and Trails, 1: Family Camps, Short Hikes, and View Roads in the North Cascades and Olympics

Trips and Trails, 2: Family Camps, Short Hikes, and View Roads in Mt. Rainier and the South Cascades

The two companion volumes are the basic introduction to car travel and car camping, essential for every visitor. They include scores of hikes up to several miles in length—shorter and easier than those in the present book. Text by E.M. Sterling, photos by Bob and Ira Spring, maps by Marge Mueller. Published by The Mountaineers.

50 Hikes in Mount Rainier National Park

Photos by Bob and Ira Spring, text by Ira Spring and Harvey Manning, maps by Marge Mueller. Published by the Mount Rainier Natural History Association and The Mountaineers.

Cascade Alpine Guide—Climbing and High Routes: Columbia River to Stevens Pass

By Fred Beckey, published by The Mountaineers.

The Pacific Crest Trail—Volume 2: Oregon and Washington

By Jeff Schaffer and Bev and Fred Hartline. Includes 140 full-page topographic maps of the trail route. Published by Wilderness Press.

The Cascade Crest Trail

By Louise Marshall. Published by Signpost Publications.

Trail Country: Olympic National Park

Comprehensive description of the Park and a foot-by-foot log of all its trails, by Robert L. Wood. Published by The Mountaineers. The trail log section is available in paperback, titled **Wilderness Trails of Olympic National Park.**

Exploring the Olympic Peninsula

An introduction to car travel and walking by Ruth Kirk. Published by University of Washington Press.

The Olympic Seashore

An introduction to the beaches by Ruth Kirk. Published by Olympic Natural History Association.

Climbers' Guide to the Olympic Mountains

By a committee of the Olympic Mountain Rescue Council. Published by The Mountaineers.

MORE HIKES

The 102 hikes are, in the judgment of the authors and The Mountaineers, most of the best remaining in the Alpine Lakes and South Cascades, and a sampling of the best in the Olympics. Below are listed some 160 other hikes —in addition to those described in books noted above—that are worthy of consideration.

To take the following hikes, consult the books referred to, if any, or else obtain the applicable maps and make your own way. The lack of detailed "recipes"—or in some cases, of a trail—may be compensated for by a greater degree of solitude. (Indeed, more and more hikers are avoiding trails recommended in guidebooks. —and abandoning trails altogether—in their quest for lonesomeness.)

Skykomish River

West Fork Miller River: An abandoned road, now a pleasant forest trail beside the stream.

Hope Lake: 2 miles up North Fork Tunnel Creek to Crest Trail and the lake.

Nason Creek

Lanham Lake trail No. 1589: 1¾ miles to lake under cliffs of Jim Hill Mountain. (Closed to bikes and horses.)

Glacier Creek trail No. 1573: An access via Chiwaukum Creek to meadows on east side of Chiwaukum Mountains. A dead-end trail after 1½ miles—needs maintenance.

Lake Ethel trail No. 1585: Steep 4½ miles. Passes through a grove of lodgepole pine with contorted trunks.

Painter Creek trail No. 1575: Pleasant forest and meadows—long hike.

Hatchery Creek trail No. 1577: Access to Icicle Ridge trail.

McCue Ridge trail No. 1574: From trail No. 1584A to trail No. 1591.

White Pine Creek: From White Pine Creek road to Icicle trail No. 1551.

Icicle Creek

Icicle Ridge trail No. 1570: 25-mile ridge walk with lots of ups and downs and lots of views. 4-5 day hike.

Fourth of July Creek trail No. 1579: 5 miles to an old lookout site and Icicle Ridge trail.

Trout Lake trail No. 1555: 5 miles to shallow Trout Lake. Trail goes on to Windy Pass and Eight Mile Creek.

Icicle Creek trail No. 1551: 12-mile access to Crest Trail past Lake Josephine.

Jack Creek trail No. 1558: 11½ miles to meadows and Stuart Pass.

Solomon Creek trail No. 1593: Meadows. Long trail via Jack Creek or shorter from Cle Elum River.

Cradle Lake trail No. 1560: Long loop trip to meadows.

French Creek trail No. 1595: 12 miles to Paddy-Go-Easy Pass. Good trail in timber but boggy in meadows. Trail not maintained between Klonaqua Lakes junction and Meadows Creek trail junction.

French Ridge trail No. 1564: Open meadows on a steep loop trail.

Lake Leland trail No. 1566: Long hike in woods to lake on edge of meadow country.

Square Lake trail No. 1567: Interesting trail past a canyon, meadows, and views.

Chain Lakes trail No. 1569: Very steep trail from 10 miles up Icicle Creek trail to above timberline. View of spires on Bulls Tooth from hill north of lakes. Map shows loop via Doughgod Creek but trail is in very poor condition.

Klonaqua Lakes trail No. 1563: Steep trail (and long access) to two alpine lakes.

Mission Ridge Area

Devils Gulch trail No. 1220: Good trail 12 miles up Mission Creek to Beehive road and return on ridge via trail No. 1201. Good in May.

Red Hill trail No. 1223: Hike to top of 3800-foot hill in May.

Squilchuck trail No. 1200: 2-mile hike through alpine forest. Access to Clara and Marion Lakes.

Ingalls Creek

Hansel Creek Ridge and return to Ingalls Creek.

Negro Creek and Three Brothers Mountain.

Falls Creek trail and trail along ridge dividing the Teanaway River and Ingalls Creek.

North Bend Area

Bare Mountain from Lennox Creek: Stiff climb to lookout site on little-used trail.

Mt. Teneriffe: 7 miles up a jeep road from valley and then ¾-mile trail to summit.

Granite Creek: Abandoned road and fishermen's path to Granite Lakes and Lake Thompson and connection with Defiance trail No. 1007.

Lake Thompson: From Granite Creek road and trail.

Pratt River: Possible for 7 miles but must first ford the Middle Fork Snoqualmie River.

Rainy Lake trail (not a trail) from Camp Brown: Route very difficult to find. 6 or 7 hours to lake.

Quartz Creek: Very difficult route to Rainy Lake or a ¾-mile fishermen's trail to Blethan Lake.

Nordrum Lake: Rough trail around logs and up creek beds from Taylor River to Nordrum Lake. Gateway to alpine country.

Middle Fork Snoqualmie valley trail: Unmaintained trail across river from road. Forest Service plans to rebuild this trail when money is available.

Rock Creek trail: Unusual approach from valley trail to Snow Lake (Hike 27). Trail not used much because of difficult river crossing.

Mt. Washington: Gated logging road through clear-cuts to outpost summit (4400 feet) with grand views.

Mason Lake-Mt. Defiance: From Mason Creek on road No. 2218A, a rude path to lake. From Mason Lake, intersect Defiance trail (Hike 26). 5584-foot summit of Mt. Defiance easily reached.

Trail No. 1018 from Silver Peak to Hanson Creek: Presently closed through watershed and unmaintained for 15 years or more.

Cle Elum Area

Roaring Ridge: Find abandoned road near Lost Lake. Follow it to road-end, then take a short trail to old lookout site.

Snowshoe Butte: Cross-country travel from road No. 204B or from Cascade Crest Trail between Tacoma Pass and Stampede Pass.

Lookout Mountain: Inquire at Ellensburg Ranger Station.

Cole Butte: Begins on the High Line Canal near Easton to Goat Peak and along jeep road to saddle between Log Creek and Big Creek.

Silver Creek: 16 miles to hanging valley, a beautiful meadow of berries and subalpine timber. Can also be reached from Cooper Pass.

Kachess Ridge trail No. 1315: Passes through Silver Creek drainage under Thorpe Mountain to No Name Ridge and then to road at Cooper Pass.

Thorpe Mountain trail No. 1316: One of five routes to the lookout. 3½ miles from Thorpe Creek road.

Knox Creek trail No. 1315A: 2½ miles to Thorpe Mountain lookout.

Red Mountain trail No. 1330: 7 miles long, connecting with the Kachess Ridge trail a mile short of the Thorpe Mountain lookout.

Davis Peak trail No. 1324: Steep 5½ miles to an old lookout site and broad views. Possible roaming out along Goat Ridge.

Paris Creek trail No. 1393: A short 8 miles to open basin where trail is difficult to follow. One could spend a week here without retracing path, since the trail joins the Teanaway, Jolly Mountain, and Boulder-De Roux trails.

Boulder-De Roux trail No. 1392: 4-mile jeep trail connecting to the Paris Creek trail and others.

South Fortune Creek trail No. 1335: 4-mile jeep trail to mining claim and south to Boulder Creek, Paris Creek, Jolly Mountain, and Sasse Ridge.

Fortune Creek spur trail No. 2342: Jeep trail from Van Epps Pass.

County Line trail No. 1342: Links Fortune Creek with Scatter Creek and the Teanaway.

Trail Creek trail No. 1322: From Waptus River to Fish Lake. Must ford the river.

Michael Lake trail No. 1336: Side-trip from Trail Creek trail. Best reached from the Fish Lake end.

White River

Noble Knob trail No. 1184: From Corral Pass, 8½ miles in alpine trees and meadows with grand views of Mt. Rainier to road No. 196.

Dalles Ridge trail No. 1173: Starts from trail No. 1184. 2½ miles of scenic trail with views of Mt. Rainier.

Ranger Creek trail No. 1197: Being constructed by volunteers of the Boy Scouts of America. 8 miles to Dalles Ridge trail No. 1173. Good view overlooking White River in 2¼ miles.

Crystal Mountain trail No. 1163: 8½ miles from Silver Creek trail No. 1192 past Hen Skin Lake over top of Crystal Mountain (also reached by chairlift) down the ridge to Crystal Mountain highway.

White River trail No. 1199: 4-mile lowland trail in big timber paralleling US 410.

Deep Creek trail No. 1196: A steep 5 miles to Noble Knob trail No. 1184. Last ½ mile in open alpine country.

Greenwater trail No. 1176: Scenic trail following the Greenwater River 12½ miles. Passes 4 lakes.

Lost Lake trail No. 1185: Starts 3¼ miles up the Greenwater trail. Passes Quinn Lake, Lost Lake, and goes through alpine country to join the Noble Knob trail. Trail is 5½ miles long.

Maggie Creek trail No. 1186: Starts 5½ miles up

the Greenwater trail. In 5¼ miles, all in timber, reaches Cascade Crest Trail.

Arch Rock trail No. 1187: Steep 3½-mile access to Cascade Crest Trail starting 7½ miles up the Greenwater trail. Last ½ mile in alpine country.

Carbon trail No. 1179: 13-mile trail from Flip-O-Way road No. 1810 to a junction with the Summit Lake trail No. 1177. Scenic around Bearhead Mountain.

Cedar Lake: Steep, 1-mile fishermen's trail to lake, then ½ mile more to Celery Meadow.

American River

Bismark Peak trail No. 983: Reached from Bumping Lake or Indian Creek trails.

Fifes Peak trail No. 954: Rough, dry horse trail around the rugged cliffs of Fifes Peak.

Richmond Mine trail No. 973: Long route from Bumping River to Rattlesnake Creek.

Bumping River trail No. 971: Long access to Crest Trail.

Mt. Aix trail No. 982: From Rattlesnake Creek road to Mt. Aix.

Rattlesnake trail No. 981: Long route to the headwaters of Hindoo Creek.

Randle Area

Strawberry Mountain trail No. 220: Long and scenic ridge walk. Very little water.

Langills Peak trail: Long scenic ridge walk. Water at Grasshopper Lake and Bear Creek.

Upper Green River trail No. 213: Woods walk to Norway Pass or Meta Lake.

Green River trail No. 213: O.K. to National Forest boundary, then contact Weyerhaeuser Company for conditions on its land.

Vanson Peak trail No. 217: Best reached from Ryan Lake over Goat Mountain. North end of trail is in private land (U.S. Plywood-Champion Papers).

Tongue Mountain Trail 294: Early season hike from road 111 or 123.

Trail No. 119: 3½-mile ridgetop trail from Blue Lake to Mid Lake.

Packwood Area

Lake Christine trail No. 249A (901A on old maps): Near southwest corner of Mt. Rainier National Park.

Puyallup trail No. 248 (900 on old maps): On west side of Mt. Rainier National Park.

Tatoosh trail No. 161: Long, spectacular meadow walk, best in late July when flowers are blooming. Carry water.

Carlton Ridge trail No. 42: Old-growth Douglas fir, views of narrow valley, and access to Crest Trail at Fish Lake.

Cowlitz and Jug Lake trails, Nos. 44 and 43: Access to Crest Trail and shallow Jug and Fryingpan Lakes. Many marshy meadows.

Sand Lake trail No. 60: A way to Crest Trail.

Cartright Creek trail No. 57: Access to Crest Trail.

Bluff Lake trail No. 65: Long route to Coyote Ridge and Goat Rocks Wilderness.

Clear Fork trail No. 61: River access to Goat Rocks Wilderness.

5030 trail No. 83: On Snyder Mountain, joining trail No. 86 in 1 mile.

Lily Basin trail No. 86: Ridge hike to Lily Basin and Goat Ridge trail (Hike 62).

Angry Mountain trail No. 90: Ridge hike to Lily Basin.

Jordan Creek trail No. 94: Long access route to Goat Ridge (Hike 62).

South Point trail No. 123: A lookout and a long ridge hike on a dry access route to Klickitat Trail (Hike 60).

Coleman Weed Patch trail No. 121: Access route to the Crest Trail. A timbered plateau with small lakes.

Teeley Creek trail No. 251: Can start on road No. 149 for longer hike to Granite Lake.

Tieton Area

Sand Ridge: Long, dry, flat, and wooded ridge hike from near Rimrock Reservoir to Blankenship Meadows.

Spiral Butte: A side trail from Sand Ridge to a wooded hilltop going through the site of a recent forest fire. Excellent view of Mt. Rainier and Mt. Aix area.

Bear Creek Mountain: Exciting viewpoint of the Goat Rocks reached from Section 3 Lake (see **Trips and Trails, 2**) and North Fork Tieton River road.

Tenday Creek trail No. 1134: Starts from Conrad Meadows. A long creek and ridge route to Cirque Lake. Just above lake is a fine view of Goat Rocks.

Jump-off Lookout: Trail to lookout. Jeep road on other side of ridge.

Trout Lake Area

Snipes Mountain trail No. 11: From road No. N80, trail climbs along a lava flow 5 miles to alpine meadows and a junction with Adams Highline Trail.

Cold Springs trail No. 72: 15-mile loop hike is possible by starting on trail No. 11, going to the Adams Highline Trail, following it westward to timberline, then down the timberline road to trail No. 72, to trail No. 40, and walking road No. N80 ¾ mile back to car.

Bird Lake trail No. 100: Beautiful flower walk—see **Trips and Trails, 2.**

St. Helens Area

Miners Creek trail No. 212: Lower end in poor condition with some phenomenal mudholes. Upper end is fairly good.

Trade Dollar trail No. 246: Poor condition. Used mainly by tough hunters who want to be alone.

Butte Camp trail No. 238A: Widened for jeeps during a forest fire. Now closed to jeeps, but there are enforcement problems.

Trail No. 242: Lange's Mine Trail from Boy Scout camp 2 miles to open meadows on side of Mt. Margaret.

Lewis River

Quartz Creek trail No. 5: Miles of forest and creek. The largest virgin forest in the area.

Snagtooth Creek trail No. 4: Climb from Quartz Creek to Boundary Trail.

Lava Caves: Interesting ¼-mile trail.

Wright Meadow trail No. 80: Through forest between roads N920.2 and 933.

Trail No. 17: Recently reopened from Lewis River road to Craggy Peak trail No. 3.

Wind River Area

Lost Lake trail No. 133: A small gem-like lake near Government Mineral Springs.

Observation Peak and Sister Rocks trail No. 132: Old-growth silver fir and trail to peak near Government Mineral Springs.

Falls Creek trail No. 152: 2-mile trail from road N73 to a falls in a secluded little valley.

Little Huckleberry Mountain trail No. 197: Starts from road No. 500. Camping near the top and views from the rounded 4202-foot mountain. Crossed by Crest Trail.

Silver Star Mountain: Impassable jeep road to a lookout in the Yacolt Burn. Generally closed during fire season.

Hamilton Mountain, in Beacon Rock State Park: 4-mile hike to a tremendous overlook of the Columbia River. See **Trips and Trails, 2.**

Table Mountain: 3-mile hike to views of the Oregon and Washington volcanoes.

Dog Mountain: 2½-mile hike along the Cascade Crest Trail from the Columbia River to the top of the mountain.

Thomas Lake trail: 3 miles from road No. 605 to Crest Trail and the heart of Indian Heaven.

East Side Olympic Peninsula

(See **Trail Country**)

Mt. Washington trail No. 800: Starts from Big Creek road No. 2419. An easy grade 1½ miles to ridge top. Does not go to summit of mountain.

Mt. Rose trail No. 814: Steep, strenuous climb 3 miles to within ¼ mile of the 4301-foot summit. For experienced hikers only.

Dry Creek trail No. 872: Starts from road No. 2357 near the Park boundary. The first 1½ miles are along the shores of Lake Cushman. Ideal for family hiking.

Wagon Wheel Lake trail: Located near Staircase. Trail is a steep (12 to 15 percent) 3-mile climb to a small tarn. Good views of Mt. Lincoln and upper Slate Creek Basin.

Six Ridge trail: From North Fork Skokomish River trail. Long, steep, dry way trail to subalpine meadows, elk country.

Putvin trail No. 813: Starts at head of Hamma Hamma valley near Boulder Creek. A long-abandoned trapper's trail to alpine country. Very steep but offers access to Mt. Stone, Mt. Skokomish, and acres of flowers and wildlife.

Constance Pass: Scenic route between the Dosewallips and Dungeness valleys.

Graywolf trail: 20-mile hike to 6150-foot Graywolf Pass and descent to Dosewallips. Can be shortened by starting at Deer Park.

Cameron Creek trail: Reached from the Graywolf trail. A very long hike to 6400-foot Cameron Pass and on over Lost Pass to Dose Meadows.

North Side Olympic Peninsula

(See **Trail Country**)

Grand Ridge trail: 8-mile ridge walk from Deer Park to Obstruction Point. Splendid alpine hike. Carry water.

Little River trail: Lovely and little-traveled 8-mile route to Hurricane Ridge.

Lake Creek: Begins at Heart O'the Hills Campground, Loop E. 2-mile woods walk, no lake.

Cox Valley trail: Starts 1 mile along Obstruction Point road. Trailhead not marked. Goes into Cox Valley.

P.J. Lake: Starts at base of Eagle Mountain on the Obstruction Point road. ½ mile down to lake. Trail not marked.

Pyramid Peak trail: Great viewpoint of Lake Crescent. 3½-mile climb.

Storm King trail: 1½-mile steep trail to viewpoint of Lake Crescent on side of Mt. Storm King.

Barnes Creek trail: Indistinct way trail through forest to Aurora Ridge trail. Fades out as it reaches 5000-foot Lookout Dome.

Aurora Creek trail: 3½-mile shortcut to Aurora Ridge trail. Very steep.

Aurora Ridge trail: 16-mile ridge walk, mostly in trees, then down to Olympic Hot Springs. Some good views of Mt. Olympus.

Long Ridge trail: From the Elwha trail to Dodger Point, a long, dry ridge with views. Ends in scenic meadows. Route to Bailey Range. Good trail.

Appleton Pass: 8-mile hike from Olympic Hot Springs to the Soleduck trail over a 5000-foot pass. Elk are often seen.

Boulder Lake trail: 3½ miles from Olympic Hot Springs to Lake Crescent.

Happy Lake Ridge trail: Long hike with views and a lake, starting from Olympic Hot Springs road. Can be a loop with the Boulder Lake trail. 3½ miles between trailheads.

Martins Park trail: 2-mile side-trip from the Elwha trail at Low Divide to glorious meadows and views.

North Fork Soleduck trail: Woods walk 9 miles to dead-end.

West Side Olympic Peninsula

(See **Trail Country**)

Geodetic Hill trail: Very indistinct route, abandoned in 1945, from the Bogachiel to forested Spruce Mountain.

Hoh-Bogachiel trail: Follows the Park boundary from the Hoh over and down into the Bogachiel at Flapjack Shelter.

Indian Pass trail: Forested route from the Bogachiel River to Calawah River and on to Rugged Ridge and Forest Service road.

South Fork Hoh trail: Short trail to canyon. Very easy. Fades out in unspoiled rain forest.

Mt. Tom Creek trail: A difficult ford of the Hoh River leads to seldom-visited forest.

Queets River trail: A difficult ford of the Queets River leads to 15-plus miles of primitive rain forest.

Kloochman Rock trail: From Queets trail past largest Douglas-fir tree to lookout site.

Tshletshy Creek trail: From the Queets to Quinault.

Higley Peak trail: 3-mile climb from Lake Quinault or a short walk from logging road. View of lake. See **Trips and Trails, 1.**

Mt. Colonel Bob trail: 6½-mile climb, gaining 400 feet, to viewpoint of Lake Quinault and mountains.

Elip Creek trail: Intersects the Skyline Trail from North Fork Quinault. 4½ miles.

Skyline Trail: Long, strenuous, scenic route to Low Divide. A late-summer trip, since snow obscures route at head of Promise Creek.

Three Lakes trail: Starts at North Fork Quinault Ranger Station. A 7-mile trail connects at divide above Three Lakes with Tshletshy Creek trail. 18 miles from Three Lakes to Queets River.

Graves Creek trail: 9-mile hike from the Quinault to Six Ridge Pass and Sundown Lake.

Second Beach (near LaPush): See **Trips and Trails, 1.**

Ruby Beach to Hoh River: Hike under a steep bank to the mouth of the Hoh River. Half the way is on the Hoh Indian Reservation. Very narrow beach is feasible only on low or minus tides. No escape from incoming tides.

INDEX

OTHER BOOKS FROM THE MOUNTAINEERS

THE HIKES SERIES

50 Hikes in Mount Rainier National Park

Companion volume to this book. A comprehensive guide to hiking in the Park. Text by Ira Spring and Harvey Manning, photos by Bob and Ira Spring, maps by Marge Mueller. Published jointly with the Mount Rainier Natural History Association.

101 Hikes in the North Cascades

Companion volume to this book.

Trips and Trails, 1: Family Camps, Short Hikes, and View Roads in the North Cascades and Olympics

Mountain and beach recreation for the entire family. 106 maps by Marge Mueller, 128 photos by Bob and Ira Spring, text by E.M. Sterling.

Trips and Trails, 2: Family Camps, Short Hikes, and View Roads in the South Cascades and Mt. Rainier

Companion volume to the above. Features a coding to separate the easier hikes from the more difficult, the smooth roads from the bumpier.

Bicycling the Back Roads Around Puget Sound

Full details, maps on 54 cycle tours on quiet back roads, including descriptions of scenery, mileage, elevation change, estimated times. By Bill and Erin Woods.

Footloose Around Puget Sound: 100 Walks on Beaches, Lowlands, and Foothills

Afternoon strolls in city parks, beaches to wander, lonely roads and easy trails in the front range of the Cascades. Walks for winter Sundays and summer evenings. Each walk with text by Janice Krenmayr, map by Helen Sherman, photo by Bob and Ira Spring.

55 Ways to the Wilderness in Southcentral Alaska

Explore this great wilderness by foot, canoe, kayak, ski and snowshoe with this guide prepared by the Mountaineering Club of Alaska. Detailed text, scenic photos, maps.

OTHER GUIDES

Routes and Rocks: Hiker's Guide to the North Cascades from Glacier Peak to Lake Chelan

Trails and off-trail high routes in and around the Glacier Peak Wilderness Area, with notes on geology. 96 drawings and maps, 8 photos, 3 quadrangle maps in back pocket. By D.F. Crowder and R.W. Tabor.

Hiker's Map to the North Cascades: Routes and Rocks in the Mt. Challenger Quadrangle

Also by Crowder and Tabor, covering the Picket Range and Custer Ridge.

Trail Country: Olympic National Park

Mile-by-mile guide to every trail in the park, with chapters on natural and human history. 25 photographs, 25 maps. By Robert L. Wood.

Wilderness Trails of Olympic National Park

Paperback reprint of the trails section from Trail Country.

Guide to Leavenworth Rock Climbing Areas

Complete descriptions of routes, difficult moves, hardware used, etc. 10 sketches, 2 sketch maps. By Fred Beckey and Eric Bjornstad.

Snowshoe Hikes in the Cascades and Olympics

Easy walks for the beginner, strenuous ascents for the winter mountaineer. More than 80 trips, each with sketch map. 13 photos. By Gene Prater.

Climbers Guide to the Olympic Mountains

By Olympic Mountain Rescue. All approach and climbing routes for Olympic peaks, plus high alpine traverses, ski and snowshoe tours. Photos and maps.